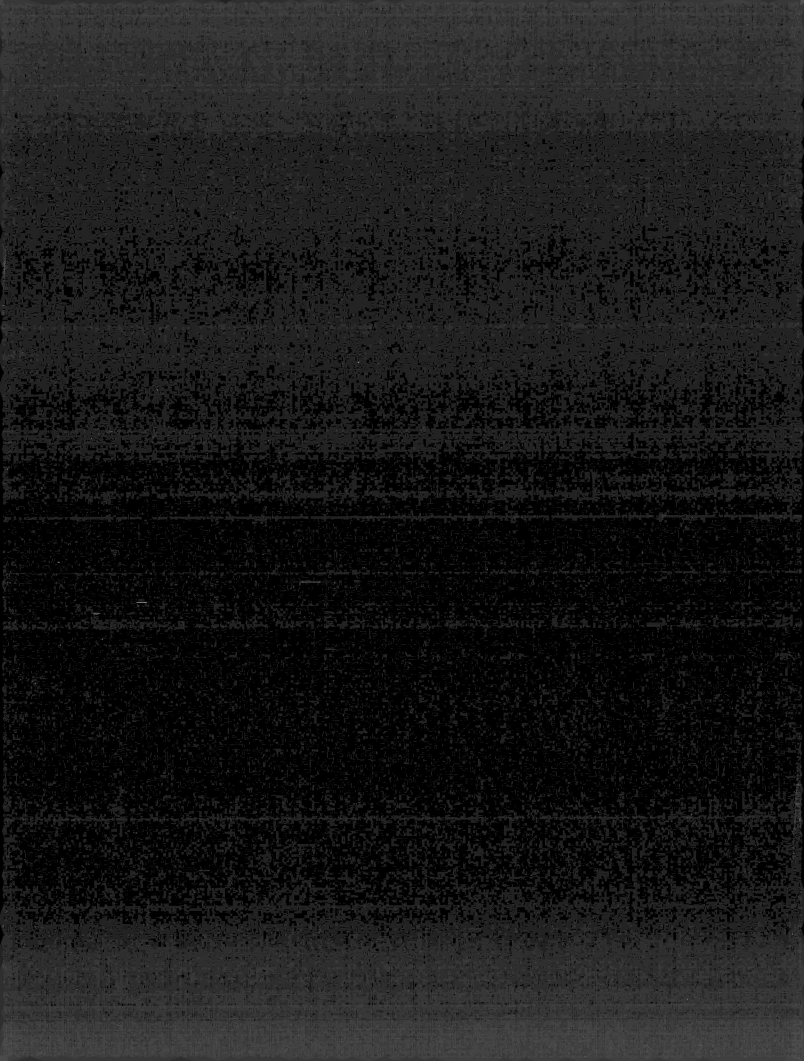

WONDER WOOD

Barbara Glasner, Stephan Ott

# WONDER WOOD

*A FAVORITE MATERIAL FOR DESIGN, ARCHITECTURE AND ART*

Birkhäuser
Basel

# INTRODUCTION

6 *In the Wonderland of Wood*

# PROJECTS
# AND PROCESSES

*CONTEMPORARY PROJECTS, PRODUCTS, EXPERIMENTS, MAKING-OFS, AND
NEW DIMENSIONS FOR WOOD IN DESIGN, ARCHITECTURE, AND ART*

11 *24H >architecture*
12 *Werner Aisslinger*
14 *ALICE*
16 *Architekten Martenson und Nagel-Theissen*
20 *Yemi Awosile*
24 *Shin Azumi*
25 *Maarten Baas*
28 *Bernardo Bader*
30 *Aldo Bakker*
32 *Stephan Balkenhol* › INTERVIEW
36 *Bamboosero*
37 *Shigeru Ban Architects*
40 *Bark Cloth, Barktex*
42 *Georg Baselitz*
43 *Baubotanik*
48 *BCXSY*
50 *Bernath+Widmer*
52 *Beton*
54 *Patrick Blanchard*
56 *Jörg Boner* › INTERVIEW
60 *Tord Boontje*
62 *Gion A. Caminada* › INTERVIEW
68 *Nick Cave*
69 *Gehard Demetz*
72 *Marco Dessí*
74 *Stefan Diez* › INTERVIEW
78 *Doshi Levien*
80 *Dutch Invertuals*
81 *Piet Hein Eek*
84 *Fehling & Peiz*
85 *Hans-Peter Feldmann*
86 *Laetitia Florin / ECAL*
88 *Malcolm Fraser Architects*
89 *Front*
90 *Terunobu Fujimori*
92 *Elise Gabriel*
93 *Martino Gamper*
96 *Liam Gillick*
98 *Glass Hill*
100 *GRAFT* › INTERVIEW
104 *Gramazio & Kohler*
106 *Konstantin Grcic* › INTERVIEW

112 *Guallart Architects*
114 *Max and Hannes Gumpp*
115 *Florian Hauswirth* › INTERVIEW
120 *Stuart Haygarth*
121 *Heide und von Beckerath Architekten*
122 *Staffan Holm*
124 *Benjamin Hubert*
126 *Enrique Illánez Schoenenberger / ECAL*
127 *INCHfurniture* › INTERVIEW
132 *ICD, Institute for Computational Design
(Prof. Achim Menges) and ITKE, Institute of
Building Structures and Structural Design
(Prof. Jan Knippers), University of Stuttgart*
134 *ICD, Institute for Computational Design
(Prof. Achim Menges), University of
Stuttgart*
136 *IwamotoScott Architecture with Buro
Happold*
137 *Hella Jongerius* › INTERVIEW
142 *Cordula Kehrer*
144 *Steffen Kehrle*
148 *Ko-Ho*
150 *Kraus Schönberg Architekten*
152 *Kengo Kuma & Associates*
154 *Maya Lahmy*
156 *Lassila Hirvilammi Arkkitehdit*
158 *Le Briccole di Venezia*
160 *Seongyong Lee*
161 *Hans Lemmen*
162 *Khai Liew*
163 *Kai Linke*
166 *Idee Liu*
167 *localarchitecture*
170 *Paul Loebach*
174 *Philippe Malouin*
175 *Enzo Mari*
176 *Michael Marriott*
177 *Jürgen Mayer H.* › INTERVIEW
182 *Junichi Mori*
184 *Paola Navone*
185 *Nendo*
187 *Sascha Nordmeyer*

188 *Henrique Oliveira*
190 *Jens Otten*
191 *Harry Parr-Young*
192 *Patternity*
194 *Lex Pott*
196 *Ray Power*
197 *Philippe Rahm architectes*
198 *Raw Edges*
202 *Steffen Reichert*
203 *Steffen Reichert with Prof. Achim Menges
and Florian Krampe at the ICD,
Institute for Computational Design,
University of Stuttgart*
204 *ROLU, rosenlof/lucas, ro/lu*
206 *Adrien Rovero*
208 *Marc Sadler*
209 *Stefan Sagmeister* › INTERVIEW
214 *Colin Schaelli*
216 *Albrecht Schäfer*
217 *Scholten & Baijings*
219 *Franziska Schreiber*
220 *Tilo Schulz* › INTERVIEW
224 *Jerszy Seymour*
225 *DJ Simpson*
226 *Ernst Stark*
228 *Wolfgang Stehle*
230 *Elisa Strozyk* › INTERVIEW
236 *Studio Formafantasma*
237 *Studio Jens Praet*
238 *Studio Job*
239 *Tb&Ajkay with Karl-Johan Hjerling
and Karin Widmark*
240 *The Medley Institute by Jana Patz*
242 *Katharina Trudzinski*
244 *Xavier Veilhan*
245 *Charlotte Wagemaker*
248 *Waugh Thistleton Architects*
250 *Ai Weiwei*
252 *Wingårdh Arkitektkontor*
253 *Martin Wöhrl*
254 *Bethan Laura Wood*
255 *Richard Woods*

# MATERIAL AND TECHNOLOGY GUIDE

*ELEMENTARY PRINCIPLES AND INNOVATIVE DEVELOPMENTS IN THE AREAS OF WOOD AND WOOD-BASED MATERIALS, PRODUCTION PROCESSES, AND CONSTRUCTION PRINCIPLES IN TIMBER BUILDING*

**I MATERIAL**
260 *1 Wood—definition and characteristics*
261 *2 Solid wood*
263 *3 Veneer*
264 *4 Wood-based materials*

**II TECHNOLOGY: PRODUCTION PROCESSES**
270 *1 Reshaping*
270 *2 Separating*
271 *3 Joining*
273 *4 Coatings*
273 *5 Changing the characteristics of materials*

**III TECHNOLOGY: THE PRINCIPLES OF TIMBER CONSTRUCTION**
276 *1 Timber frame construction*
276 *2 Solid timber construction*
276 *3 Natural building processes*

# APPENDIX

278 *Biographies*
284 *Index*
290 *Picture credits*
294 *Bibliography and sources (selection)*
295 *Acknowledgments / The Authors*

# IN THE WONDERLAND OF WOOD

*"FOREST, TIMBER FOREST, TREE FELLING, AS IT HAS ALWAYS BEEN."*
THOMAS BERNHARD, *HOLZFÄLLEN. EINE ERREGUNG* (CUTTING TIMBER. AN IRRITATION), 1984

1   SEE HANS-JÖRG MODLMAYR, *SPEERSPITZE DER ARCHÄOLOGIE
    – DIE ERFORSCHUNG DER HOLZ-ZEIT* (SPEAR THROWER OF
    ARCHEOLOGY—RESEARCHING THE WOOD AGE. TRANSCRIPT OF
    A RADIO BROADCAST, DEUTSCHLANDRADIO KULTUR—FOR-
    SCHUNG UND GESELLSCHAFT), AUGUST 27, 2009.

2   WWW.UN.ORG/EN/EVENTS/IYOF2011/RESOLUTION.SHTML
    ACCESSED JUNE 28, 2011.

3   SEE ALSO BURKHARD MÜLLER, "DIE SCHÖNHEIT DES WALD-
    BAUS. DIE FORSTAKADEMIE THARANDT FEIERT IHREN ZWEI-
    HUNDERTSTEN GEBURTSTAG — UND DIE ENTDECKUNG
    DER NACHHALTIGKEIT" (THE BEAUTY OF THE FOREST. THE
    THARANDT FORESTRY ACADEMY CELEBRATES ITS 200TH
    BIRTHDAY—AND THE DISCOVERY OF SUSTAINABILITY).
    IN: *SÜDDEUTSCHE ZEITUNG NO. 140*, P. 9, JUNE 20, 2011.

4   SEE STEFFEN UHLMANN, "LUXUSYACHTEN STATT SCHRANK-
    WÄNDE. DER TRADITIONSREICHE MÖBELHERSTELLER DEUTSCHE
    WERKSTÄTTEN HELLERAU MUSSTE SICH NEU ERFINDEN,
    UM IN DER HART UMKÄMPFTEN BRANCHE ZU ÜBERLEBEN"
    (LUXURY YACHTS INSTEAD OF WALL UNITS. THE FURNITURE
    MANUFACTURER DEUTSCHE WERKSTÄTTEN HELLERAU,
    RICH-IN-TRADITION, NEEDS TO REINVENT ITSELF TO STAY AHEAD
    OF THE GAME IN THE HIGHLY COMPETITIVE BRANCH OF
    FURNITURE MAKING). IN: *SÜDDEUTSCHE ZEITUNG NO. 14*,
    P. 21, JANUARY 19, 2011.

5   CHRISTOPH SCHINDLER, *EIN ARCHITEKTONISCHES PERIODI-
    SIERUNGSMODELL ANHAND FERTIGUNGSTECHNISCHER
    KRITERIEN, DARGESTELLT AM BEISPIEL EINES HOLZBAUS* (AN
    ARCHITECTURAL PERIODIZATION MODEL USING PRODUCTION
    TECHNIQUE CRITERIA, ILLUSTRATED WITH AN EXAMPLE OF
    A WOODEN STRUCTURE), PH.D. DISSERTATION, ZURICH, 2009.

**First and foremost, the most fascinating and wonderful fact:**
*Wood is irreplaceable, but it grows back.*
This fact alone makes wood a unique and sustainable material.
It may also be the reason why many disciplines continue to use wood,
and also why it has continued to accompany us through the ages.
Archeologists now speak of the Wood Age as an enduring historical
age of mankind. The Stone or Bronze Ages, for example, would
not have been possible without the existence of wood or its application as a building or heating material. New findings show that even
the Neanderthals had discovered how to fix a flint blade into a wooden
handle by using heated birch-bark tar.[1]

### Woods and Forest. The Raw Material

2011 was named the International Year of Forests by the United
Nations. Which is ultimately unnerving, because whenever something
has a year dedicated to it, it usually means that it is in need of attention, care, and that we need to be reminded of its value. However,
UN Resolution 61/193 reassures us that forests are given great
importance as climate protection and providers of a vital, perhaps
even the most important raw material in the world.[2] Because, different
to other raw materials such as oil, coal, or ore, wood grows back in
a reasonable amount of time, remaining consistent in quality.
In Germany and in Switzerland, forests comprise approximately thirty
percent of their national area, in Austria, they comprise as much as
forty-eight percent. This percentage remains stable due to efforts by
forest management, which was established two hundred years ago
in Germany.[3] Without the intensive commitment and research of this
discipline—despite some rather damaging forest management aberra-
tions such as the planting of monocultures and clearcutting—the
outlook for forests would be much more dire, and the same would be
true for wood as a construction material and for by-products manufactured from wood. An additional, important contribution is the
increasing requirement to certify wood products with labels such as
PEFC (Programme for the Endorsement of Forest Certification Systems)
and FSC (Forest Stewardship Council).

### More than Wood. The Construction Material

Wood is a multifunctional material that is particularly exciting because
it can be used in more areas and in more forms—from roughly sawn
construction wood to oiled parquet flooring and luxurious furniture—
than any other material. Moreover, because it is also available regionally—which is an additional valuable advantage over other raw materials—people from all over the world have been building with wood
for thousands and thousands of years. It was therefore logical that
the material was developed from a raw material into a construction
material: the specific modification, meaning that wood began to be
industrialized at the latest in the nineteenth century, with the steam
bending process invented by Michael Thonet, was continued at the
beginning of the twentieth century with the invention of the laminated wood panel by furniture maker Karl Schmidt, co-founder of the
German Hellerau Workshops, and artist, graphic designer, and interior
architect Johannes Joseph Vincenz Cissarz.[4] There are more and more
new wood construction materials being developed today, and wood
is capable of ever more innovative possibilities that were previously
ascribed to other materials: today, for example, it is possible to
injection mold plastic in the form of Wood Plastic Composites (WPC).
In structural timber engineering, modern wood plastics are now a
standard in many fields alongside concrete and steel (construction,
fire prevention, and so on). In some cases they are even preferred.
There are a number of research institutes focused on developing new
ways of modifying wood, and based on the knowledge we have today,
we can assume that one of the most important construction materials of the past will be one of the most important of the future.

### Old Connections and New Technology. The Resource Material

Wood not only grows back and is $CO_2$ neutral, it can also be recycled
100 percent into the ecological cycle—without downcycling or producing non-biodegradable residual waste. It is one of the few
technical construction materials that truly holds to the cradle-to-
cradle principle, meaning it can qualify as a resource material.

Because it is extraordinarily adaptable, wood is also an excellent
basic material for new technical developments. A current example
of this are the most recent CNC processing centers. "The steel
joint initially superseded the wood-to-wood joint because it was not
sufficiently cost-effective. But now, CNC technology is helping the
wood-to-wood joint regain its territory as a cost-effective alternative."[5] That's why wood qualifies as a valuable technological material
for the twenty-first century.

### Felled, Comforting. The Vital Material

Wood is created when a tree grows. However, when we speak of wood,
we are usually referring to the dead material. In German, the word
*Holz* (wood) is derived from the Old High German word "felled." Nonetheless, this felled material has more life in it than plastic. Even long
after it has been felled, wood continues to expand and contract, it
ages with dignity, it warms, is insulated, has a pleasant scent, and it
gives us advance warning by making creaking sounds before it breaks.
They even say that Swiss pine has a heartbeat-slowing effect and is
supposed to calm and soothe—a quality greatly appreciated by many
innkeepers in the Alps region, who traditionally panel their pubs with
Swiss pine. There are even political decision makers who take advantage of the calming effect of this wood. The top floor of the Bavarian
State Chancellery is paneled with Swiss pine.

### WonderWood. The Reading Material

This book is a compilation of over a hundred current projects and
"making-ofs," from the fields of design, architecture, and art, that work
with wood as a material in varied and extraordinary ways. We also
had the opportunity to interview thirteen internationally acclaimed
designers, architects, and artists about their work(s). The discussions
illustrate in detail the different approaches used by the three disciplines, but also reveal the designers' and artists' enthusiasm for the diverse material and the intense ways of working with the material.

Readers who would like to research the subject further can look at
the material and technological guide in the second part of the book.
This section is designed as a reference handbook, providing a glimpse
of the complex world of wood and its manufacturing processes, as
well as tips on constructing with wood.

Those who would like to research even further can refer to the final
service section, where you will find information about further litera-
ture, essays, magazines, and websites that specialize in the subject.

We will continue to be committed to the subject of wood in the future,
because we're convinced that we're in store for many more surprises
from this raw, construction, resource, and vital material:
www.wonder-wood.de

Barbara Glasner and Stephan Ott

# PROJECTS AND PROCESSES

*CONTEMPORARY PROJECTS, PRODUCTS, EXPERIMENTS, MAKING-OFS, AND NEW DIMENSIONS FOR WOOD IN DESIGN, ARCHITECTURE, AND ART*

# 24H > ARCHITECTURE

The organic structure of this house is ideally adapted to its natural forest setting. A section of the house is mounted on castors, allowing it to be slid in and out like a drawer. The roofing shingles, a traditional material used for roofs in Sweden, are made from Western Red Cedar, a wood that requires no further maintenance.

# WERNER AISSLINGER

**HEMP CHAIR**, 2012
STACKABLE CHAIR
HEMP, KENAF (MALVACEAE FAMILY), WATER-BASED
THERMOSET BINDER ACRODUR® BASF
DEPTH 50 × WIDTH 65 × HEIGHT 75 CM, WEIGHT: 15 KG
MANUFACTURER: MOROSO

The Hemp Chair belongs to the tradition of stackable, manufactured monobloc chairs, usually made of reinforced plastics such as polypropylene. Unlike these, however, it is made exclusively from the natural fibers hemp and Malvaceae kenaf. The fibers are formed by heat treatment, and bonded using Acrodur®,

a formaldehyde-free, water-based thermoset binder. The manufacturing process, which was borrowed from the automotive industry, gives the Hemp Chair an extraordinary high stability and low weight.

# ALICE
## (ATELIER DE LA CONCEPTION DE L'ESPACE)

STUDENTS AT THE ÉCOLE POLYTECHNIQUE FÉDÉRALE DE LAUSANNE (ALICE 2009: AHMED BELKHODJA, AUGUSTIN CLEMENT, NICOLAS FEIHL, OLIVIER DI GIAMBATTISTA, EVELINE JOB, MARTIN LEPOUTRE, SAMUEL MAIRE, BENJAMIN MELLY, ADRIAN LLEWELYN MEREDITH, FRANÇOIS NANTERMOD); PROFESSOR: DIETER DIETZ, ZURICH; TEAM: KATIA RITZ, DANIEL POKORA, OLIVIER OTTEVAERE, ALINE DUBACH, ISABELLA PASQUALINI, EVELINE GALATIS.

EVOLVER, 2009
STELLISEE, ZERMATT, SWITZERLAND
SPRUCE
Ø 8.8 M, HEIGHT 5 M

The walk-in sculpture was originally conceived as a temporary installation for the 2009 Zermatt Festival of Chamber Music. For this reason, it was to be a relatively low-tech construction that could be easily installed and then dismantled at the end of the festival. "Evolver" references the panoramic view from Zermatt of the Matterhorn and the Monte Rosa Massif. The sculpture consists of twenty-four, spiral-shaped wooden frames, that open toward a 720° panorama of extraordinary perspectives.

# ARCHITEKTEN MARTENSON UND NAGEL-THEISSEN

**JUST K**, 2009
TÜBINGEN, GERMANY
DWELLING HOUSE
INTERNAL AND EXTERNAL WALLS OF SPRUCE
AND CROSS-LAMINATED PINE, TIMBER
FLOORS OF SILVER FIR
FLOOR AREA: 138 M²

This building constructed of solid timber elements was prefabricated in modules, assembled on site, and completely covered with a roof foil of synthetic rubber. The house consists of a total of 136 individual elements. Before being assembled, rebates were made in them for the joinery and carpentry work, and channels and holes bored for the electrical services. The interior fitting out including furniture and stairs is integrated in the architecture, the wood for these was sanded, leached, and soaped to preserve its light color.

# YEMI
# AWOSILE

CORK FABRIC, 2008
FURNITURE UPHOLSTERED WITH CORK AND
POLYMER FIBER
STOOL: Ø 40 CM, HEIGHT 30 CM
PROTOTYPES

This extremely lightweight fabric is a mixture of shelled, treated cork
and an elastic polymer fiber (elastic). It is an extraordinary fabric
above all because of its excellent thermal and acoustic insulation qualities. Its elasticity and flexibility make the fabric perfect for a variety
of interior uses, such as wall-coverings or upholstery.

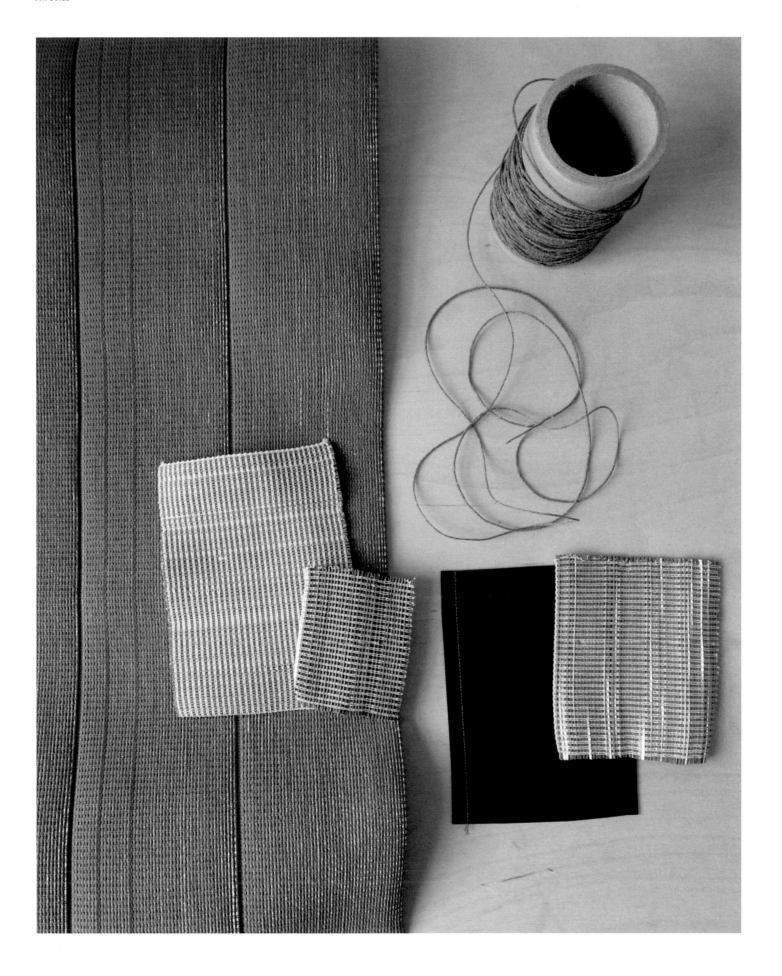

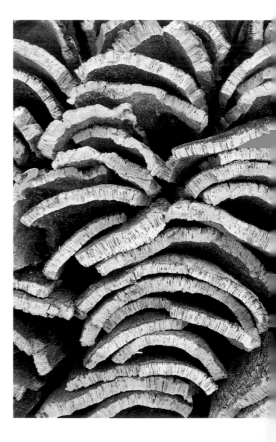

**SURFACE PATTERN**, 2010
LASER-CUT CORK MATS
PROTOTYPE

The cork mats are a by-product of wine cork production and are
suitable for use in interiors as wall paneling or room dividers.
The laser-cut mats are available in a wide variety of sizes and shapes
and can be coated in different metallic varnishes, such as silver,
copper, or gold.

# SHIN AZUMI

**AP**, 2010
STACKABLE STOOLS
MULTIPLEX (OAK, BLEACHED OR BLACK
STAINED)
DEPTH 37 × WIDTH 47 × HEIGHT 50 CM
MANUFACTURER: LAPALMA

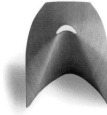

The stackable stool is a monocoque construction made
from a piece of plywood, with no joining bolts or screws.
Its form is derived from origami, follows ergonomic
requirements, and is also highly stable.

# MAARTEN BAAS

**CHINESE OBJECTS OBJECT**, 2008
CARVED CAMPHORWOOD, VARNISH
DEPTH 120 × WIDTH 120 × HEIGHT 195 CM
CREATED DURING THE CONTRASTS GALLERY
"ARTIST IN RESIDENCE" PROGRAM
COURTESY CONTRASTS GALLERY, SHANGHAI

Within the framework of the Artist in Residence program, Western designers were given the opportunity to engage with local cultural traditions and artistic processes in Shanghai. The assemblage of different Chinese wooden objects was carved from solid wood by Chinese artisans.

The design classics in the "Smoke" collection were first
burned with a gas burner and then coated with epoxy
resin. This preserves the pitch-black burnt wood. The
concept is based on Maarten Baas' final thesis work at
the Design Academy Eindhoven from 2003.

*MAARTEN BAAS*

**SMOKE**, 2004–2009
BURNED FURNITURE DESIGN CLASSICS WITH
AN EPOXY COATING AND TRANSPARENT
POLYURETHANE AND UV-FILTER,
COURTESY MOSS, NEW YORK

**"WOODEN CHAIR"**
BY MARC NEWSON, 1992
DEPTH 74.9 × WIDTH 74.9 × HEIGHT 99.7 CM

**"RED AND BLUE CHAIR"**
BY GERRIT T. RIETVELD, 1918
DEPTH 88 × WIDTH 66 × HEIGHT 83 CM

**"FAVELA CHAIR"**
BY FERNANDO AND HUMBERTO
CAMPANA, 2003
DEPTH 61 × WIDTH 67 × HEIGHT 74 CM

**"ZIG ZAG CHAIR"**
BY GERRIT T. RIETVELD, 1934
DEPTH 42 × WIDTH 38 × HEIGHT 75 CM

# BERNARDO BADER

.EMA HAUS, 2008
FELDKIRCH-NOFELS, AUSTRIA
FACADE OF ROUGH SAWN FIR
FOOTPRINT: 57 M², FLOOR AREA: 90 M²

The rear-ventilated facade of this three-storey house consists of rough-sawn fir wood boards that can be fitted when still moist, thanks to a vertical tongue and groove joint. The prefabricated wooden substructure meant that the entire assembly, including the fitting-out of the interior with birch plywood paneling, could be completed in a day and a half—allowing the building costs to be substantially reduced.

# ALDO BAKKER

**STOOL**, 2009
COLLECTION OF STOOLS MADE FROM
RECYCLED WOOD
STOOL: HONEY LOCUST (*GLEDITSIA
TRIACANTHOS*), ELM, ASH OR BEECH,
TRANSPARENT VARNISH
DEPTH 35 × WIDTH 36 × HEIGHT 34 CM
PRODUCTION: KUPERUS & GARDENIER
LIMITED EDITION OF 15 PIECES

**STOOL URUSHI**, 2006
STOOL COLLECTION OF ABACHI WOOD
URUSHI LACQUERER: MARIKO NISHIDE
LACQUER SUPPLIER: TAKUO MATSUZAWA,
JOBOJI URUSHI SANGYO
DEPTH 36 × WIDTH 36 × HEIGHT 34 CM
LIMITED EDITION OF 7 PIECES
CLIENT: PARTICLES GALLERY

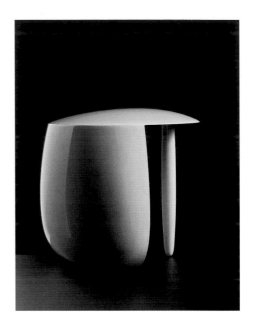

Each of the stools consists of one leg, a curved base, and a top seat that are constructed from eight layers of the same piece of wood, a process that protects the wood from splitting. The "Urushi Stool" is made from different pieces of wood and is an intricately crafted construction. It is treated with 30 individually sanded layers of Urushi varnish, a traditional Japanese varnish made from resin derived from the lacquer tree (*Rhus vernicifera*). The varnish is highly durable; 9,000-year-old, well-preserved examples exist of objects painted using the Urushi method.

# STEPHAN BALKENHOL

**SEMPRE PIÚ (MORE AND MORE)**, 2009
ROME, ITALY
CEDAR
DEPTH 100 × WIDTH 150 × HEIGHT 500 CM
© 2012, PROLITTERIS, ZURICH

The larger than life-sized torso made from cedar was
installed from October 2009 to February 2010 at the
Forum Romanum in Rome amid fake coins—which was a
metaphor for the Forum in ancient times being both
a place of worship and trade, which is why it still serves
as a symbol of human excess.

# "WOOD REFLECTS MY OWN CHARACTER"

*You like working in wood more than other materials. What is it about wood that fascinates you so much?*
I can work in a direct and immediate way with wood, meaning I don't have to first work with a casting process, as is the case with clay or plaster. For this reason, the artistic process is completely legible on the surface of the work. I work on a scale of one to one. What I do is the result itself. At the same time, this way of working allows the greatest level of freedom and independence. I can work alone, without assistants and without specialist companies, such as a foundry; I can also work in sync with my own artistic decisions, meaning I don't have to depend on anyone to make a sculpture.

*What, in your opinion, is the difference between wood and other traditional sculpture materials?*
Each material dictates the speed with which you can work: clay is fast, stone is hard and requires more time. Wood is somewhere in-between and exactly reflects my own character. The type of sculpture I want to create is also best realized with wood, because it can be painted.

*When you are working, does wood still confront you with surprises or tricks, despite your many years of experience? Or is this even a necessary aspect?*
Wood is a living material that is subject to constant change—even after years. The experience that I have gained taught me how to avoid unwanted changes and how to incorporate the inevitable ones. Because wood shrinks when it dries, radial cracks form toward the center. This is why I usually use tree trunk halves, because the core is exposed and the wood can work without forming extreme cracks. The sculpture can handle the cracks that form, but they close again when the trunk is completely dry. You also always have to consider knotholes, hollow cavities, parasites, mold, and so on …

*In what context did you make the sculpture "Sempre più" in Rome?*
I was invited to make a sculpture by the Italian curator Ludovico Pratesi for a temporary project for an area inside the Forum Romanum, the Caesar Forum. It was a special challenge for me to accept the invitation and create a work, which would somehow link the history with the present, for such a history-laden site.

*What role did the choice of wood as a material play for the sculpture? What kind of wood did you choose, and did you paint it or treat it somehow?*
I've had a large trunk of cedar wood in my storeroom for a while. I just didn't have an exciting idea for the wood. The Rome project came at the perfect time, because the trunk had exactly the right dimensions. Cedar wood is also very weather resistant. The surface is oiled, which is also an additional protection against weather and erosion.

*The sculpture is very large. What necessary structural aspects did you have to consider for the work?*
The sculpture consists of a trunk that has been halved lengthwise. Both parts were straightened and placed side by side, creating a volume of 3×5×1.5 meters. The sculpture is only worked on one side; the two halves are bolted together at the back. On site in Rome, the work was fixed to a metal plate.

*How long did you work on the sculpture?*
All together for about three months.

# BAMBOOSERO

**BAMBOO BICYCLES**, 2010 (PROJECT START 1995)
GHANA, AFRICA
FRAME MADE OF BAMBOO
DIFFERENT MODELS: TRANSPORT BICYCLES,
MOUNTAIN BIKES, CITY BIKES, RACING BIKES

The bicycle frame manufacturer Craig Calfee initiated the "Bamboosero" project, in which bicycle frames are produced from bamboo in their own factory. Choosing the unusual, regionally available, and natural material of bamboo for this bicycle construction is an ecologically and socially excellent solution.

# SHIGERU BAN ARCHITECTS

**HASLEY NINE BRIDGES GOLF RESORT**, 2008
YEOJU, SOUTH KOREA
BUILT-UP AREA: 5,420 M²
3D PLANNING: DESIGNTOPRODUCTION
ENGINEERS: SJB.KEMPTER.FITZE AG
TIMBER CONSTRUCTION: BLUMER-LEHMANN AG
TECHNICAL DEVELOPMENT: CRÉATION HOLZ

A baldachin woven from timber beams carries the roof of the clubhouse that Shigeru Ban designed for the Hasley Nine Bridges Golf Resort in Yeoju (South Korea). A total of 21 slender columns carry 32 roof elements made up of over 3,500 complexly detailed glulam timber segments that were produced in Switzerland using CNC technology.

**CENTRE POMPIDOU**, 2010
METZ, FRANCE
SHIGERU BAN ARCHITECTS WITH
JEAN DE GASTINES
GLULAM PLYWOOD
TEFLON-FIBERGLASS COMPOSITE
TOTAL HEIGHT (INCLUSIVELY METAL MAST): 77M
ROOF CONSTRUCTION: HEIGHT CA. 36 M
SURFACE AREA: 8,000 M²
3D PLANNING: DESIGNTOPRODUCTION
ENGINEERS: SJB.KEMPTER.FITZE AG
TIMBER CONSTRUCTION: HOLZBAU
AMANN GMBH

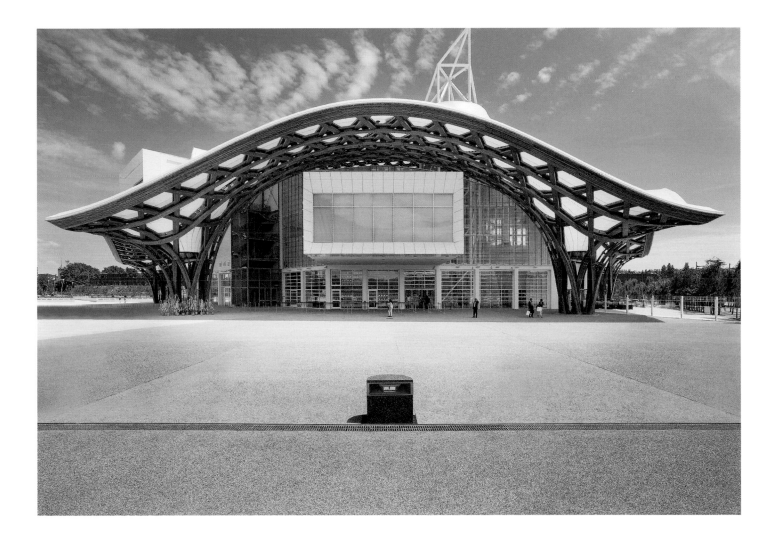

The double curved superstructure of the Centre Pompidou in Metz consists of 1,800 individually produced glulam beams that are connected at the junctions using wooden dowels and slotted metal plates. The beams, at distances of 2.90 meters apart, form a typical Shigeru Ban hexagonal grid that is derived from a straw hat. A metal mast at the center and four conically shaped columns support the entire building. A polytetrafluorethylene (PTFE) membrane, a water-tight, teflon-fiberglass composite, is stretched above the timber construction; the facades consist of retractable louvers and large windows that are made of polycarbonate.

# BARK CLOTH

**BARK CLOTH®, BARKTEX®**, 2009
TEXTILES FROM BAST FIBERS
PRODUCER: BARK CLOTH UGANDA LTD.
BARKTEX STRIPES 'N' SPRINKLES
ARTE WALLCOVERINGS

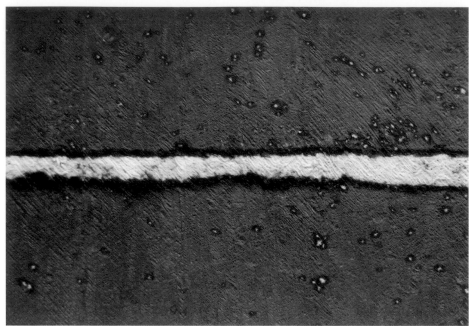

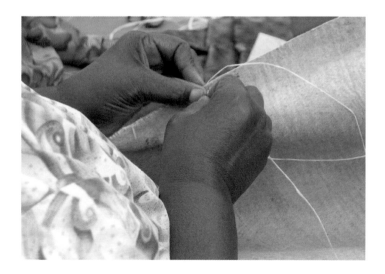

Bark Cloth is produced from bast fibers derived from the east African Mutuba fig tree. The fleece is created by means of complex handwork and is one of the oldest textiles in the history of mankind. Depending on the lighting situation and the angle it is viewed from, the material can take on the appearance of leather or that of the lightness and transparence of organza. When covered with textiles such as silk, or coated with water- or fireproof material, Bark Cloth goes under the brand name of Barktex, and is used, for example, for clothing or as a technical fleece in product and interior design.

# GEORG BASELITZ

**VOLK DING ZERO**, 2009
CEDAR, OIL PAINT, PAPER, AND NAILS
DEPTH 125 × WIDTH 120 × HEIGHT 308 CM
© GEORG BASELITZ, PRIVATE COLLECTION

Georg Baselitz works with chainsaws, axes, and chisels on mainly maple, lime-wood, red beech, or cedar to make his sculptural works. The sculpture "Volk Ding Zero" is made from cedar and served as the model for Baselitz's first outdoor sculpture, a bronze cast of the figure, for the Convent Garden of the former Augustinian Monastery of Dalheim.

# BAUBOTANIK

**STEG** (ELEVATED WALKWAY), WALD-RUHESTETTEN (LAKE CONSTANCE), GERMANY, FROM 2005
FERDINAND LUDWIG, OLIVER STORZ/BUREAU BAUBOTANIK
LIVING PLANT LOAD BEARING STRUCTURE OF WILLOW RODS
(TEST SYSTEM WITH 300 WILLOW PLANTS)
DECK: STEEL CONSTRUCTION: GALVANIZED
LADDERS AND HANDRAILS: STAINLESS STEEL
DIMENSIONS: HEIGHT CA. 3 M × LENGTH, CA. 22 M

Under the heading "botany building", the elevated walkway and the tower represent the first architectural prototypes in which woody plants and inorganic materials such as steel are combined with each other. Fast-growing plants such as willows or plane trees provide the structure. This concept makes three-dimensional park structures possible even in densely built up cities.

TOWER, FROM 2009
WALD-RUHESTETTEN (LAKE CONSTANCE), GERMANY
FERDINAND LUDWIG, CORNELIUS HACKENBRACHT
LIVING PLANT LOAD BEARING STRUCTURE OF WILLOW RODS
FROM ONE-YEAR-OLD WILLOW SHOOTS THAT ARE
CONNECTED USING A PLANT ADDITION PROCESS
DECK: STEEL CONSTRUCTION, GALVANIZED
HEIGHT CA. 9 M, FOOTPRINT CA. 3 × 3 M

Botany building clearly reveals two botanical phenomena: firstly the ability of plants to grow together and secondly their ability to "incorporate" foreign objects. The 22-meter-long deck of the elevated walkway grows together with the 64 "bundled" columns, in much the same way the three accessible floor levels of the tower "fuse" with the external mesh structure.

46    **BAUBOTANIK**    GROWTH HANDRAIL (WALKWAY) 2005–2010    WILLOW GROWTH TEST (TEST INSTALLATION DIRECTLY AFTER PLANTING) / TEST SYSTEM

WILLOW GROWTH TEST (ANNUAL) / TEST SYSTEM    WILLOW GROWTH TEST (BIENNIAL) / TEST SYSTEM

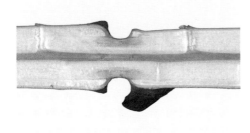

Incorporating technical constructions: if a tree is in mechanical contact with a foreign body, it will increase its surface at the point of contact and ultimately enclose the form. This growth process allows the connection points of structural botanical support frames, between plants and technical construction components, to become stronger with time.

The platform in the Steveraue is the first living plant load-bearing structure to include a temporary support structure, as part of the design concept. This indicates that plants that have not yet grown together or covered building elements will eventually be able to form jointly an independent load-bearing structure. The increasing stability of the plants will allow the botany building support structures to be removed successively. This resembles the practice of espalier training used in gardening, where a trellis provides support for plants that are still young and fragile or have become so. It allows the current strength to be judged, although in fact it represents a promise of the plants' growing stability.

# BCXSY

**JOIN**, 2010
COLLECTION OF FOLDING WOODEN SPACE-DIVIDERS
HINOKI (JAPANESE CYPRESS)
EACH SCREEN CA. WIDTH 1.55 × HEIGHT 1.65 M
LIMITED EDITION OF THE THREE SCREEN SECTIONS OF 8
PIECES EACH
MADE BY HAND IN JAPAN BY THE *TATEGU* MASTER,
MR. TANAKA

The design of the folding screens is based on the aesthetic and crafts-manship traditions of Japanese sliding doors. They are produced according to the principles of *tategu*, the traditional Japanese art of woodworking, from Japanese cypress, a pleasant scented wood that is highly resistant to rot and hence does not require additional treatment with wax or oils.

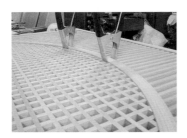

# BERNATH+ WIDMER

**BÜTTENHARDT VACATION HOME**, 2010
SCHAFFHAUSEN, SWITZERLAND
POST AND BEAM CONSTRUCTION OF
HEART-FREE OAK,
PLANKS WITH PINE INFILL
FOOTPRINT (INCL. COTTAGE): 150 M²

Hardwood is the most common wood used for furniture making. However, buildings and other structures made from wood need to be built using hardwood trees with thick trunk diameters, which are uncommon in Europe. For the Büttenhardt vacation home, which was built using the traditional post and beam construction technique, hardwood that has been freed of its heartwood was used as an

alternative. The trunks were split from their heartwood lengthwise, without having to saw them open, by a drilling system specially developed by Bernath+Widmer, in collaboration with other experts in the field (Hermann Blumer, Michael Koller, Bergauer Holzbau GmbH, Heiri Bührer). The advantage of this method is that regionally available hardwood, which had previously been processed only for heating or

industrial purposes, could now be used as valuable hardwood, and a
plank could even be cut from a trunk with a relatively small diameter.
In addition, planks without the heartwood are much less likely to
develop shrinkage cracks, which increases the durability and simplifies
processing of the wood.

# BETON

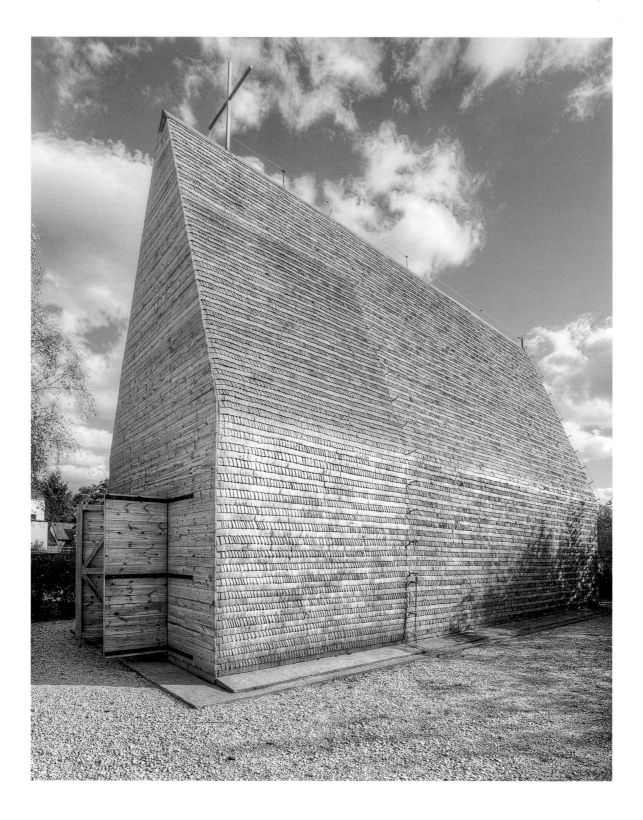

In this church built entirely of wood there is a flowing harmonious transition between the shingle covered roof and wall surfaces. The building was deliberately based on the simplest construction principles, as it was to be erected by amateur local workers. The acrylic glass area at one gable end of the building (which otherwise has no windows) serves as a light source and background for the altar.

# PATRICK BLANCHARD

**ACANTHUS**, 2008
TABLE LAMP
LIME WOOD, SYCAMORE, ALDER, OR
MAHOGANY
DEPTH 24 × WIDTH 24 × HEIGHT 70 CM
MANUFACTURER: META

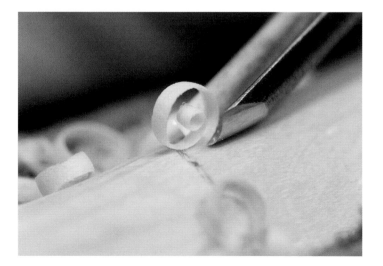

The form of the table lamp is inspired by the world of plants and reminiscent of intricate goldsmith work of the Jugendstil era. Cabinet-maker Patrick Blanchard, beautifully hand carved the lampshade from lime, sycamore, alder, and mahogany, which allows it to create a candle-like light effect.

# JÖRG BONER

The stackable chair is an example of a successful combination of
a traditional material, such as molded plywood, and contemporary
production technologies. Modern CNC milling technology creates
complex molded parts that can be inserted into the pressing tool and
pressed directly with the plywood. The structural center of the chair
is the pressed core under the curved seat surface.

# "WOOD IS TRICKY"

**What fascinates you about working with wood as a material?**
The most interesting thing about it is that it's renewable. I also think the surface and haptic qualities of wood and wood-based materials are excellent. This is a quality that's hard to match using other materials.

I think there's a clear difference: plastic can help realize certain specific ideas. Wood might be relatively limited in what is offers, but it's renewable. A good example here is Fritz Becker KG who make molded plywood. They manufacture their product very close to Europe's largest birch tree forest.

**So, does that mean your first concern is that of ecology?**
Yes, that too.

**Is there anything about the technical or processing aspects that fascinates or excites you about wood?**
Of course. With our new chair for WOGG, the WOGG 50, we learned the hard way how tricky wood actually is.

**Can you give us more detail?**
When a material is invented, for example a new plastic, it can lead to a completely original formal language. Or, another example is the demise of the light bulb in favor of LED and OLED technology, which is triggering substantial changes in form. None of this happens or will probably ever happen to wood. Technologically speaking, wood or wood-based materials do not and probably never will undergo novel advancements. There are no wood or wood-based materials invented on a yearly basis, which are easy to work with. The step-by-step processing of wood is fairly predefined. CNC technology has actually opened a new field in the area of formal design, but, on the whole, wood remains fairly antiquated. It is still a process that involves skilled craftsmanship, even though it can now be processed in a more industrial manner than previously. But I think this long tradition of woodworking is precisely that, which poses a challenge to designers to find new ways of working with a material that does not per se make great technological strides.

**The WOGG 50 chair could not have been produced without the modern technology you mentioned. What was the challenge involved in this process?**
With the previous chair, the WOGG 42, the focus was clearly on the combination of seat, textile seat surface, and backrest, this also posed the greatest challenge. The frame is pure old-fashioned joinery work: old joints, doweled, milled, and planed—basically the same process used to make furniture by hand. The WOGG 50, however, requires the industrial phase of wood processing, because the design would be impossible without the very particular deformation and CNC cutting

technology. The CNC technology allows, for instance, the molding cutter to revolve around the molded part. This creates forms that would never have been feasible using classic, manual woodworking techniques. The challenge we faced making the WOGG 50 chair, was to push the production technology to its limits and to design a contemporary form for the year 2010, and not a chair that could have been produced just as easily in the 1950s. Charles and Ray Eames achieved excellent results with molded plywood.

**What were the technological and formal crunch points for you?**
The price range for this chair was set very low, which was related to it being mass-produced. Combining price, technology, and the formal aspects—which is why I said that wood is tricky—was very challenging.

The critical situation popped up exactly where we thought we'd have absolutely no problems. From a technical point of view, everything was fine, but the price ended up a third higher than we originally calculated.

Much is known today about molded plywood, and we didn't really understand at the beginning why two solutions, which were not even very technically or, for that matter, formally different from one another, would differ so greatly in price. Almost everything can be made technically, but you have access to a lot of knowledge when working in the world of mass-produced products.

**Did you have any experience with plywood before making the chair?**
Well I thought I had experience with the material. But we soon found out that we'd practically have to start from the beginning for this task. We had meetings with the company Fritz Becker KG where, I believed, we were presenting a functioning product. But they explained that the production of the pressing tool would be so complex and expensive that it would make the price of the chair skyrocket. For instance, the number of layers of wood you have is crucial to calculating a price.

**Is it necessary to team up with technological experts when working with wood?**
For the WOGG 50 chair, it was very important: in contrast to other projects, I had the impression here that we were working with experts highly experienced in molded plywood, but who were not really able to communicate this experience because the different phases of the procedure and their results are not as easy to predict as with other materials.

For instance, it's far easier to predict the results of working with plastic. You can say plastic has to maintain a certain thickness or strength or it will break. With molded plywood, you have to say that you cannot go under a certain thickness if you do this or that. But if you make something else simultaneously, then it's OK.

I found this transfer of knowhow difficult but fascinating. There were meetings with Becker, when I had absolutely no idea whether they would say, "this is no problem," or "this won't work at all."

**Can you explain that, using a detail of the WOGG 50?**
I can explain it using the backrest as an example. I was always worried that a backrest that is too thin looks cheap. So we clearly wanted a backrest of a certain thickness. But then Becker said that the three or four additional layers of wood required for this idea would almost double the price.

**How did you arrive at the final, thinner solution? And are you satisfied with this result formally?**
Yes, very much so. Because then something happened which is so obvious that I'm almost afraid to admit it. Becker's technological experts asked why we weren't exploiting the flexibility of molded plywood. This was such an obvious idea that it never even occurred to us. But from then on, it was obvious that we would utilize this aspect of the material for the backrest, which would never have been possible for the thicker design. We immediately assumed that a thicker backrest would automatically mean more value, and disregarded the unique qualities of the material.

**There is another innovative detail in your chair regarding the joint between the seat and legs. Can you tell us something about that?**
What is new is that we didn't glue the relatively large joint connecting the seat and the legs to the shell afterwards, as is normally the case. We inserted it into the device and grouted it into the shell in one step. Once again, CNC technology—a relatively new technology that differs fundamentally from the usual handcrafted process that required two steps—made it possible to fit this complex joint exactly into the device.

**How long did it take to develop the chair?**
Two years. Originally, we wanted to develop the chair based on the WOGG 42 and use wood instead of fabric. But we quickly realized that that would formally compromise the WOGG 42, and that it would not function as easily technically.

In the second phase, when we decided to use molded plywood as a material, we realized that it wouldn't make any sense to use solid wood, except for the straight-cut, very simple solid wood legs. Especially because we would have needed to work with two different manufacturers—since the molded plywood experts know little about solid wood and the solid wood people little about molded plywood. They are two completely different, highly specialized industries.

# GION A. CAMINADA

**MORTUARY**, 2002
VRIN, SWITZERLAND
SPRUCE, PAINTED EXTERNALLY WITH LIME
CASEIN
FOOTPRINT: CA. 61 M²

This *stiva da morts* (village mortuary) is the first of a number of buildings that Gion A. Caminada designed in his native village of Vrin (Les Grisons) based on traditional timber building methods (log cabin construction). The facade is painted with a mixture of milk proteins and shell limestone, known as lime casein; the entire interior was given a coat of shellac.

*GION A.
CAMINADA*

**BALLENBERG ADMINISTRATION BUILDING**, 2010
HOFSTETTEN, SWITZERLAND
FACADE OF UNTREATED SPRUCE
FOOTPRINT: CA. 285 M²

This new building for the administration of the Ballenberg outdoor museum is a three-storey timber structure constructed on a grid system. After the completion of the timber construction, the exposed-concrete floor slabs were inserted between the timber elements. The primary structure (columns and downstand beams) is of spruce.

For the facade, the architect chose untreated, especially wide spruce boards that are visibly screwed in place and overlap to create layers. The interior can be laid out flexibly thanks to lightweight, jute-covered partitions; all the other elements are made of oak.

# "MODERN ARCHITECTURE CONSUMES PLACES"

**How would you define your job as an architect?**

My main concern is to adopt a clear position on the world, to define an idea of how the world could be. As an architect, I have to deal with social, cultural, and even economic issues as a matter of course. Or at least that's how I describe architecture. I don't only need to have a good idea, I have to develop it in a way that others can derive pleasure from it. That's the only way to create something that has a value or meaning beyond that of a pure object. The architecture itself is purely the vessel.

**When you build a house, do you (as an architect) always change the cultural context?**

Yes, of course. The Vrin Mortuary is a good example of that. Before mortuaries existed, people died at home where their loved ones said goodbye to them. But nowadays people here in Vrin, like people all over the world, are trying to censor death, to hide it, because we feel it isn't supposed to be a part of life.

This idea of censoring is the reason we developed the building. We created a new place of mourning, because mourning is important for those left behind. Whether they want to ignore the notion of death or not.

**What role did the smallness of a village such as Vrin play in the project?**

When someone dies in a village, everyone is always somehow involved. However, I believe that smallness is relevant, and not only regarding how we deal with death and not only in a small village. That's how I see the project "Making Places," which we developed in the context of my professorship at ETH Zurich. The project focuses on the creation of small places. Because people are only ready and willing to take responsibility when places are, and remain, small enough. It's a dialog between science, politics, economics, architecture, and craft.

**Your work often deals with the relationship between the periphery and the supposedly stronger center. Is the concept of smallness something that the center could learn from the periphery?**

Not as a model, but the concept can easily be conveyed. We never intended to develop Vrin as a model, and I would also hope that architectural concepts cannot easily be transported to other fields. Our idea is far more about reinforcing differences by developing one's own potential. I think it's important to emphasize the character of a place. However, modern architecture tends to "consume" places nowadays, which is the exact opposite. You can do very little to stop this trend. Exploiting the power of a site for your own purpose is a legitimate approach, but there should be an equal concern for how the neighbors respond to the intervention.

**In the sixth of your nine theses about designing the cultural landscape, you write that, "Universal standards and mass-production are the greatest enemies of culture." Does this concur with what you just mentioned?**

The French sociologist, Henri Lefebvre, states in his concept of space, I believe, aptly, that a combination of both products and knowledge is necessary to develop spaces to live in; only then can meaning be produced. This triangle is very important to me. Nowadays, we are fed product after product, which is a system that doesn't produce knowledge; it only produces disputed spaces.

**How does this relate to your work in Vrin?**

My experience with production, for example with building in *Strickbau* (a method popular in Alpine regions of "knitting" together layers of wooden beams or logs), created first knowledge and then meaning. I can draw from the intensity of my experience with *Strickbau* when I work with other techniques or materials.

**Can you describe this intensity?**

When I was designing my first Vrin houses, I made some minor changes to the basic ground plan, because living habits have also changed. For instance, we made the hallway wider so it could also be used as a room. After a while, I realized that it is possible to think of *Strickbau* three-dimensionally. I can, as when I build with concrete, place walls wherever I want .... OK, they can't exceed a certain length or everything will fall apart. One of our newest *Strickbau* buildings is the house of Kübler and Beckel in Fürstenaubruck. We played a lot more with mass for this design. Few wooden constructions exude such a power and weight. We were thinking about Eduardo Chillida's sculptures, which give the impression that empty space is almost denser than mass. That fascinated me. We applied this principle to the design for the house and created a building that seemed not to need any walls at all.

**Was it obvious to you from the start that you would use the Strickbau technique?**

No, not in the least. Before I studied architecture, I trained as a carpenter, which is where I learned the technique of *Strickbau*. Later, as an architect, many colleagues said, "Forget that practice, it's old fashioned." For a while I made post and beam constructions, but it quickly became clear that that method didn't interest me, simply because I saw more potential in *Strickbau*. We then developed the Vrin typology further, and realized that *Strickbau* had its own typology and its own rules and principles. From that moment on, we believed we could use the *Strickbau* technique even on Paradeplatz in Zurich, which has absolutely nothing to do with Vrin.

**Strickbau or log cabins require a lot of wood. Do you think there is a danger of waste here?**

For one, the price of wood in the Vrin region is very low. Why should we only export the material cheaply, and not use it ourselves? Moreover, solid constructions also have the advantage of being naturally well insulated. And, it doesn't really require that much more material. We don't always build using the double *Strickbau* technique, as we used for the Vrin Mortuary. It's often a single shell with an interior constructed using a different material. The cost of material is relatively low compared with the cost of labor.

**What criteria do you use to select the materials for your buildings?**

For the "Making Places" project, I was concerned with emphasizing the effects of certain places. Everyone is moved by impressive and expressive places, and I believe repetition is important. Sometimes the structure emphasizes the effect of a room, sometimes the material—so, I obviously don't use wood as a raw material for everything. In Vrin, it's a clear choice because there's nothing else. Wood is abundantly available and people like it.

# NICK CAVE

**SOUNDSUIT**, 2010
DIFFERENT MATERIALS, BRANCHES FROM THE
DOGWOOD TREE (*CORNUS*)
DEPTH 55.9 × WIDTH 83.8 × HEIGHT 243 CM
COURTESY NICK CAVE AND JACK SHAINMAN
GALLERY, NEW YORK

The sculptural "Soundsuit" is part of a series that was inspired by African tribal rituals and Tibetan textiles. The costumes are made from sewn (not glued) wooden branches, pearls, buttons, sequins, real hair, feathers, and old spinning tops and are presented in exhibitions as well as used in the artist's dance performances.

# GEHARD DEMETZ

**YOUR MONSTERS ARE JUST LIKE MINE**, 2006
LIME-WOOD
DEPTH 35 × WIDTH 38 × HEIGHT 168.5 CM
COURTESY GALERIE BECK & EGGELING NEW
QUARTERS, DÜSSELDORF AND GALLERIA
RUBIN, MILAN

The works of Gehard Demetz are characterized by their highly precise workmanship. The figures are made using traditional woodworking techniques, and are assembled from small wooden pieces rather than cut from one block of wood. Their particular aesthetic appeal is the result of a combination of raw, open seams and cracks, and perfectly sanded, smooth areas.

**YOUR SWEAT IS SALTY**, 2005
LIME-WOOD
DEPTH 35 × WIDTH 38 × HEIGHT 172 CM
COURTESY GALERIE BECK & EGGELING NEW
QUARTERS, DÜSSELDORF AND GALLERIA
RUBIN, MILAN

**EVERYTHING HE LIED WAS TRUE**, 2006
LIME-WOOD
DEPTH 50 × WIDTH 37.5 × HEIGHT 166 CM
COURTESY GALERIE BECK & EGGELING NEW
QUARTERS, DÜSSELDORF AND GALLERIA
RUBIN, MILAN

**A SOFT DISTORTION**, 2008
LIME-WOOD
DEPTH 28 × WIDTH 31.5 × HEIGHT 162 CM
COURTESY GALERIE BECK & EGGELING NEW
QUARTERS, DÜSSELDORF AND GALLERIA
RUBIN, MILAN

# MARCO
# DESSÍ

**PRATER CHAIR**, 2009
BIRCH PLYWOOD SHEETS
WATERPROOF BLACK PHENOL RESIN BOND
DEPTH 45 × WIDTH 52 × HEIGHT 79 CM
MANUFACTURER: RICHARD LAMPERT

The stackable "Prater chair" is formally based on the famous Vienna coffee house chairs, but is constructed in an entirely different manner: the sections of the chair are made from birch plywood and grouted with black phenol resin glue, then processed with a CNC-milling machine at a very flat angle. This allows the glue between the individual layers of wood to remain visible and gives the chair its unique surface. The black phenol resin bond cannot be stained and hence does not take on color, which allows a strong contrast to emerge in the yellow stained models, and the black stained chairs to assume an almost brocade textile-like effect.

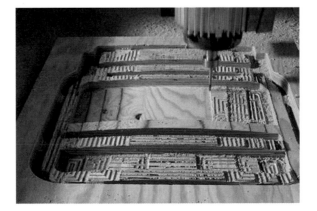

# STEFAN DIEZ

**HOUDINI**, 2009
PLYWOOD CHAIR
OAK-VENEERED PLYWOOD
(VARIATIONS: CLEAR VARNISH, JET BLACK, SIGNAL WHITE,
TRAFFIC GRAY)
DEPTH 50 × WIDTH 57.5 × HEIGHT 80 CM
(WITH ARMS: DEPTH 57 × WIDTH 53 × HEIGHT 78 CM)
MANUFACTURER: E15

A model airplane building technique was used to produce this chair.
The two-dimensional plywood panels used for the seat and the
back were pulled by hand around a milled solid wood ring. All of the
joints are glued and reinforced with wood dowels at only a few points.

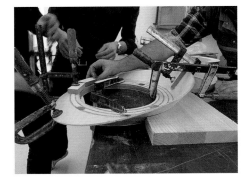

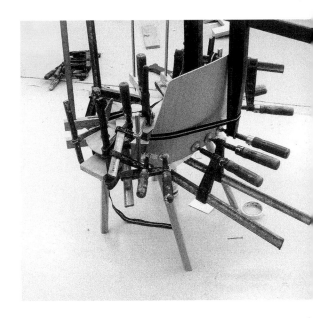

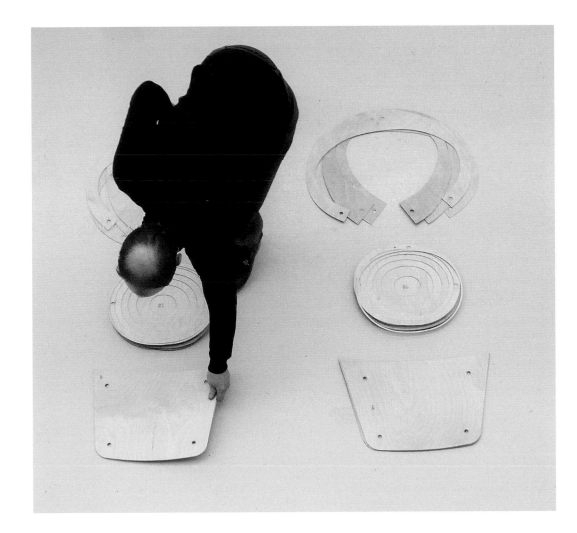

*STEFAN*
*DIEZ*

**THONET 404**, 2007
BENTWOOD CHAIR
BEECH PLYWOOD
CHAIR: DEPTH 51 × WIDTH 49 × HEIGHT 78 CM
MANUFACTURER: THONET

**THONET 404 H**, 2009
BAR STOOL
BEECH PLYWOOD
BAR STOOL: DEPTH 46 × WIDTH 46 × HEIGHT 77 CM
MANUFACTURER: THONET

"Thonet 404" is an aesthetic and technological interpretation of the classic bentwood chair. The curved chair legs and arms merge together to form a type of knot, and are inserted from below into the ergonomically formed seat. Seat and back elements consist of molded plywood, the leg and back struts of glulam.

# "A CHAIR IS NOT A SPACE SHIP"

*You trained to be a carpenter before studying industrial design. Is that why you prefer wood as a material?*
We worked with many different materials besides wood when I was learning carpentry, and I also later worked at a mechanical engineering company. But my relationship to wood and my experience of it as a material began long ago in my parents' carpentry workshop. It is a very agreeable material. It can be sanded, glued, bent, cut. It has excellent structural properties. It is both light and stable. It grows again and again and is readily available; but furthermore, the process from tree to a piece of furniture is something very modern in my opinion.

*How do you choose a material for your designs?*
It depends on the manufacturer, on the brief. If you are designing a chair for Wilkhahn, for example, it has to be able to be produced in large numbers in a short period of time. Moreover, as a special-purpose chair, it has to fulfill very different criteria. It also depends on how much money can be invested in a product. For instance, most of the work that goes into industrial products is done before the actual production phase begins, so for the most part a tool or a machine has to be developed and built. In contrast, an e15 chair can be constructed by a skilled craftsman who builds one an hour. In this case most of the budget goes on the craftsman and not on manufacturing a tool.

*If one has a background in craftsmanship, as you do, and uses wood as a material for a mass-produced product, what difficulties can arise?*
The fact is, very little mass-produced furniture is made of wood. The only companies that come to mind right now are Thonet, who actually manufactured tools, and of course Fritz Becker KG. Most products made from wood are prefabricated constructions, but are still very craft based although they're produced in large numbers.

*Despite CNC technology and new wood materials?*
CNC technology is more like a rapid prototyping process. The wood doesn't grow into the desired form, it has to be cut. And regarding wood materials: we regularly deal with WPC (wood plastic composite). But this material is still work intensive and time consuming when it comes to tool manufacturing—moreover, the material is nowhere near as stable as plastic. You also have to consider that you are "only" dealing with a chair, or a table, or a shelf, which doesn't require an entire arsenal of high technology, because it wouldn't be worth the effort. A chair is not a spaceship. We're interested mainly in the potential changes regarding typology, perception, or quality that go along with developing a new material. Using a new technique just for the sake of it is not our objective.

*Typology is a good catchword here: the "Houdini" chair is formally very different from the other products usually associated with e15.*
Being able to work with such a bold and reduced vocabulary was a stroke of luck—the furniture all looks like it was designed by an architect, which is mainly the case anyway. So we were able to design the exact opposite: the "Houdinis" are formally complex and lightweight.

*But doesn't that pose a slight risk for a company, if a design diverges completely from the norm?*
No, because in essence that's exactly what you want: a new product that makes a bold break from the norm. It's much more difficult to tolerate tactics if creative freedom becomes more and more restricted. It's easier to make a radical change and go forward. We never questioned the typical design style at e15, we simply added something new. This occurred to us while browsing through the e15 catalog. The lightweights were all there: the Eames, the Saarinen, the Wegner. So it didn't make sense to me to design a chair that looked like a baby elephant.

*Did e15's competency in wood play a role in developing the Houdini?*
No, because the problem of joining the different sections of the back of the chair was new to e15: almost all of the suppliers said that our design would be impossible to build. We didn't want to glue layers or produce complex tools—and not just because of cost issues. I wasn't that keen on a solution involving 3D wood, an idea that some suppliers suggested. I'm not really a friend of 3D wood because it is too removed from the natural material. If that's the case, then I'd rather have plastic.

*How did you arrive at a solution?*
By trial and error. We built many prototypes and found out that a material thickness of 4 millimeters was the best. If we were to increase this to 5 millimeters it would break if it were bent in a narrow radius. If we decreased it, it would be too unstable. The direction of the grain of sliced veneer is also important. At the beginning the chairs broke if they fell over. We were able to solve this problem by using plywood reinforced with fiberglass, which we manufactured ourselves. This is basically the material masons use to make crack-resistant walls. It's used whenever there is a risk of too much tensile stress.

*How big is the difference between the last prototype and the final chair?*
There is not a very big difference at all. But we needed a lot of models before we arrived at the correct details and proportions.

*What do you think the biggest difference is between that and the 404 chair for Thonet?*
The work involved in building the tools for the Thonet chair is much more time-consuming and complex. We have individual components that are constructed by using templates and that can be assembled with relative ease.

*How is the seat of the Thonet chair constructed?*
Sliced veneer is produced by gluing numerous layers of veneer together. These are then layered by hand and put through a press. You can design the layers so that they decrease in size as they build up. The uppermost layer would have the full thickness again. This allows for different material strengths or thickness within the component—the seat is approximately 4 centimeters thick at the center and only 5 millimeters at the edge, obviously much thinner. The seat is a kind of saddle that is thick enough underneath and in the middle to attach the legs to it.

# DOSHI LEVIEN

**IMPOSSIBLE WOOD**, 2011
OUTDOOR CHAIR
SEAT SHELL MADE OF WPC (WOOD PLASTIC COMPOSITE)
DEPTH 45 × WIDTH 65 × HEIGHT 75 CM
MANUFACTURER: MOROSO

The seat of the chair is made from WPC (Wood Plastic Composite), which consists of 80 percent wood fibers and 20 percent polypropylene, and was produced using a standard injection molding technique. The stripes of the chair are reminiscent of the installation *Cedar Lodge* (1977) by Afro-American sculptor Martin Puryear, in which parallel, overlapping strips of red cedar and pine are held together, reminiscent of a barrel, by horizontal rings.

# DUTCH INVERTUALS

**MATTER OF TIME**, 2010
EINDHOVEN, THE NETHERLANDS
EXHIBITION OF DESIGN OBJECTS MADE FROM
600-YEAR-OLD OAK
INITIATED AND CURATED BY WENDY PLOMP,
SPONSORED BY THE EINDHOVEN
ARCHAEOLOGY CENTRE AND THE CITY OF
EINDHOVEN

TOP RIGHT AND LEFT:
EXHIBITION OBJECT BY RAW COLOR

BOTTOM RIGHT:
EXHIBITION OBJECT BY JULIEN CARRETERO

BOTTOM LEFT:
EXCAVATION

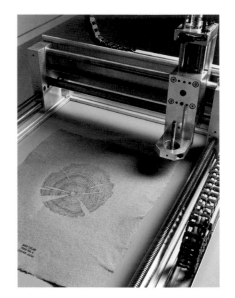

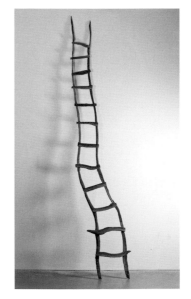

Modern objects were created from the 600-year-old oak from the ancient city wall of Eindhoven, discovered during an archeological excavation. The exciting conceptual and aesthetic aspect here is the modern processing of a historical material by young designers and artists.

# PIET HEIN EEK

**FAIR TRADE ORIGINAL**, 2009
PALM WOOD
HIGH BASKET: Ø 37 CM, HEIGHT 47 CM
MANUFACTURER: FAIR TRADE ORIGINAL

The collection of different sized baskets is made from palm wood and in accordance with Fair Trade principles. They were produced in collaboration with Vietnamese artisans using traditional production techniques. Working with various small pieces of wood reduces the possibility of cracks developing, which is typical of the fast-growing palm wood.

# LAETITIA FLORIN

*ECAL*

**PLASTIC SURGERY,** 2010
FIVE-PART SERIES OF BOXES
SOLID MAPLE, FOREX® DISKS
DEPTH × WIDTH × HEIGHT: 20 × 20 × 25 CM, 25 × 25 × 17 CM,
30 × 30 × 11 CM, 37 × 37 × 7.5 CM, 40 × 40 × 5 CM
PROTOTYPES, PRODUCED WITHIN THE FRAMEWORK OF
A WORKSHOP AT THE ÉCOLE CANTONALE D'ART DE
LAUSANNE (ECAL)

The metaphorical name of the series "Plastic Surgery" refers to the unique way in which the individual boxes are assembled: the solid wood components are joined by means of plastic disks. The remaining, projecting ends of the disks are capped and sanded along with the rest of the piece.

# TERUNOBU FUJIMORI

**YAKISUGI HOUSE (CHARRED CEDAR HOUSE)**, 2007
NAGANO, JAPAN
DWELLING HOUSE
FACADE CLADDING OF 400 CHARRED CEDAR
BOARDS, EACH 7.6 M LONG
FOOTPRINT 167 M²

To protect this house made of cedar, from the elements, the traditional process of charring was used. By briefly setting the surface of the wood on fire and then extinguishing the fire with water, a waterproof charcoal layer is produced. This charring process also releases tar-like substances within the wood which prevent the development of mold.

**CONRAN INSPIRATIONS,** 2008
CHAIRS MADE FROM BENTWOOD PARTS
BACK OF THE CHAIRS: DEPTH 48 × WIDTH 45 × HEIGHT 68 CM
CHAIR OF THE RINGS: DEPTH 50 × WIDTH 53 × HEIGHT 130 CM
MANUFACTURER: CONRAN SHOP

The chair series pays homage to the classic bentwood chair by Thonet.
Martino Gamper used about one hundred individual components—
seating surfaces, chair legs, arms, or backs—all from the Croatian
Mundus factory, to assemble new furniture, and in so doing, created
an individual interpretation of the classic original.

# LIAM GILLICK

POURQUOI TRAVAILLER?, 2012
15 HAND-CARVED OAK BOARDS, OIL PAINT
WIDTH 39.5 × HEIGHT 59 CM
EACH BOARD IS LIMITED TO 4 COPIES,
1 ARTIST'S PROOF, AND 1 "HORS COMMERCE"
COURTESY THREE STAR BOOKS, PARIS

The edition of wood panels is part of Liam Gillick's book project "Pourquoi Travailler" (Why work?). The artist selected fifteen motifs from previous publications for the oak panels of this "sculptural" edition. He was then able to commission six, hand-carved positives—as opposed to printing techniques, in which the printing plates show a reversed image. This reversal means that the final images are already created by means of carving and application of paint. At the same time, this approach also answers the titular question, "Why (keep) working?"

# GLASS HILL

**ICA**, 2010
BENCH
YELLOW PINE, BIRCH, PINE
LENGTH 4 M
OWN PRODUCTION

The surfaces of the benches were designed for a charity event at the Institute of Contemporary Arts (ICA) in London and are made from yellow pine, the material that is also often used to make parquet flooring. Legs made from pine are screwed into the underside of the attached blocks of solid birch. These can be removed if necessary. The entire bench is treated with an organically produced hard wax oil.

**GLASS HILL & DAVID DAVID CHAIR**, 2011
CHAIR
HORNBEAM
DEPTH 36 × WIDTH 32 × HEIGHT 76 CM
LIMITED EDITION OF 25 EXAMPLES

This chair is the first result of the collaboration between Glass Hill and the fashion label David David. The geometrical pattern on the seat and back were drawn by hand using colored pencils. Glass Hill originally designed the chair in 2010 in ponderosa pine—also in an edition of twenty-five examples—for the salesroom of the London auction house Phillips De Pury & Co in the Saatchi Gallery.

# GRAFT

This loft is characterized by the great diversity of materials used. The surfaces of the furniture are of walnut, lacquered MDF, stainless steel, strips of slate, tiles, leather, and textiles. The wall covering is of Bark Cloth®, a bast fiber material that was widely used for clothing in various areas of Africa into the nineteenth century, particularly before the mass import of cotton fabrics.

The ceiling in this restaurant is clad with precisely milled, curved battens made of padouk, which comes from the Pterocarpus tree, different kinds of which are found in Africa, Southeast Asia, and America. By working in collaboration with the services engineers, the air vents could be fitted precisely in the joints between the battens.

# "WOOD, DIGITAL"

*In relation to other materials, what role does wood play for you in general as a material? Do you work with wood because it's the wish of a client or because of the region?*

Basically, we want to abandon the Bauhaus classical canon of steel-glass-concrete and so on. We're working on developing a narrative architectural language, a scenographic narration that we intensify atmospherically through certain materials. There are various ways in which architects can tweak visual and perceptive routines in order to make their conceptual idea clear. Wood has structural properties that can be compared to the qualities of integrated material systems. For the last few years, wood has played a role in most of our experiments in form. It can be used to make sure that a formal or conceptual idea remains accessible.

*What do you mean by accessible?*

Wood makes both the experienced professional and the layman feel good and comfortable. Moreover, people are drawn to touching it more than other materials, because it has the great advantage of a natural surface finish.

*In your opinion, what are wood's disadvantages?*

For the most part, using it outdoors. We've only ever used wood in other climate regions, such as that in Las Vegas, which has a different drying cycle. At the moment we're experimenting with bamboo structures in South Africa and Ethiopia, where we are planning a clinic in Addis Ababa. But we're just at the beginning because, first of all, there is no bamboo available in Ethiopia. We're considering setting up a bamboo farm, but before bamboo can be used, it has to be chemically treated for up to half a year before being harvested, to guarantee it against decay. It's a relatively uncomplicated process, but is time-consuming.

*But climatic or geographic situations do play a large role in your work, don't they?*

Yes, we're always on the look out for local wood sources, but of course we're also concerned with finding unique or surprising types of wood or techniques. For instance, we used padouk, which has a striking reddish orange color, for Fix Restaurant in Las Vegas. At first you think the wood is painted, but it's not, it is the natural color of the material. For structural reasons, we used veneer rather than solid wood. Padouk is not really a hardwood, but its color has made it very popular and scarce.

In another situation, we wanted to build a bathroom completely out of charcoal, but the client decided against it. That would have been a strong metaphorical image: a large black room made of wood that calls to mind a burnt tree trunk on the beach.

*How important are digital tools to your design process?*

We went to the States at the end of the 1990s, partly for this reason. We wanted to learn how to progress directly from two-dimensional plans to production.

*Which three-dimensional processes is wood best suited for?*

It is very good for sectioning, forming, and contouring. Sectioning is basically the division of a three-dimensional form into cut layers. This is an essential part of the formal process, because wood is mainly manufactured in panel form—which serves a construction industry that unfortunately works entirely with two-dimensional board production. Forming is a process used to produce organic shapes. Here we try to work more with wood because the most complex forms can be produced in a relatively sustainable manner. Wood is always good for contouring. Most students begin with the subtraction woodworking technique, which creates forms by gradually removing wood from a larger mass.

*The subject of wood is always directly related to that of joinery. What role does wood joinery play for you?*

That depends on whether you see it from the formal or the technological aspect. Visible joints don't play much of a role in our work at the moment. As far as form is concerned, we are more interested in an optimal flow of surface, the overcoming of—or let's say the overriding of—classic curves. However, technologically, we're very interested in joints, especially regarding efficiency. For our projects in the USA, we often work with classical wooden structures, and here optimal efficiency in the sense of optimal sustainability plays a vital role.

With our non-profit reconstruction project for New Orleans, for instance, we developed and patented a special metal nail that has a large saving potential.

*What is special about the nail?*

The nail has a unique ribbing around the shaft, which means it can be driven to a certain depth and the head of the nail can be sunk to an optimal level. Because of this, it requires less corrective work than traditional nails, which makes it thirty percent more efficient.

*And this nail was developed specifically for the New Orleans project?*

In our Make It Right Foundation, we have an autonomous department called "Construction" that focuses specifically on optimization and preproduction processes. In addition to the nail, we also developed a wall module made of plasterboard insulated with wood, which we're using to build housing in New Orleans, and also further afield for American Indians and military veterans. These are classic minority groups in the States, who of course have needs and standards, but who can barely afford a product such as a home with the little money available to them.

*Can you say something about the Hamburg Loft, where you used Bark Cloth?*

For that project, it was important to us to use wood as a material in a way not typically associated with its usual characteristics and applications. The Bark Cloth "lines" the architectural body like a skin or leather. It also has a particular haptic quality and looks very soft. In contrast to pure cut veneer, Bark Cloth is reminiscent of the warmth and the gleam of Japanese mulberry paper.

# GRAMAZIO & KOHLER

**SUPERWOOD**, 2009
DIGITAL CARVINGS IN THE DINING AREA OF
THE NEW MONTE ROSA HUT, SAC, ZERMATT,
SWITZERLAND
CLIENT: ETH ZURICH AND SWISS ALPINE
CLUB (SAC)

In this interior the woodcarving work traditionally used to decorate the insides of mountain huts was reinterpreted using digital design and fabrication methods and directly applied to the structure. The carvings follow the lines of the architectural elements in the dining area and at the same time extend as a design element throughout the entire floor. Like force fields, the lines are drawn across the ceiling and the structural elements, break at the edges and thus flow through the entire space.

*GRAMAZIO &*
*KOHLER*

**DWELLING HOUSE**, 2009
RIEDIKON, SWITZERLAND
SPRUCE
FOOTPRINT: 134 M²

The continuous cladding of the pentagonal house consists of a total of 315 vertical timber battens, their narrow sides fixed vertically to the wall surface. They not only refer to the facade structure of the nearby stables but the specially milled battens also provide shade from the sun and visual privacy. The CAD data for the timber cladding were translated, using a specially developed software program, into the code for the CNC mill (file-to-factory production process).

# KONSTANTIN GRCIC

**43**, 2008
CHAIR OF BAMBOO
DEPTH 55 × WIDTH 53 × HEIGHT 77 CM
BAMBOO ARTISAN: KAO-MING CHEN
INITIATED BY YII, A COLLABORATIVE PROJECT
OF NTCRI (NATIONAL TAIWAN CRAFTS
RESEARCH INSTITUTE) AND TDC (TAIWAN
DESIGN CENTER)
MANUFACTURER: SKITSCH

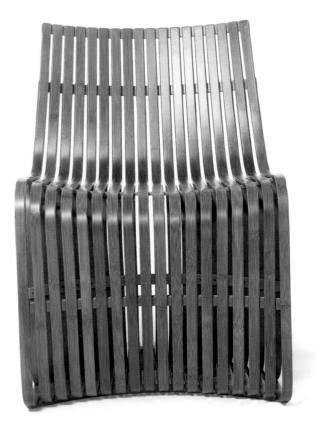

The name of the cantilever chair refers to the forty-three bamboo lathes from which it is produced. The chair was made within the framework of the "Yii" workshop and combines traditional Taiwanese craft methods with contemporary design.

**CHAIR_B**, 2010
FOLDING WOODEN CHAIR
ASH (LEGS, BACK), ASH PLYWOOD VENEER
(SEAT), LAMINATE OR ALUMINUM
(UNDERSIDE OF SEAT)
DEPTH 48 × WIDTH 56 × HEIGHT 77 CM
MANUFACTURER: BD BARCELONA

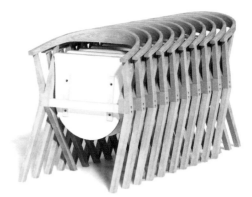

The X-shaped legs of the chair are characteristic of this
particular design; they and the back of the chair are both
made from solid ash. The ash plywood seat surface folds,
meaning the chair can be stacked.

**MEDICI**, 2012
LOW CHAIR
OUTDOOR VERSION OF THERMO-TREATED ASH
INDOOR VERSION OF AMERICAN WALNUT (BLACK WALNUT),
DOUGLAS FIR (NATURAL, STAINED YELLOW OR GRAY)
DEPTH 73.3 × WIDTH 68.4 × HEIGHT 81.8 CM
MANUFACTURER: MATTIAZZI

Medici phenomenologically follows two self-imposed guide-lines of the designer. Firstly, the chair was only to consist of wooden boards, as these constitute for Konstantin Grcic the archetypal, typological shape of the timber. Secondly, there were to be no flush connections between the individual boards, because they are contrary to the natural process of wood shrinkage.

The wood used comes primarily from the Udine region of Italy, the main headquarters of the manufacturing firm, Mattiazzi. It is processed on site using the latest CNC technology and without chemical treatment.

**MONZA CHAIR**, 2010
STACKABLE WOODEN CHAIR
ASH, POLYPROPYLENE (BACK)
DEPTH 47 × WIDTH 53 × HEIGHT 76 CM
MANUFACTURER: PLANK

The ash frame is either coated in a clear varnish or stained black. The back of the chair is made from reinforced polypropylene and is available in black, gray white, traffic red, wine red, light blue, and yellow green.

# "SOMETIMES WOOD RESTRICTS ME"

*You once said that you believed wood
to have more future potential than other
materials. Why?*
There are still many arguments in favor of
wood. It has a good temperature and a good
sound. It is relatively lightweight, and it becomes increasingly beautiful as it ages, which
is particularly important to me. The plastics
industry has a massive problem, because it
still cannot produce a material that ages well.
Wood is an old material, but I think it's very
contemporary for different reasons. It is more
appropriate for the furniture industry, as far
as cost and performance are concerned, compared with other materials. Wood is amaz-
ingly versatile and, regarding construction,
has the just the right level of stability, which is
another aspect I like. Steel tubes for instance
are too stable.

*What do you mean by "wood is
appropriate"?*
With furniture, I think it is good to know when
you've reached a limit. The construction is alive
in the Thonet chair, it is still working, sometimes the screws might loosen a bit, but somehow it all still functions well. I am a qualified
furniture restorer, and when you are restoring
a piece of furniture you quickly realize that
quality old furniture was built very intelligent-
ly, that it is constructed so rationally and is
reduced to only that which is absolutely necessary, and that the material will last. Another
example is a project we are working on at
the moment for Herzog & de Meuron, a design
for a museum on Long Island. The furniture
we are building for the project is made exclusively from very old wood, called "reclaimed
wood," which was taken from old barns. This
means that the wood is reclaimed by the
production process—which again is possible
with this material.

*Does appropriate also mean that some
designs must be made from wood and no
other material, for example in your project
"Missing Object" for Galerie Kreo?*
Yes, "Missing Object" was about the original,
elementary material, about the weight of
volume, the solidity. I could not even imagine
a different material for that object—maybe
marble, but then the edges would have been
too vulnerable. And, the user would approach
the object very differently. It was clear to
me from the beginning that it had to be made
of wood. It is bonded wood, not carved from
a solid piece of wood as a sculptor might
do. The entire object plays with ideas involving
proportion, sound, and volume. It is also a
type of solidity study.

*What role does craft play for you as a
designer?*
Craft plays a very important role for me per-
sonally, because I come from the craft side of
things. Carpentry in particular taught me a
lot about construction, design, and basically
furniture. But I very consciously abandoned
craft, because I was simply more interested in
the planning and the design of furniture, as
well as in different materials.

*What do you think are the greatest differ-
ences between wood and other materials?*
Quality standards are still not yet established
for woodworking, which means it's much
more difficult to define them than it is for other
materials. Wood is always associated with
a type of romanticism; but you have to be
able to forget that sometimes. I'm still amazed
at how difficult it is to do certain things, despite new technologies and machines, For
instance, with the "Monza" chair for Plank,
we reduced the wood part of the chair to an
absolute minimum. Nonetheless, it took a
long time to find a manufacturer that met
our expectations of price and quality. We first
had to point out to the manufacturer that
someone had to sort the legs, so that the legs
of a particular chair would have the same
wood grain. You have to deal with issues that
would not even come up if you were using a
different material. In addition, wood works, it
shrinks. Structural and even required joints in
the joint details have to be minimized by choosing the right kind of wood. Unless you want
to go for a '70s chair aesthetic, which developed a true "joint language."

*You designed a chair made from bamboo
in 2008. What are the most important
differences between working with wood
and working with wood-related or other
materials?*
The bamboo chair was created for a project
initiated by the Taiwan Design Center and
Taiwanese craftsmen. Taiwan is one of the
regions in the world that grows bamboo, and
that also has a longstanding tradition of
working with the material. It was a very interesting experience for me, because I had the
feeling that I did not really understand the
material, even though it is related to wood

in certain aspects. This made bamboo seem
like a type of counterpart to wood, a material
about which I have a lot of knowledge, but
I realized that precisely this knowledge hinders
me in my work sometimes, and takes an
element of freedom away.
    Because bamboo grows so quickly, it has
very long fibers, which makes it extremely
elastic and stable. It was perfect for an experiment, and we designed a cantilever chair.
However, to work with the material at a higher
standard of quality than is normally done in
the industry, meaning to shred the material
and then use this to produce boards, you
have to be experienced and knowledgeable
about the material. There are nevertheless
very beautiful examples of bamboo furniture,
such as designs by Charlotte Perriand, who
worked with bamboo while she was in Japan.

*How did you process the dimensioning of
the individual battens of the chair?*
We had test pieces and sent the translator a
list of questions that the craftsman answered.
These dealt with the climatic vulnerability of
the battens, their load-bearing ability, and so
on. We could not send any three-dimensional
data, so we broke down the construction of
the chair into single battens and reduced it to
a two-dimensional drawing. This was then
used by a craftsman to build a template on
a board of nails and then bending the lathes.
Actually, it was a very typical design process:
to realize a design within certain parameters
or guidelines.

*Would you like to work with bamboo
again, based on this more experimental
experience?*
Absolutely. I would especially be interested in
how you could industrially manufacture bamboo while still being responsible to the material. Because the complicated method of
industrially manufacturing the boards takes
you farther and farther away from the original material, the bamboo tube. There are
a few architectural projects now, which unfortunately use synthetic resin and other environmentally unsound bonds. I prefer joints
that are typical of the bamboo furniture made
by artisans. They are more honest, because
the tubes are visible and joined using a traditional method. For instance, there is a lot
to learn from Asian scaffolding builders, especially about how to work with the characteristics and tolerances inherent in the material.

# GUALLART ARCHITECTS

**VINARÒS MICROCOASTS**, 2007
VINARÒS, SPAIN
PERMANENT INSTALLATION ON THE
MEDITERRANEAN COAST BETWEEN
BARCELONA AND VALENCIA
STRUCTURE AND FLOOR COVERING MADE
FROM IPÉ WOOD (IRONWOOD)
EACH ELEMENT: 4.40 × 3.80 M, LENGTH OF THE
INSTALLATION: CA. 1 KM
IN COLLABORATION WITH MARTA MALÉ
ALEMANY

The architectural installation entitled "Microcoasts"
stretched along approximately one kilometer of the south
coast of the Mediterranean city Vinaròs. The hexagonal
wooden platforms form artificial islands that are sometimes flat and sometimes pyramid-shaped and extend
over cliffs and large stones.

# MAX AND HANNES GUMPP

**LATHES**, 2008
STACKABLE CHAIRS
HDF PINE, MDF (COLORFUL SEAT SURFACES
IN MDF AND FORMICA® SYNTHETIC
LAMINATE)
SURFACE TREATMENT: UNTREATED PINE,
FINISHED AND SANDED
DEPTH 45 × WIDTH 45 × HEIGHT 80 CM,
WEIGHT: 3 KG
MANUFACTURER: ABR

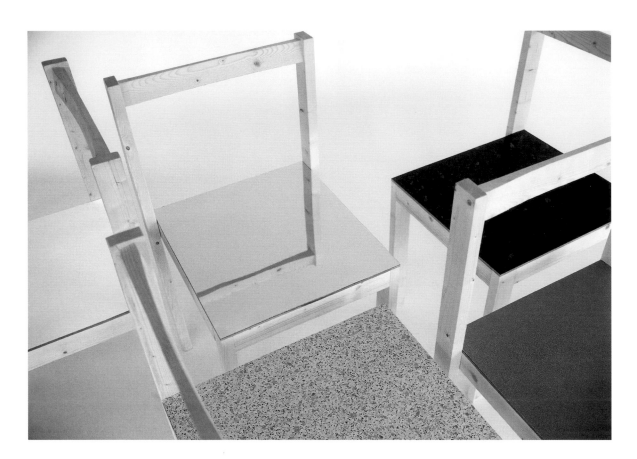

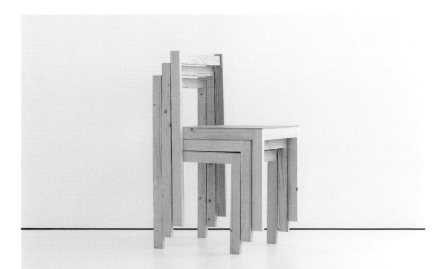

The 24 × 48 millimeter lathes that make up the chair are cut exclusively at right angles. The license agreement with ABR allows the chairs to be produced in different regions using lathes made from the best possible, locally available wood. This means there are inevitable variations of the stackable chair regarding color, surface structure, and material composites for the high-density fiberboards (HDF).

# FLORIAN HAUSWIRTH

**DOUBLEFACE AND DOUBLEFACETTE**, 2009
VASE AND FRUIT BOWL, AND SALT AND PEPPER MILLS
CHERRYWOOD AND CERAMIC
VASE: Ø 9 CM, HEIGHT 27 CM
BOWL: Ø 24.5 CM, HEIGHT 10.5 CM
PEPPER MILL: Ø 7 CM, HEIGHT 10 CM
SALT MILL: Ø 5 CM, HEIGHT 9.8 CM
PROTOTYPES (SOME ALREADY IN PRODUCTION)

With "doubleface" and "doublefacette," the functional areas are defined according to materiality and form, whereby the forms complement one another. The underside of the fruit bowl can also be used as a cutting board and the lower section of the ceramic vase can be filled with water.

**JUST WOOD CHAIR** (JWC) 2, 2010
STACKABLE WOODEN CHAIR
ASH
DEPTH 59 × WIDTH 55 × HEIGHT 79 CM
TECHNICAL IMPLEMENTATION OF THE PROTOTYPES IN
COLLABORATION WITH SEBASTIAN KRAFT (BFH-AHB, BERN
UNIVERSITY OF APPLIED SCIENCES—ARCHITECTURE, WOOD
AND CIVIL ENGINEERING)

All of the chair's components are joined using a technique known as friction welding, which bores wood dowels, at a certain speed of revolutions into predrilled holes. The heat created by the friction releases the wood's natural lignin and hemicellulose and bonds them to create a stable joint without the need for glue or screws.

MINIMAL WOOD CHAIR
(MWC) (FROM THE "FHNY" COLLECTION), 2010
CHAIR WITH ADJUSTABLE BACK
ASH, SOLID
DEPTH 58 × WIDTH 50 × HEIGHT 88 CM
PROTOTYPE

The unique aspect of this chair is its adjustable back, which features
a joint entirely constructed from glued pieces of wood. It is a technique that refers to the "Minimal Chair," a unique experimental piece
created in 1948 by Charles and Ray Eames exhibiting the high quality
of Shaker workmanship.

# "THE DOWEL PASSED THE REFRIGERATION TEST WITH FLYING COLORS"

*Your "Just Wood Chair" (JWC)—as the name suggests—is made purely of wood, even the joints. Why do you find wood an exciting material?*
I think it is primarily because of my general affinity for natural materials and secondly due to my training as a technical model builder. I worked in that profession for several years, most recently for three years at Vitra, the furniture company in Birsfelden. I built numerous demonstration and functional chair models there and of course worked extensively with wood. Later, while I was studying, I did a lot of material research for Vitra, in which wood played an important role again. Collaborating with Sebastian Kraft, the wood engineer at the woodworking technical school here in Biel, where I live and work, is another important reason why I started working in wood.

*How did you start developing the "Just Wood Chair"?*
I always wanted to make a chair, but I waited a long time because I knew from working at Vitra that designing and building a chair required a lot of knowledge. Moreover, it was an exciting challenge to develop a chair made exclusively of wood and wooden joints, without glue or screws.

*You arrived rather quickly at friction- or dowel welding. Can you explain how that works?*
The technique of friction welding is not particularly new, especially in plastics. The friction creates heat that melts the material; after it cools, the material is just as stable as it was in its original form. What is relatively new, however, is the knowledge that this technology can also be applied to wood joints. The frictional warmth releases lignin and hemicellulose, which in a matter of seconds creates a fabric-like welded connection (the wood's own binding agents melt together again). The woodworking technical school in Biel, Switzerland and the one in Nancy, France have been doing research in this area for some time. But it has yet to make its way into practice.

*What is the difficulty of this technique?*
First of all it is crucial that the wooden dowels are screwed into the hole at the right speed. If the speed is too slow, the bonding will not occur, but if it is too fast, the wood will not only burn but also it won't bond. You also have to make sure that the thickness of the dowels corresponds as well as possible to the size of the holes to ensure a good bond. Moreover, you have to be careful to increase the effort or number of revolutions with the size. The dowel has to be strong enough not to break.

*Do you use normal wooden dowels?*
At the beginning, we worked with a standard dowel made of beech. Beech is used a lot for chairs, but the way it behaves when it comes into contact with moisture makes it unsuitable for this technique. A chair has to remain stable in different climate conditions (temperature, moisture). The chair simply has to function well regardless of climatic conditions. So, I later commissioned a woodturner to make dowels out of ash wood and maple. Acorn is the best wood for welded joints.

*But it is possible to use different woods for the dowels?*
Yes, although it would have to be a hardwood. A softwood, for instance pine, would not create enough friction.

*Can you tell us something about the development of the form of the chair? Did the technology lead to any restrictions?*
I first started developing a much larger chair with strong overlaps. This was due to structural and static concerns, because you have to think about the direction of the wood's grain when you are dowel welding. Only very limited angles can be realized. The joint construction functions like that of a half-timbered construction.

However, the chair reflects the character of the technique, a formal aspect that I have always liked. The second version of the JWC no longer has the massive cover structure, the forms interweave more; and except for the fact that it can be stacked, it looks very different formally. It appears much lighter and more delicate.

*Could you imagine mass-producing the chair?*
Yes, I could. I'm already pretty far along with the prototype. The assessment performed by the woodworking technical school makes a piece of furniture very feasible. Stability is not a problem and the dowel passed the refrigeration test with flying colors.

# STUART HAYGARTH

**FRAMED,** 2010
INSTALLATION AT THE VICTORIA & ALBERT
MUSEUM, LONDON
WOODEN FRAME: CA. 600 M IN LENGTH
IN COLLABORATION WITH FRAMER JOHN
JONES, LONDON

For a temporary installation for the London Design Festival in 2010,
the marble stairs at the London Victoria & Albert Museum were clad
and framed in 600 meter long, zigzag profiles. The profiles were cut,
mitered, assembled, and sanded before being decoratively painted
and adorned in gold leaf.

# HEIDE UND VON BECKERATH ARCHITEKTEN

The building consists of a timber-frame construction with a back venti-lated, tongue and groove formwork spruce facade. Four large windows, two in the pitched roof, two in the long side walls, can be closed by wooden sliding doors that have vertical light slits. The entire facade is painted in an anthracite gray Falun wash. The floors of the bedrooms and the rooms on the upper level as well as the kitchen and bathroom are of oak.

# STAFFAN HOLM

**SPIN**, 2011
(FROM THE "MILANO" FURNITURE COLLECTION)
STACKABLE STOOLS
ASH VENEER
Ø 32 CM, HEIGHT 44 CM, WEIGHT: CA.1 KG
MANUFACTURER: SWEDESE

The design of the stool is based on Alvar Aalto's classic design from the 1930s. The legs of the laminated ash stool were bent in two directions, which is a highly complex process requiring skilled workmanship. The spiral-shaped stool is part of the 2010 "Milano" collection that was presented at the Milan Furniture Fair in 2010.

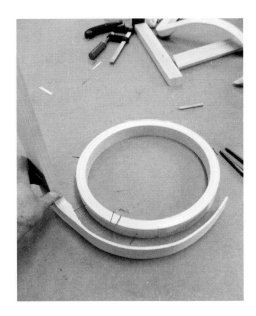
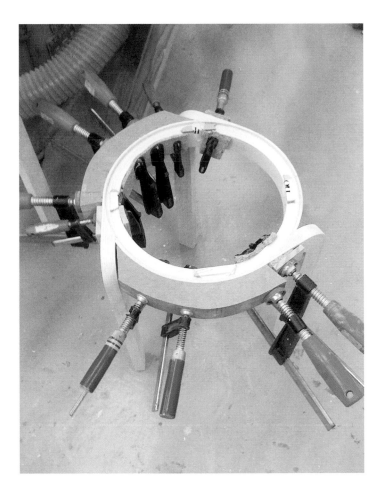
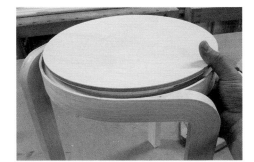

# BENJAMIN HUBERT

**FLOAT**, 2009
LAMP COLLECTION
OAK CORK
Ø 25/40/60 CM, HEIGHT 20/30/40 CM
MANUFACTURER: BENJAMIN HUBERT STUDIO

The shades of the lamps were produced by hand from residual cork from the production of wine bottle corks. The cork is pressed to form blocks and then processed using a traditional lathe process. The slivers left over from this process can be used in turn to produce new blocks of cork.

# ENRIQUE ILLÁNEZ SCHOENENBERGER

*ECAL*

**BRIGITTE**, 2010
OUTDOOR FURNITURE
SPRUCE SHINGLES SEWN
DEPTH 2.20 × WIDTH 1.60 × HEIGHT 1.90 M
PROTOTYPE

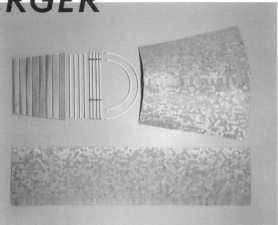

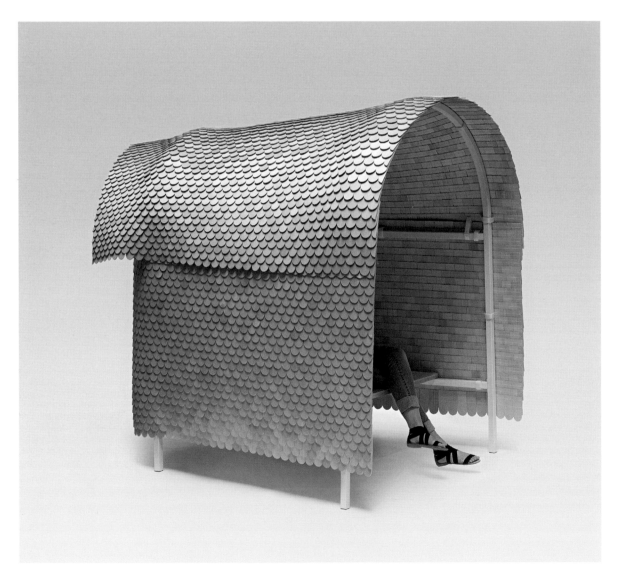

This shelter made of small spruce shingles sewn together is a private space to withdraw to that can be used outdoors. "Brigitte" uses a technique, traditionally employed in Alpine countries, in particular, of covering the facades and roofs of houses with several overlapping layers of wooden shingles. This metal-framed refuge is given structural stability by a bench inside that braces it.

# INCHFURNITURE

**SEPULUH**, 2008
SIDEBOARD
SOLID TEAK, OILED
DEPTH 48 × WIDTH 193 × HEIGHT 61 CM
PRODUCED BY THE TECHNICAL SCHOOL OF WOODWORKING
PIKA (PENDIDIKAN INDUSTRI KAYU ATAS)

All furniture by INCH is produced by an Indonesian wood-working manufacturer, called PIKA, using sustainable teak. Because mass production methods of the solid wood furniture can only be applied to a certain extent—due, for one, to the different growth of the wood and the unique grain pattern and color of the wood—each individual chair component is produced on site in accordance with specific, prescribed structural and aesthetic requirements.

**SHANGHAI CHAIR,** 2010
SOLID TEAK, OILED
DEPTH 56 × WIDTH 44 × HEIGHT 81 CM
PRODUCED FOR THE SWISS PAVILION AT THE
EXPO IN SHANGHAI 2010

**SHANGHAI CHAIR,** 2010
SOLID TEAK, OILED
DEPTH 56 × WIDTH 44 × HEIGHT 81 CM
PRODUCED FOR THE SWISS PAVILION AT THE
EXPO IN SHANGHAI 2010

**SHANGHAI TABLE**, 2010
SOLID TEAK, OILED
DEPTH 54 × WIDTH 61 × HEIGHT 35 CM
PRODUCED FOR THE SWISS PAVILION AT THE
EXPO IN SHANGHAI 2010

SHANGHAI TABLE, 2010
SOLID TEAK, OILED
DEPTH 54 × WIDTH 61 × HEIGHT 35 CM
PRODUCED FOR THE SWISS PAVILION AT THE
EXPO IN SHANGHAI 2010

# "WE REPRESENT A NEW GENERATION"

**Your furniture is produced in Indonesia. How did that come about?**

In 2004, we were both looking for a place where we could do our alternative military service. We saw a classified ad looking for two product designers for a foreign assignment in Kalimantan, the Indonesian part of Borneo. We were very interested in the opportunity. Positions like these usually go to doctors or teachers. The job was to develop new products together with students at a woodworking technical school, and to investigate whether professional handcraft vocations still existed in central Kalimantan, and if so, to identify them and research whether they were sustainable.

**Who was the client?**

The Basler Mission, which is called Mission 21 today. This mission founded the woodworking technical school in the 1950s.

**Did you establish INCHfurniture during your stay in Kalimantan?**

No, after a month-long intensive language course, we worked at the woodworking technical school for half a year. This quickly opened up a completely new world for us. We saw what could be produced there and were excited about how receptive the people were. We established INCHfurniture when we got back from Indonesia.

**What does INCH mean?**

INCH stands for Indonesia (IN) and Switzerland (CH), and the name should clearly imply that this is a collaboration between Indonesia and Switzerland.

**Who are your partners there?**

While we were in Kalimantan, we opened a similar woodworking technical school on Java called PIKA. We have been working with them for the past five years. PIKA is an educational facility but also a large production facility that employs approximately one hundred people.

**So, what did you do?**

We had three, difficult to implement designs built there and soon realized we still had a long way to go before we would reach an acceptable standard of quality. We calculated the furniture for the European market and checked export formalities, and so on. It took a total of three years, from 2004 to 2007. Then, in the autumn of 2007, we presented our collection at the "Neue Räume" furniture trade fair in Zurich.

**How often have you been on Java at the time?**

Two or three times a year. At the moment, we're there more often to oversee production. Not only for quality control, but also because we value the personal exchange with the skilled workers and the place. Real knowledge transfer only happens when we are there and working with our partners on a standard of quality that will also be satisfactory for Europe, because ultimately we want to bring the furniture to Europe. The exchange is very direct and affects both the technical and administrative aspects. For instance, the FSC label for sustainable forestry is not very well known there, and we plan to have PIKA certified in the near future. To get the FSC accreditation, every single link of your production chain has to be certified, one by one. Otherwise you can't use the label. PIKA will most likely be the first school and production facility in Southeast Asia to be FSC certified.

**Do you work exclusively with teak?**

It's important for us to work with sustainable and renewably farmed wood. Because teak is a very hard wood, it is naturally excellent for furniture production; moreover, we work with certified plantation wood, which is important to us because *certified forest management* is rare in Indonesia. We chose to use teak when the WWF in Jakarta suggested it while we were collaborating with them, and we don't regret the decision in the least. On the contrary.

**Do the climatic conditions there cause problems with your adhesive bonding?**

No, we use a German glue that is produced specifically for oily woods and is easily available in Indonesia.

**Has PIKA ever expressed a desire to design their own furniture?**

Not really. This would be the case in Europe too. The people at PIKA are craftsmen who are more interested in detail than design. It's a vocational school and not a design academy. We plan to work with a contemporary Indonesian designer, but that will most likely take place outside the school.

**How many pieces can be produced by PIKA?**

This can be illustrated using a specific example. In September 2009, we were awarded the contract for the Swiss Pavilion at the Expo in Shanghai, and the pavilion had to be furnished by March 2010. We only had half a year to wrap up the design process, then the production of one hundred and thirty chairs, thirty tables, and twenty lounge chairs, and finally the four and a half week long shipping period from Indonesia to Shanghai. That was a

crucial test, which we passed—the quality was good and we honored our deadlines. It can't be compared with mass-production of course, but our furniture should not and will never be mass-produced products.

**Do you have all your furniture produced by PIKA?**

PIKA is our exclusive manufacturer. The surface finishing is done in Indonesia, but the final assembly work is done here in Basel. We only touch up the surface finish during the final assembly. Production is less expensive in Indonesia, which means that there is less pressure to produce as quickly as possible in order to keep costs at a minimum. This allows much more freedom to design. In return, PIKA benefits from collaborating with us by increasing their quality standard, even if it does already have the best reputation within Indonesia. In addition to the increased quality standard, PIKA gains from our workshops and lectures on topics such as sustainability and contemporary product design.

**What makes you different, for instance, from the many garden furniture manufacturers who have been producing their furniture in Indonesia for decades?**

Our observation—and we know that PIKA experienced the same—is that these manufacturers do not work with the Indonesians on a collaborative basis, but still harbor a post-colonial patronizing attitude. We represent a new generation. PIKA is our partner and manufacturer, which directly results in high quality. Maximal profit is no longer the prime objective.

**Is this also how PIKA sees it?**

Two school principals came to Switzerland last summer. We took them to the exclusive shops that sell our furniture. That was an extremely important experience for them, because they were able to understand that, if we want our furniture to exist in this context, the quality must be guaranteed.

**How did shops react to your furniture?**

There has to be an equal amount of trust on the commercial side of the business as there is on the production side of things. There is, of course, resistance. A shop owner once told us that, "We watch you for about four years before we place an order." But there are also shop owners who already like our products very much.

# ICD + ITKE

## INSTITUTE FOR COMPUTATIONAL DESIGN AND INSTITUTE OF BUILDING STRUCTURES AND STRUCTURAL DESIGN, UNIVERSITY OF STUTTGART

PROF. ACHIM MENGES (ICD), PROF. JAN KNIPPERS (ITKE)

**ICD/ITKE RESEARCH PAVILION** 2010
CAMPUS OF UNIVERSITY OF STUTTGART,
GERMANY
TEMPORARY PAVILION
BIRCH PLYWOOD
EXTERNAL DIAMETER 10 M, SPAN 3.5 M

The temporary pavilion is made up of eighty 6.5 millimeter-thick and 10-meter-long strips of birch. The flexible plywood strips were spatially shaped—following precise calculations and simulations of the performance of the material—and achieved the necessary stability through the way they are fixed. For the robot-controlled production, the data and results provided by the digital information model and the simulation were directly translated into the machine code (file-to-factory process).

# *ICD*

## *INSTITUTE FOR COMPUTATIONAL DESIGN,*
## *UNIVERSITY OF STUTTGART*

PROF. ACHIM MENGES

ADAPTIVE BENDING THROUGH SECTIONAL
VARIATION, 2009
LAMINATED SPRUCE
DIMENSIONS SYSTEM STUDY: 1×2 M
DIMENSIONS ELEMENTS STUDY: 0.5×1.5 M
PROTOTYPE
PROJECT PARTICIPANTS: MORITZ
FLEISCHMANN, OLIVER DAVID KRIEG, PROF.
ACHIM MENGES, CHRISTOPHER ROBELLER

The aim of this project was to develop other possibilities of integrating computer-based methods into architectural and design production processes. First, the strips of plywood were cut to allow the module to be deformed through the impact of external force. Ultimately, this deformation is what develops the shape of the structure as a whole.

The cross sections of the module were at first identical, before conducting experiments using symmetrical and asymmetrical cross sections. To illustrate the experiment's complexity and wealth of variation more clearly, it was set up as a "meso-structure," according to a digital parametric model manufactured prototype.

**RIGID STRUCTURE OF LAMINATED RULED
SURFACES**, 2009
SYCAMORE
DIMENSIONS: 1.5 × 2.2 M
PROTOTYPE
PROJECT PARTICIPANTS: MARCO BAUR,
FRED ERNST, MORITZ FLEISCHMANN,
PROF. ACHIM MENGES, CHRISTOPHER
ROBELLER, MAX VOMHOF

This project set out to develop a system, using wood veneer, which could easily adapt to external influences such
as heat or moisture. The experiment examined different
parameters such as hygroscopic und hydrophobic qualities
of the veneer, the influence of the thickness of the
material, and the effect of computer-aided production
methods. In this case as well, the prototype presents
a model that allows the results of the project to be
self-evident.

# IWAMOTOSCOTT ARCHITECTURE

## WITH BURO HAPPOLD

**VOUSSOIR CLOUD**, 2008
EXHIBITION IN THE GALLERY OF THE
SOUTHERN CALIFORNIA INSTITUTE OF
ARCHITECTURE (SCI-ARC), LOS ANGELES, USA
ULTRA-LIGHT VENEER

The construction model for this architecture installation was provided by voussoirs, the wedge-shaped masonry blocks that make up an arch. The paper thin, laser cut veneers were folded along the curved joints and connected by cable ties. The veneer construction gives the installation its special, cloud-like appearance.

# HELLA
# JONGERIUS

**FROG TABLE**, 2009
(FROM THE "NATURA DESIGN MAGISTRA" COLLECTION)
WALNUT, BLUE, SEMITRANSPARENT COATING
DEPTH 1.05 × WIDTH 2.10 × HEIGHT 1.20 M (OVERALL SIZE)
LIMITED, NUMBERED EDITION OF 8 + 2 A.P. + 2 PROTOTYPES
MUSEUM BOIJMANS VAN BEUNINGEN, ROTTERDAM, PRIVATE
COLLECTION
COURTESY GALERIE KREO, PARIS

**MIROIRS ANIMAUX**, 2007
FENNEC (FOX), RHINOCÉROS, VAUTOUR (VULTURE),
AMERICAN WALNUT VENEER, METAL, MIRRORS
FENNEC: WIDTH 45, HEIGHT 24 CM
RHINOCÉROS: WIDTH 115 CM, HEIGHT 72 CM
VAUTOUR: WIDTH 88 CM, HEIGHT 60 CM
DRAWINGS: ROGIER WALRECH
LIMITED AND NUMBERED EDITION OF 8 + 2 A.P. + 2
PROTOTYPES PER MOTIF
COURTESY GALERIE KREO, PARIS

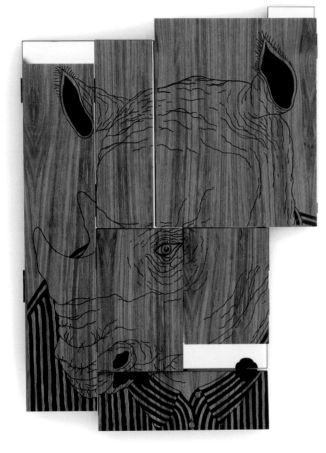

With the series of mirrors, the animal motif was first carved into the
wood and then filled with cast black resin. The design plays with
the notion of two reflections, that of the viewer's face and that of
the fragmented animal's face.

*HELLA
JONGERIUS*

**TURTLE TABLE** 2009
(FROM THE "NATURA DESIGN MAGISTRA" COLLECTION)
LAYERED WOOD AND MULTICOLORED CAST RESIN
DEPTH 93 × WIDTH 115 × HEIGHT 63 CM (OVERALL SIZE)
LIMITED, NUMBERED EDITION OF 8 + 2 A.P. + 2 PROTOTYPES
COURTESY GALERIE KREO, PARIS

**SWATCH TABLE**, 2008
AMERICAN WALNUT, MULTICOLORED CAST RESIN ELEMENTS
DEPTH 85 × WIDTH 162 × HEIGHT 35 CM, LIMITED AND
NUMBERED EDITION OF 8 + 2 A.P. + 2 PROTOTYPES
COURTESY GALERIE KREO, PARIS

**MINI SWATCH TABLE**, 2009
AMERICAN WALNUT, MULTICOLORED CAST RESIN ELEMENTS
DEPTH 47 × WIDTH 60 × HEIGHT 40 CM
LIMITED AND NUMBERED EDITION OF 20 + 2 A.P.
+ 2 PROTOTYPES
COURTESY GALERIE KREO, PARIS

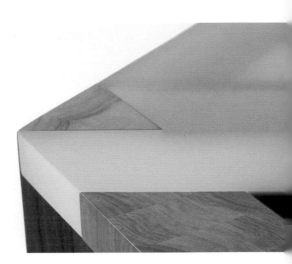

The "Swatch Table" is the contemporary interpretation of
a colorful mosaic. The exciting aspect of its design is the
combination of walnut, inlay, cast resin elements, and
different surface structures.

# "A LIVING MATERIAL"

**Could you say in a few words what wood means for you in comparison with other materials?**

Wood is a material that has its own voice, even before the designer starts to work with it. I'm always interested in materials that have a history, that contain references, for instance to the past or to specific contexts. A design benefits if a material or the employment of a material contains many layers of meanings. The nice thing about wood is that, while it is naked as it is, it already has a voice. If I compare it for instance with porcelain or textiles, which in their final expressions also contain many references to tradition, wood starts with meaning. In the initial phase porcelain is just powder, only in the design and making process does it gain meaning and character. Wood is likewise fit for many applications. But at the same time it's alive. It has a character to start with, whereas porcelain needs the hand of the designer and the hand of the maker to give it meaning and context.

**And in comparison with new materials, like plastics?**

Plastic is a fairly young material. There is no age-old knowledge, almost no tradition. Although one might argue that by now Tupperware products have added something of a history to the material. If I work with plastics, the challenge is different from working with an old material like wood. The attractiveness of plastic cannot be found in its many references to craftsmanship, but rather in its being deployed in specific contexts. The language of young materials is limited. This means you have almost nothing to build upon, whereas in age-old crafts such as woodworking you build upon knowledge. As a designer you start with endless sheets of meanings, contexts, history.

**Plastic production always requires a mold, but not so wood. What about the costs?**

Take care, molds are also used in working with wood! But the differences in costs are substantial. Apart from the additional costs to take care of the waste of discarded plastics, plastic is predictable, cheap and easy to form and there's no scarcity of the material. Wood is a life material, which we cannot produce in endless quantities and the material itself is hard to manipulate. I know from the furniture company Vitra that it's not easy

to work with wood in an industrial process. A carpenter might produce a one-off wooden chair, but for the industry, which aims to produce series of chairs, the challenges are more complex: How to control the wood itself in the making process, the finish, how to connect the various parts, how to combine the wood with other materials such as aluminum or steel. A plastic chair can be poured in one production process, wood necessarily needs more operations and more decisions along the way and, due to that, the industrial process becomes very expensive. Almost as expensive as the work of a carpenter.

**What about the combination and connection of materials. Regarding your "Swatch Table," we were wondering how the more or less transparent resin and the wood are fixed together. With glue?**

No, there are aluminum strips inside with a little space for expansion and shrinkage because they are different for resin and wood. My ambition was to hide any fixing points between the two very different materials to give the table a magic appearance. It seems to be a contradiction to my usual way of working. In many works I overtly show the traces of the making process. But in this product the overall impression counted foremost, not so much the "how" of the process.

**Who would you ask if you intended to work with wood, a craftsman or a technologist?**

That's not how it works. That's not how I think. While experimenting with forms, materials and function I research all the possibilities. Sometimes also the production conditions of a specific company and the price parameters count from the very start. In the design process the question of who am I working with, a craftsman or another expert, comes naturally. Wood is often rejected by companies because it's a labour-intensive and expensive material. For Galerie kreo I did a few things in wood, because it was not a large production. So it was easier for them to accept wood.

**Because it's for an edition?**

That's not the only reason. They also applauded wood because the craftsmanship and the inherent meanings of the material played such an important role in the experimental projects I did for them. In working on these projects I don't have to limit myself in costs, that offers freedom. Wood is a high-quality material. But wood alone can also become very conservative. So you have to do something special with it, you have to ennoble it or

work with its meanings in a new form. Galerie kreo has always offered me the opportunity to do just that.

**Can you give us an example?**

The "Frog Table" is probably a good example. As in the porcelain "Animal Bowls," which I created for Nymphenburg Porcelain Manufactory in Munich, I experimented with the imaginative power of decoration. Decoration usually works as a communication bridge between a human being and an object, which in fact is my overall theme in design: how to create a close relationship between users and products. Decoration is the mediation because it offers more meaning to a functional object. To represent that view on decoration I wanted to test how far I could go. How autonomous could decoration become, how much could this 3D creature loosen itself from the flat surface and still remain closely linked, thereby stressing its expression? Creating this sculptural object in wood was quite costly and required a lot of craftsmanship. But Galerie kreo liked the idea immediately and we pulled it off to create "Frog Table." If you imagine sitting at this table with somebody else, it's obvious: not two, but three creatures are sitting at the table! The usage of wood is most important. The archetypal table is a wooden table. But even more importantly, the frog needed to be crafted of the same material. Content, form, function, and the material have to match. This weird, almost living creature now merges with a living material. Nature and culture have become one.

# CORDULA KEHRER

**BOW BINS**, 2010
PAPER BASKETS F.L.T.R.
BOW BIN # 04: PLASTIC, WICKER WEAVE, Ø 34 CM, HEIGHT 50 CM
BOW BIN # 05: PLASTIC, BAST WEAVE, Ø 86 CM, HEIGHT 86 CM
BOW BIN # 06: PLASTIC, RATTAN WEAVE, Ø 26 CM, HEIGHT 31 CM
BOW BIN # 07: PLASTIC, WICKER WEAVE, Ø 26 CM, HEIGHT 29 CM
UNIQUE PIECES

The combination of contrasting materials is the exciting design aspect of these paper baskets. Combining broken plastic buckets or bowls with natural materials such as wicker, bast, or rattan creates new products that can be used for everyday functions and that possess a unique aesthetic. At the same time, the "Bow Bins" also promote the use of sustainable materials.

# STEFFEN KEHRLE

**PLUG SHELF**, 2012
PLUG-IN SHELF SYSTEM
NATURAL OAK, PAINTED ASH WITH
WATER-BASED STAIN (ANTHRACITE, WHITE,
RED, GREEN)
SIZE VERSION OF S (3 SHELVES):
DEPTH 32 × WIDTH 80 × HEIGHT 87 CM,
WEIGHT: 9.4 KG
SIZE VERSION OF M (4 SHELVES):
DEPTH 32 × WIDTH 80 × HEIGHT 124 CM,
WEIGHT: 12.6 KG
SIZE VERSION OF L (5 SHELVES):
DEPTH 32 × WIDTH 80 × HEIGHT 160 CM,
WEIGHT: 15.8 KG
MANUFACTURER: STATTMANN NEUE MOEBEL

Plug Shelf consists of only two components—shelves and poles—and can be easily assembled and disassembled thanks to an intelligent plug-in design. The stability of the shelves is due to the extremely precise manufacturing process. The diagonal dowels are firmly connected to the poles, and can be precisely inserted into the milled hollows of the shelves, without tools and without bonding. The pigments are based on color codes from the Pantone system, and are applied by spray gun on the sanded surface of the wood. This ensures a more even application of coloring than by using a brush or cloth.

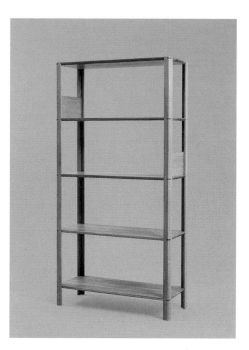

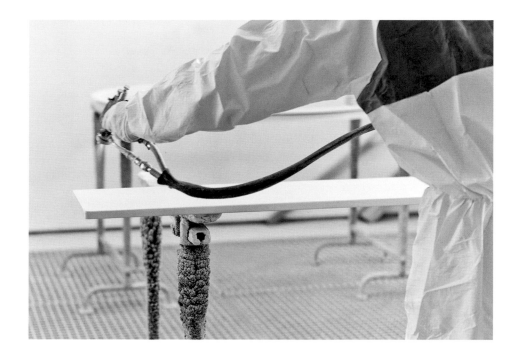

# KO-HO

**GEOMETRIC**, 2012
STACKABLE CHAIR
COMPOSITE OF FINNISH, WINTER DOUSED
HEMP FIBERS
DEPTH 50 × WIDTH 54 × HEIGHT 74 CM,
WEIGHT: 4.5 KG
PROTOTYPE

Geometric is the prototype of a monobloc chair, which stands out mainly due to its material. It is made from hemp, which is not harvested in autumn, which is usually the case, but remains in the soil throughout the winter. In the harsh winters in Finland, the plants are covered by a thick layer of snow. The increasing sun exposure and the onset of melting snow in spring sets a natural process in motion, which allows pectin to be extracted from the hemp fibers. Without additional energy consumption and emissions, this ensures a quality of fiber that is perfect for the further forming process.

# KRAUS SCHÖNBERG ARCHITEKTEN

**HOUSE W.,** 2007
HAMBURG, GERMANY
SINGLE-FAMILY HOUSE
STRUCTURE OF CROSS-LAMINATED TIMBER
(THICKNESS 11.7 CM), FACADE CLADDING OF
WHITE PAINTED DOUGLAS FIR
FOOTPRINT: 105 M²

The load bearing structure of the house is made of cross-laminated timber. The ceilings, external and internal walls support each other in a composite system. This structure rests on circular columns that are anchored to the in-situ walls of the lower floor. For the building, solid wood panels the size of an entire wall, complete with door and window openings, were prefabricated in the factory and clad externally with white painted Douglas fir. This house was awarded the German Timber Building Prize in 2009.

# KENGO KUMA & ASSOCIATES

GC PROSTHO MUSEUM AND RESEARCH
CENTER, 2010
AICHI, JAPAN
NONCOMBUSTIBLE CYPRESS
FOOTPRINT: 626.5 M²

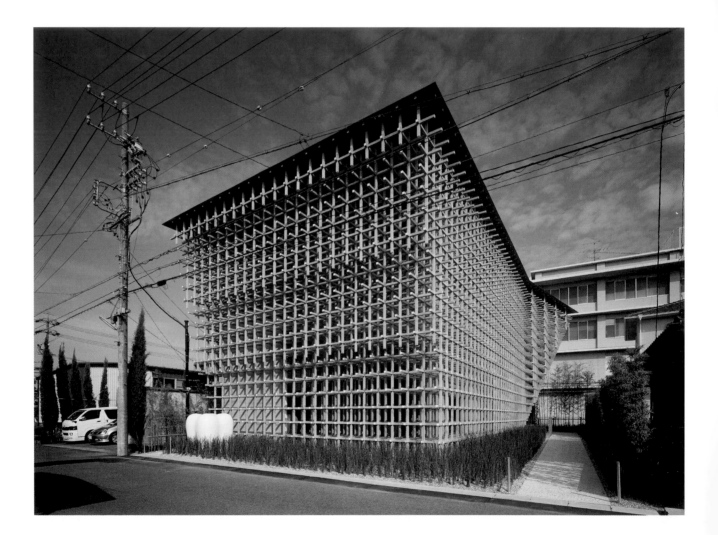

This museum of dentistry is made up of six thousand cypress wood elements. The building's structure relates to *cidori*, a traditional Japanese wooden toy. Increasing the size of the individual elements from sides measuring 12 × 12 to 60 × 60 millimeters on the one hand creates the impression of a grille structure made up of thousands of *cidori* toys, while on the other hand, it made it possible to erect a stable, 9-meter-high facade without the use of screws, nails, or adhesives.

# MAYA
# LAHMY

**POROUS WALL**, 2010
WALL PANELS
LASER-CUT PLYWOOD
1.5 M²
PROTOTYPE

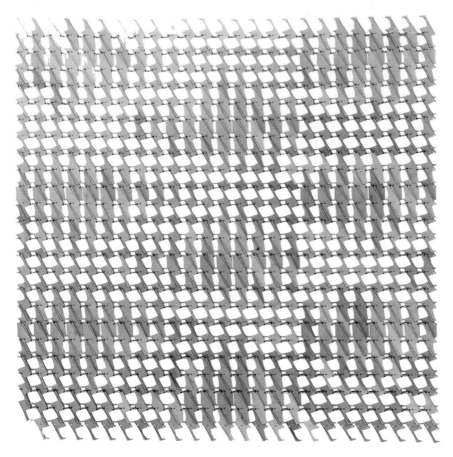

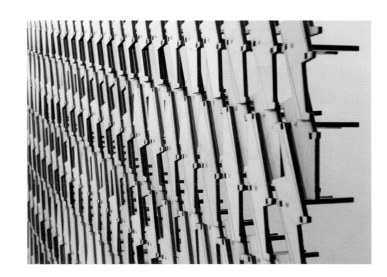

All 600, practically identical individual sections of the wooden wall-covering were cut from 5-square-meter large, 3-millimeter thick plywood board using a digital laser. The entire cutting process took only five hours in total. The wall was designed and produced in 2010 on the occasion of the Copenhagen "Laser Works" competition for innovative prototyping application.

# LASSILA
# HIRVILAMMI
# ARKKITEHDIT

**KUOKKALA CHURCH**, 2010
JYVÄSKYLÄ, FINLAND
SPRUCE, ASH, LIME-WOOD
FOOTPRINT: 1,250 M²

A glued laminated timber frame forms the basic structure of the church roof. Externally, the church is clad with overlapping slate tiles. Inside, the wooden battens form an exposed space frame that was mounted on site in three stages. The wooden frame and the load bearing structure are of local spruce, the church pews are of ash, and the altar is made of lime-wood.

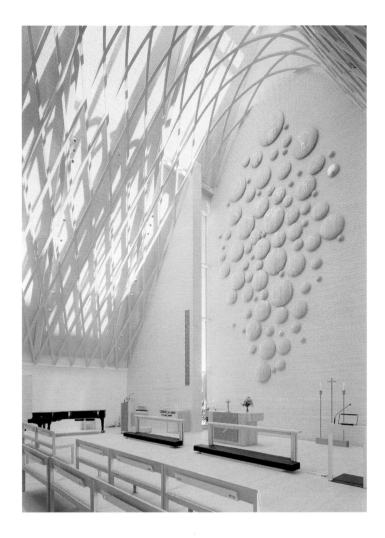

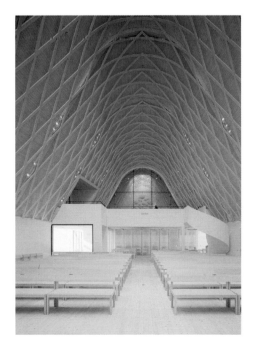

# LE BRICCOLE DI VENEZIA

**LE BRICCOLE DI VENEZIA**, 2010
FURNITURE AND OBJECT COLLECTION
OLD VENETIAN OAK PILASTERS
LENGTH 10 M
MANUFACTURER: RIVA1920

**ANTONIO CITTERIO**, ROOM DIVIDER
**MATTEO THUN**, "BRICCOLE VENEZIA"

For this collection, twenty-nine designers were commissioned to design furniture and objects using worn-out Venetian pilasters (Italian *briccole*). The oak pilasters were as long as 10 meters in length and originally served as docking stations or buoys in the canals. Because they quickly decompose in the water, they have to be replaced by new posts every five to ten years.

**LE BRICCOLE**
**DI VENEZIA**

**DAVID CHIPPERFIELD**, BOOKSHELF
**PAOLA NAVONE**, "BRICIOLE"

**PHILIPPE STARCK**, "SLICE OF BRICCOLE"
**MARIO BOTTA**, "BRICOLAGES"

# SEONGYONG LEE

**PLYTUBE**, 2010
FURNITURE COLLECTION
PLYWOOD, VENEER
STOOL: Ø 36, HEIGHT 47 CM

"Plytube" is the name of a new industrial production method for wooden tubes. The construction principle is similar to that used in cardboard tube production; the only difference being in the final curing process. A meticulous process is used to produce the very lightweight, stable, and durable tubes, which resemble the texture and qualities of plywood. The original size of the stable stool weighs 820 grams.

# HANS
# LEMMEN

GOLDEN BOY, FROM 2009
PARK KALKRIESE (NEAR OSNABRÜCK),
GERMANY
GOLD LEAF ON SIX TREES
HEIGHT CA. 8 M
COURTESY HANS LEMMEN AND THE
LANDSCHAFTSVERBAND OSNABRÜCKER
LAND E.V.

For the 2009 art project entitled "Colossal," which com-
memorated the 2,000th anniversary of the Battle of Varus
in the Teutoburg Forest, the Dutch artist Hans Lemmen
created a larger than life-size, headless figure by applying
gold leaf to six tree trunks. The figure is only visible from
a specific standpoint. It was inspired by the Arminius Monu-
ment in Hiddesen near Detmold.

# KHAI LIEW

**MINTON**, 2007
CABINET
LIME-WOOD
DEPTH 49 × WIDTH 84 × HEIGHT 168.5 CM
LIMITED EDITION

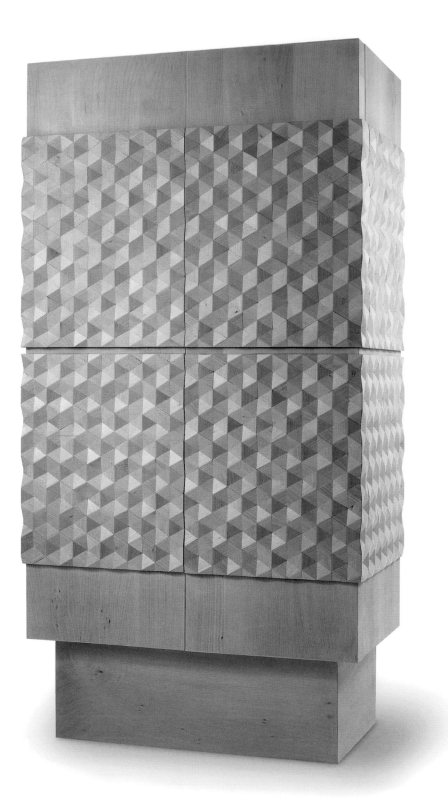

The over 2,600 three-dimensional triangles, each gradating from 3 to 10 millimeters, that decorate the cabinet were hand carved with the utmost precision. The resulting hexagonal pattern is a reference to the floor tiles of the Minton Room in the London Victoria & Albert Museum.

# KAI
# LINKE

**BLASTED W02** (FROM THE "BLASTED FAMILII" COLLECTION), 2010
WALL PANELING IN SPRUCE
OVERALL DIMENSIONS: DEPTH 0.18 × WIDTH 288 × HEIGHT 336 CM
IN COLLABORATION WITH CATRIN ALTENBRANDT AND ADRIAN NIESSLER

The wall paneling is made from twenty-nine individual spruce elements with surfaces that have been sandblasted to form various reliefs, motifs, and symbols.

The sandblasting dissolves the soft structures in the wood leaving the harder structures such as the grain, knotholes and growth rings intact. Areas not to be sandblasted are temporarily covered during the blasting process with a support material.

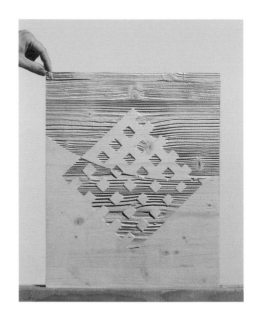

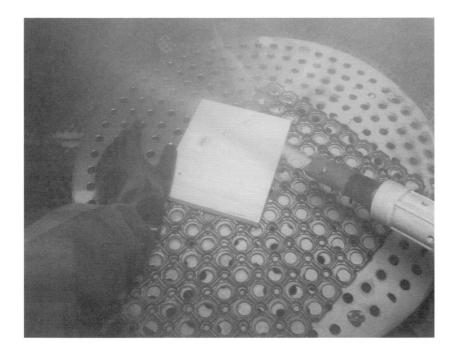

# IDEE
# LIU

**WORLD CUPS: CROAKING FROG AND REINCARNATION**, 2010
CHINESE BOXWOOD
Ø 9 CM, HEIGHT 24 CM
MASTER CRAFTSMAN: CHING-TIAN CAI
YII NO.19
INITIATED BY YII, A COLLABORATIVE PROJECT
BY NTCRI (NATIONAL TAIWAN CRAFTS
RESEARCH INSTITUTE) AND TDC (TAIWAN
DESIGN CENTER)

The objects are part of a series in which the cups and logo of Starbucks, the American coffee house chain, were reinterpreted using traditional Thai craftsmanship techniques such as woodcarving, silversmith artistry, or glassblowing. The wooden cups and the decorations were cut directly from one tree trunk, not a single element was added posthumously.

# LOCALARCHITECTURE

**FREE-STALL COWSHED**, 2005
LIGNIÈRES, SWITZERLAND
STRUCTURE OF SOLID PINE
FOOTPRINT: 470 M²
HEIGHT: BETWEEN 3.5 AND 8.2 M

This free-stall shed designed for thirty cows was built of timber from neighboring woods. Textile is used to protect the cowshed against the wind.

**CHAPEL OF SAINT-LOUP**, 2008
POMPAPLES, SWITZERLAND
CROSS-LAMINATED TIMBER, THREE-PLY PANELS
REALIZED IN COLLABORATION WITH DANILO MONDADA AND
SHEL-HANI BURI, YVES WEINAND—ARCHITECTURE,
ENGINEERING AND PRODUCTION DESIGN
FOOTPRINT: 158 M$^2$
HEIGHT: BETWEEN 3.3 AND 6.9 M

In addition to its appearance, the remarkable thing about the chapel, designed as a temporary building, is the folded structure made from 40-60 mm thick three-ply panels. The facade consists of 19 mm thick cross-laminated timber panels. The data for the structure, which were calculated with the aid of a software program, were directly transferred to a CNC mill (file-to-factory process). This allowed the different formed and differently sized building elements including the mitered joints to be sawn precisely and assembled on site using nail plates. The chapel is lit from one end.

# PAUL LOEBACH

**WOOD VASES**, 2009
VASES
MAPLE
CA. Ø 15 CM, HEIGHT 25 CM

The combination of woodworking technology and CNC technology: for these vases, blocks of solid maple were milled in half and then joined again by a visible joint that emphasized the form.

**PAUL**
**LOEBACH**

**SHELF SPACE**, 2008
WALL SHELF
LIME-WOOD
DEPTH 38 × WIDTH 114 × HEIGHT 53 CM

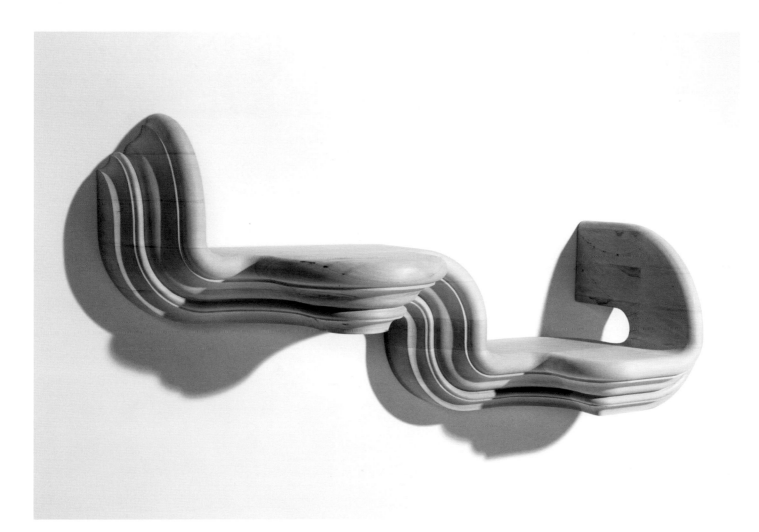

The shelf was designed in collaboration with an aerospace
company. Its form is derived from the combination of
traditional woodwork techniques and modern machine-
cutting technology.

**VASE SPACE**, 2008
TABLE OBJECT
LIME-WOOD
Ø 58 CM, HEIGHT 91 CM

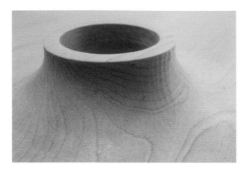

Although the three lime-wood vases were designed to look as though they flow seamlessly into the tabletop, they are completely removable. The table object was produced using multi-axis CNC technology.

# PHILIPPE MALOUIN

**EXTRUSION**, 2012
HANDMADE LOW BOWL FROM THE "EXTRUSION" OBJECT SERIES
MAPLE AND OAK
Ø 30 CM, HEIGHT 8 CM
ENTIRE SERIES OF 5 DIFFERENT OBJECTS (STOOLS, BOWLS, TABLE),
LIMITED EDITION OF 12 + 2, COMMISSIONED
BY CARWAN GALLERY, PRODUCED IN LEBANON
COURTESY CARWAN GALLERY, BEIRUT

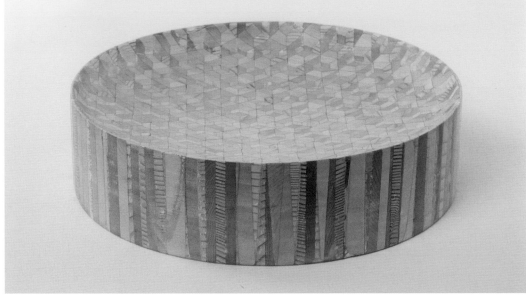

Philippe Malouin worked together with Lebanese craftsmen to combine the techniques of intarsia and lathing—two methods that emerged in approximately 1200 BC in the Middle East. The objects are composed from hundreds of individual parts to produce a tessellated pattern similar to the intarsia technique. The objects start off as chunks, which are then processed on a lathe to give them an accurate and unique shape. This is a project that experimented with two traditional woodworking processes, while presenting these traditional processes to the viewer.

# ENZO
# MARI

**SEDIA 1 CHAIR**, 2010 (DESIGN FROM 1974)
DO-IT-YOURSELF CHAIR KIT
UNTREATED PINE
DEPTH 52 × WIDTH 50 × HEIGHT 85 CM
MANUFACTURER: ARTEK

In 1974, Enzo Mari presented his designs for his nineteen-piece, self-made collection entitled "Autoprogettazione." Every purchaser can now build his or her own chair using a sheet of instructions. The "Sedia 1 Chair" is one of the objects from this collection, and is delivered as a kit consisting of prefabricated pine boards, nails, and instructions.

# MICHAEL MARRIOTT

**LUNAR CHAIR**, 2010
ARMCHAIR
BIRCH PLYWOOD
DEPTH 60 × WIDTH 45 × HEIGHT 70 CM
LIMITED EDITION OF THIRTY-THREE

**PLY STOOL FOR PAUL SMITH**, 2009
DO-IT-YOURSELF STOOL KIT
FINNISH BIRCH PLYWOOD (100% SUSTAINABLE WOOD)
DEPTH 25 × WIDTH 37 × HEIGHT 33.5 CM
LIMITED EDITION OF 100 PIECES FOR PAUL SMITH

The components of this chair were cut using CNC technology and assembled with cable ties. The pattern is applied by silkscreen. The armchair was designed and produced for the exhibition "Designer's Furniture" at the London Russian Club Gallery and was displayed for sale along with furniture by eight other designers.

This lightweight stool made from birch plywood consists of five individual components that are connected by four cable ties in eleven colors. The colorful, geometric patterns are applied using a silkscreen process.

# JÜRGEN
# MAYER H.

**MENSA MOLTKE**, 2007
KARLSRUHE, GERMANY
NEW BUILDING FOR THE KARLSRUHE UNIVERSITY OF APPLIED
SCIENCES, UNIVERSITY OF EDUCATION, AND STATE ACADEMY
OF FINE ARTS
LAMINATED SPRUCE VENEER, POLYURETHANE COATING,
REINFORCED STEEL CORE
LENGTH 55 × WIDTH 45 × HEIGHT 11 M

**METROPOL PARASOL**
2004 COMPETITION, COMPLETED 2011
SEVILLE, SPAIN
ROOF AND NEW DESIGN OF THE PLAZA DE LA ENCARNACIÓN
LAMINATED SPRUCE VENEER, POLYURETHANE COATING, REINFORCED STEEL CORE
LENGTH 150 × WIDTH 90 × HEIGHT 30 M

**RE.FLECKS**, 2010
INSTALLATION
MDF, STAINED BLACK, CNC-MACHINED
WIDTH 219 (FOLDABLE PART 97) × HEIGHT 115 CM
COURTESY GALERIE MAGNUS MÜLLER, BERLIN

The installation entitled RE.FLECKS is based on the structure of data protection patterns, which are often found on the inside surface of envelopes and conceal the envelope's contents from unwelcome eyes. The black MDF panels were cut using CNC milling technology.

# "WE WANTED A THREE-DIMENSIONAL STRUCTURE THAT SUPPORTED ITSELF"

*The Mensa in Karlsruhe and the "Metropol Parasol" project in Seville are two designs in which wood is used to construct the supporting frame. What made you choose this material?*

With the Mensa project, we were looking for a way to realize a relatively unconventional design with a limited budget. In doing so, we developed a very economic method of construction, by which a freely formed wooden body is assembled from *laminated veneer* and then spray-coated with polyurethane. Two things that this process requires are computer-aided and automated processing technology, which are relatively advanced in wood construction. Moreover, *laminated veneer* made from Finnish spruce also happens to be highly durable and good for three-dimensional processing.

We translated in principle the experiences we gathered from the Mensa project to the project in Seville. However, the Seville project involved completely different dimensions and so required a totally different construction system.

*The unique aspect of the coating is its semi-permeability. What material is this exactly, and how is it applied to the wooden structure?*

The coating is a 3-millimeter-thick outer layer of polyurethane that is spray-coated onto the mass and functions similarly to a Gore-Tex sports coat: moisture can escape from the inside to the outside, but the outer surface is completely waterproof. This helped us to take care of several functions at once: the coated and insulated supporting structure simultaneously fulfilled the roles of the facade and the roof. We were able to forgo a vapor barrier in the interior plus any gaskets on the structure's shell. This is as easy as anyone had ever hoped: you go up the facade, across the roof, and down the other side with exactly the same material.

*Is that the top surface coating, or is it also varnished?*

The PU spray-coating consists of two components that are mixed in the nozzle. Before spraying, the wood is treated with an adhesive coating. The coating hardens immediately and fulfills all of the technical requirements after only a few seconds. For optical reasons, a layer of paint is applied in any color desired to serve as UV protection. This prevents the PU layer from yellowing. In contrast to other plastics, PU does not become brittle when exposed to UV rays, meaning it is stable even without this last coat of paint.

*Are the building components now prefabricated?*

All wooden components are prefabricated according to a three-dimensional, architectural model by a computerized milling machine, and then assembled on site. Just like a kit.

*How much of the experience you gained from the Mensa project were you able to apply to the "Metropol Parasol"?*

The Mensa was a closed building with an inside and an outside, but "Metropol Parasol" was more a large bridge-like sculpture that structures the urban space. These are two very different structural requirements or demands. What the two projects have in common is the technology to freely form elements from *laminated veneer* and to spray-coat these with polyurethane.

*So the "Metropol Parasol" and the Mensa are both a kind of prototype architecture?*

Yes, they are prototypes for several reasons: from the urban-development aspect, as well as architecturally and structurally. The prototype cannot easily be categorized as a structure, sculpture, or a building. But as an urban object, it generates and integrates the most varied functions of all of these categories.

The urban context in the center of Seville is unique. There used to be a cloister there in the Middle Ages, but it has been the home of the city's market hall for the last century or so. When they were building a parking garage, they happened upon Roman artifacts that were 2,000 years old. A two-phase international competition was then announced, which called for a design concept for a large urban square with an archeological museum and a market hall.

We didn't want to construct a building by erecting a couple of poles, attaching components onto these, and then sticking on an external shell, which is what the engineers suggested. We wanted a three-dimensional structure that supported itself. For about a year, we examined complex geometric structures made from different materials. In the end, we needed to develop a completely new technique that would join the various wooden elements. Now, several engineering offices are working on this structural frame, because every joint has to be individually calculated and detailed.

*So, in other words, you weren't decided from the start about using wood?*

No. We had a budget, which was the starting point for our research into different possibilities. The first design was a steel construction, which was too expensive. And at that time there were no appropriate planning foundations or experience in relation to fiber concrete. This is why we returned to the "Mensa solution." However, of the six supporting columns, the two that extend to the archeological level and function as elevator shafts are made of concrete, because of fire protection requirements. They support a restaurant that can seat five hundred people. All other columns are self-supporting wooden constructions.

*Can you describe the construction in more detail?*

The wooden construction is made from a three-dimensional, freely formed grid framework, 150 meters long, 90 meters wide, and 30 meters tall. All of the elements and details of the supporting structure are visible. We used a new method that enabled an optimal transfer of the strongest forces at the joint points. Round steel rods were glued into the wood, and gripped the wooden elements like fingers. The "fingers" run parallel, are approximately 50 centimeters long and up to 2 centimeters thick, and follow along the direction of force.

Guidelines were introduced in Germany in late 2009, stating a maximal temperature of 60 °C. However the engineers said that, in Seville, the temperature of the components could rise above that. An experimental solution was initiated for this problem that involved several research institutes and experts in bonding technology. The bond is strengthened by preheating it in the installed condition, which allows the bond to tolerate higher temperatures. The material tests verified that the steel would crack but not the bonded area between the wood and the steel.

*So it is more an engineered construction than a building?*

This question is not easily answered, even from my perspective. Translating a complex sculptural form into a supporting structure was a task that brought many of the involved engineers to the limits of modern technology. We even doubted the feasibility of the project for a while. Of course, having engineers working on the project was essential.

# JUNICHI MORI

**DOLL, LEAVES**, 2009
JAPANESE BOXWOOD
DEPTH 20 × WIDTH 23.5 × HEIGHT 24.5 CM
© JUNICHI MORI
COURTESY MIZUMA ART GALLERY

**FLARE (BIRDS)**, 2010
JAPANESE BOXWOOD
DEPTH 37 × WIDTH 36 × HEIGHT 48 CM
© JUNICHI MORI
COURTESY MIZUMA ART GALLERY

The finely engraved motifs from Japanese boxwood were hand carved using a high-speed grinding machine. The tools used for the process resemble the attachments for dentist drills.

*JUNICHI*
*MORI*

**FLARE**, 2009
JAPANESE BOXWOOD
DEPTH 9 × WIDTH 177 × HEIGHT 177 CM
© JUNICHI MORI
COURTESY MIZUMA ART GALLERY

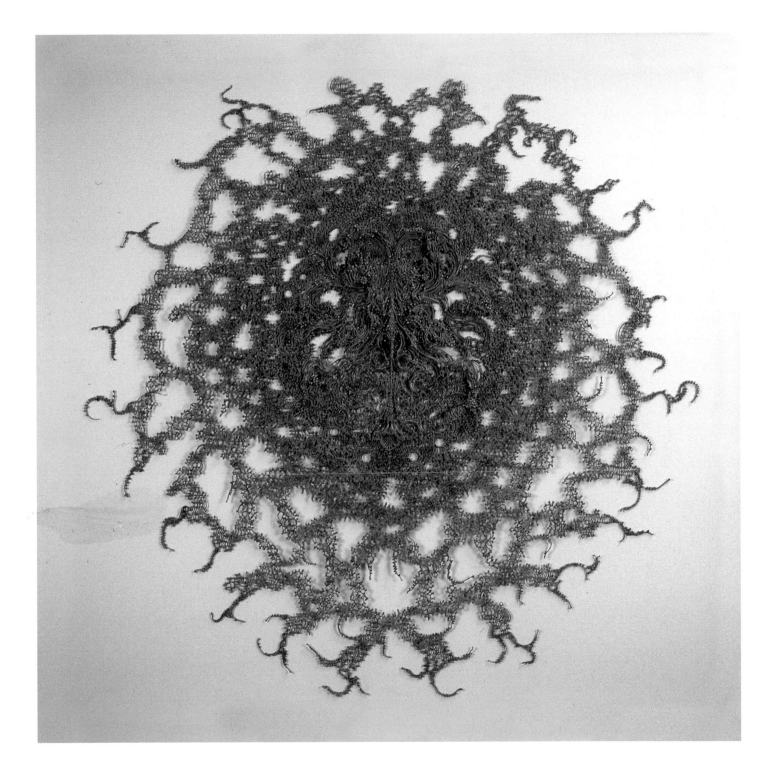

# PAOLA NAVONE

**EU/PHORIA**, 2011
OUTDOOR CHAIR
SEAT MADE FROM WOODSTOCK® WOOD
PLASTIC COMPOSITE (WPC)
FRAME FROM STEEL TUBING
DEPTH 57 × WIDTH 57 × HEIGHT 68 CM
MANUFACTURER: EUMENES

The seat of the chair is made from Woodstock, a Wood Plastic Composite (WPC) usually used in the automobile manufacturing industry, which consists of fifty percent wood scraps and fifty percent polypropylene. The material is available in boards and can be easily formed thermally and can be combined with technical textiles, weaves, or fabrics such as Alcantara during the pressing process.

# NENDO

Structurally, the chair resembles the construction of an electric cable with a rubber-sheathed conductor wire. The steel frame has a diameter of 9 millimeters and, by means of complex craftsmanship, is lined with a 3-millimeter thick tube made from maple.

# SASCHA NORDMEYER

**ECO-EFFECTIVE TABLE**, 2009
TABLE
LEGS MADE FROM ARBOFORM®
TABLETOP FROM MDF WITH BEECH VENEER
DEPTH 90 × WIDTH 150 × HEIGHT 74 CM
PROTOTYPE

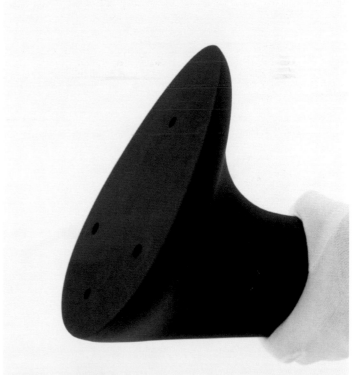

This table's design reflects a "cradle to cradle" principle, which defines the theory of the ecological cycle. Thermoplast Arboform serves as the material for the legs, and ideally also for the tabletop. It behaves in a similar manner to traditional plastic, but is completely biodegradable due to hemp fibers and lignin, which make up it main constituents.

# HENRIQUE OLIVEIRA

**TAPUMES (FENCE)—CASA DOS LEÕES**, 2009
INSTALLATION FOR THE 7TH MERCOSUR
BIENNIAL, PORTO ALEGRE, BRAZIL
ROTARY CUT OLD PLYWOOD, PVC HOSES

The installation references the provisional wooden fence that runs around the entire city of São Paulo, Henrique Oliveira's hometown. The different stages of erosion of the plywood collected from the street give the three-dimensional installations the appearance of abstract paintings. Walls or PVC hoses serve as a support structure.

**TAPUMES (FENCE)**, 2009
INSTALLATION
ROTARY CUT OLD PLYWOOD
DEPTH 2 × WIDTH 13.4 × HEIGHT 4.7 M
COURTESY RICE GALLERY, HOUSTON

# JENS OTTEN

**EXPERIMENTELLE ELASTOSTATIK,** 2008
CHAIR MADE FROM FLAT COMPONENTS
CHAIR MADE FROM CNC MILLED BIRCH,
FRAME FROM TUBULAR STEEL
DEPTH 56 × WIDTH 58 × HEIGHT 80 CM
PROTOTYPE

The prototype shows how connecting two-dimensional individual components can create a three-dimensional structure. Based on a CAD model, 1.5-millimeter thick birch plywood strips were milled using CNC technology. The ergonomic and flexible form of the chair is created by connecting the individual elements by means of screws and glue.

# HARRY PARR-YOUNG

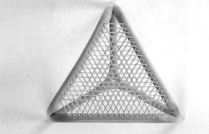

**RSM I** (RATTAN SPLICE MARK I), 2010
STOOL
RATTAN
FRAME: 45×45×45 CM,
SEAT SURFACE: 35×35×35 CM, HEIGHT 45 CM

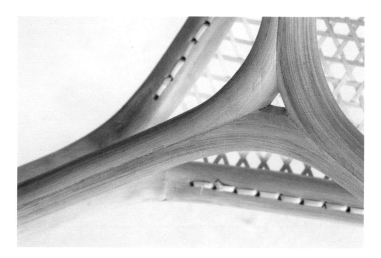

The design of the stool makes use of the exotic and outdoor look of traditional rattan furniture and translates these qualities into a contemporary seat for interiors. The frame is constructed from bent rattan tubes; the seat surface is made from woven, stripped bark from the rattan tube.

# PATTERNITY

**PHASE BUREAU**, 2010
SMOKED OAK, OAK, CEDAR, INLAYS FROM
COLORED VENEER
DEPTH 40 × WIDTH 150 × HEIGHT 120 CM
IN COLLABORATION WITH THE FURNITURE
MAKER, TOBY WINTERINGHAM

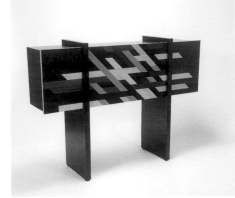

The patterns are produced using the traditional marquetry craft. They represent the transitions between cutting out and replacing, and combining the old with the new, with colorful graphic patterns slicing through natural wood.

# LEX POTT

**FRAGMENTS OF NATURE**, 2009
FURNITURE COLLECTION
DOUGLAS FIR
CUPBOARD: DEPTH 50 × WIDTH 200 × HEIGHT 180 CM
PROTOTYPE

This furniture collection combines industrial, geometric forms with the original, organic structure of a tree, from which the pieces are made. The contours of the cupboard are directly derived from the tree trunk, the legs of the table and the bench are easily perceived as tree branches.

*LEX*
*POTT*

**FRAGMENTS OF NATURE**, 2009
FURNITURE COLLECTION
DOUGLAS FIR
BENCH: DEPTH 30 × WIDTH 200 × HEIGHT 43 CM
TABLE: DEPTH 90 × WIDTH 90 × HEIGHT 74 CM
PROTOTYPES

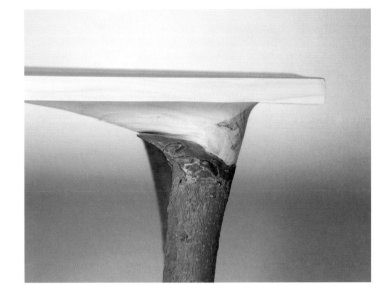

# RAW EDGES

**TAILORED WOOD BENCH TWB**, 2010
BENCH
ASH VENEER, POLYURETHANE FOAM
BENCH: DEPTH 32 × WIDTH 226 × HEIGHT 56 CM
STOOL: DEPTH 28 × WIDTH 75 × HEIGHT 56 CM
MANUFACTURER: CAPPELLINI

**TAILORED WOOD, SELF-MADE**, 2008
STOOL SERIES
TEAK VENEER, POLYURETHANE FOAM
DEPTH 20 × WIDTH 80 × HEIGHT 60 CM
OWN PRODUCTION

The wooden veneer shells are filled with polyurethane foam that increas-
es twenty-five times in volume when it hardens, giving the stool its stability. The foam does not distribute itself uniformly, and the different forms and folds that result from this mean that every piece in the collection is a unique object.

# STEFFEN REICHERT

**RESPONSIVE SURFACE STRUCTURE**, 2008
STUDY OF MOISTURE INTERACTION
MAPLE VENEER
LENGTH 1.60 × WIDTH 2.40 M
STUDY: OFFENBACH ACADEMY OF ART AND DESIGN,
DEPARTMENT OF FORM GENERATION AND MATERIALIZATION
LED BY PROF. ACHIM MENGES

The study examines the possibility of developing self-regulating, ecologically sustainable air-conditioning systems. The scale-like structure of the "Responsive Surface Structure"—a PVC film that is attached with wooden veneer elements—can adapt to the relative changes in humidity in the environment and can operate without the use of electronic or mechanical devices. Each scale reacts independently. The principle is based on the pinecone, that can continue to open and close as a response to changes in humidity even after it has fallen from the tree.

*STEFFEN REICHERT*
*WITH PROF. ACHIM MENGES AND FLORIAN KRAMPE AT THE ICD, INSTITUTE FOR COMPUTATIONAL DESIGN, UNIVERSITY OF STUTTGART*

**CLIMACTIVE SKIN**, 2010
MATERIAL EXPERIMENT
SYCAMORE VENEER
LENGTH 1 × WIDTH 1 M
PROTOTYPE

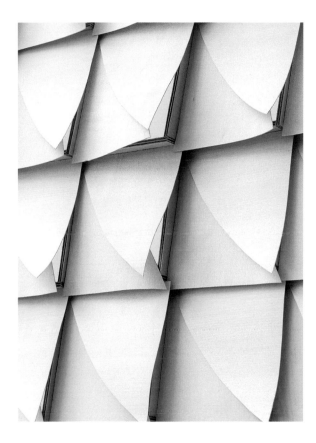

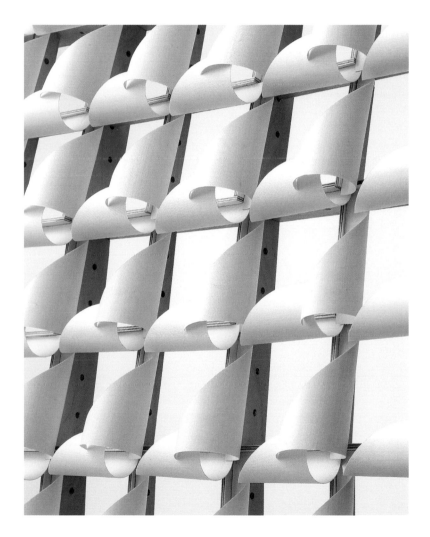

For this material experiment, a veneer composite element was developed. This allows the material to adapt to precise and various conditions of air moisture.

# ADRIEN ROVERO

**PARTICULES STOOL**, 2008
STACKABLE STOOL
WOOD SHAVINGS, STEEL JOINTS
DEPTH 34 × WIDTH 34 × HEIGHT 37 CM
PROJECT PARTNERS: VIA (VALORIZATION OF
INNOVATION IN FRENCH FURNISHING)
CREATION ASSISTANCE GRANTS 2008
BERN UNIVERSITY OF APPLIED SCIENCES,
CRITT MECA

The stackable stools are made out of compressed wood shavings, which is a process also used in manufacturing pallets. All three parts of the stool are made using the same form.

**FACETTED PANEL**, 2009
TEAK
OVERALL DIMENSIONS: LENGTH 2.59 × WIDTH 3.28 M
MANUFACTURER: PUTRA UKIR, BALI
UNIQUE PIECE

**DOG CHAIR**, 2009
ARMCHAIR
TEAK
DEPTH 96 × WIDTH 127 × HEIGHT 84 CM
MANUFACTURER: I WAYAN PASTI AND SONS,
MAS, BALI
EDITION OF 2

# COLIN
# SCHAELLI

**V30 FREITAG SKID**, 2009
SHELF SYSTEM FOR POCKET DISPLAYS
PROTOTYPE DEVELOPMENT WITH MDF, FIRST DESIGN IN
LIQUIDWOOD®, SERIAL PRODUCTION IN RECYCLED PLASTIC,
SPECIAL PRODUCTION FOR EXHIBITION PURPOSES IN
PLASTIC (RAL 1013)
MODULE: DEPTH 44 × WIDTH 27 × HEIGHT 10.5 CM

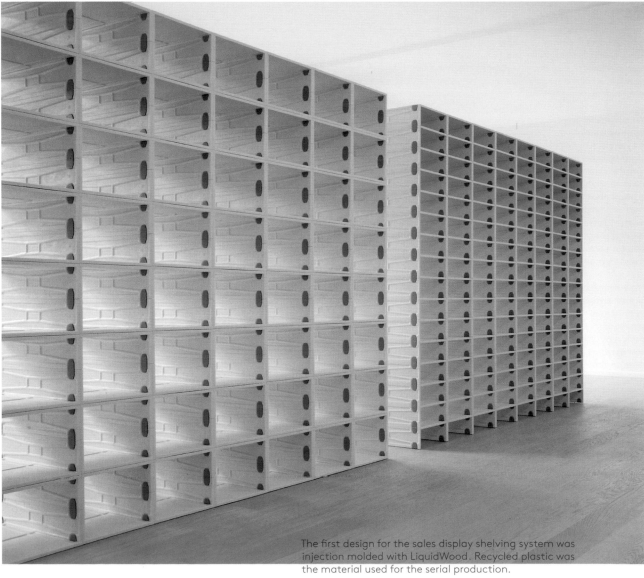

The first design for the sales display shelving system was injection molded with LiquidWood. Recycled plastic was the material used for the serial production.

*COLIN*
*SCHAELLI*

**CON.TEMPORARY FURNITURE**, 2010
FURNITURE COLLECTION
LAMINATED SPRUCE
FREESTANDING SHELVES R-1425-3-3T:
DEPTH 42.5 × WIDTH 85 × HEIGHT 142.5 CM
SIDEBOARD R-723-D-1T:
DEPTH 42.5 × WIDTH 170 × HEIGHT 72.3 CM
BOOKSHELVES R-1776-4T:
DEPTH 42.5 × WIDTH 85 × HEIGHT 177.6 CM
WORK TABLE T-723-X3:
DEPTH 85 × WIDTH 170 × HEIGHT 72.3 CM
DISTRIBUTION SHELVES R-1074-2T:
DEPTH 42.5 × WIDTH 85 × HEIGHT 107.4 CM
MANUFACTURER: CAVIEZEL AG

The basic idea of this furniture collection was that it should be easy
to transport, be able to be installed without screws, and produced by
local carpenters, which would avoid long distance shipping. The
standard module of the collection has the shipping-friendly dimensions of Japanese *tatami* mats, all the joints are a plug system, and
due to its simple construction principle, it can be manufactured
by any carpenter in the world using a CNC milling machine.

**COLOUR WOOD**, 2009
DISPLAY TABLE SERIES
STAINED AND PRINTED OAK
PLAIN GRID: Ø 71 CM, HEIGHT 32 CM
DARK GRID: Ø 60 CM, HEIGHT 39 CM
PINK: Ø 60 CM, HEIGHT 39 CM
COLOR GRID: Ø 50 CM, HEIGHT 43 CM
MANUFACTURER: KARIMOKU NEW STANDARD JAPAN

The display tables are different in size, color, and pattern.
The wooden structure of the surfaces is finished with a
coat of transparent varnish, onto which graphic patterns
have been printed. These different levels lend the narrow
tabletop an unusual depth.

# FRANZISKA SCHREIBER

The collection, which consists of twenty pieces, plays with the contrast between the stability of wood and the flexibility of textile-based materials. Most of the wooden parts are made from several layers of cold-molded zebrawood veneer with a glossy finish. Smaller pieces such as the belt buckle are made from solid zebrawood. All of the pieces are made to fit the body by means of appropriately manufactured positive forms.

# TILO
# SCHULZ

**INTARSIE**, 2010
WOOD INTARSIA
WIDTH 140 × HEIGHT 30 CM
COURTESY GALERIE JOCHEN HEMPEL, LEIPZIG

All of Tilo Schulz's wood marquetry works are intricately produced by master woodworkers after a long idea development and design process.

*TILO*
*SCHULZ*

**INTARSIE**, 2010
WOOD INTARSIA
WIDTH 1.10 × HEIGHT 1.12 M
COURTESY GALERIE JOCHEN HEMPEL, LEIPZIG

**INTARSIEN MIT TAPETE**, 2008
WOOD INTARSIA, WALLPAPER
COURTESY STEINLE CONTEMPORARY,
MUNICH, AND THE COLLECTION OF
CHRISTIAN HOSTE, MUNICH

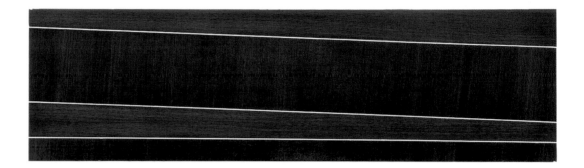

**INTARSIEN MIT TAPETE**, 2008
WOOD INTARSIA, WALLPAPER
COURTESY STEINLE CONTEMPORARY,
MUNICH, AND THE COLLECTION OF
CHRISTIAN HOSTE, MUNICH

**INTARSIE MIT TAPETE**, 2007
WOOD INTARSIA, WALLPAPER
WIDTH 1.25 × HEIGHT 2.30 M
COURTESY PRIVATE COLLECTION IN ESSEN
PART OF THE EXHIBITION CALLED
"FORMSCHÖN," MUSEUM OF
CONTEMPORARY ART, LEIPZIG

# "THE REPRESENTATIVE POWER OF WOOD INLAYS"

*You work with different materials. What criteria do you follow when you're choosing a material for a new work?*
One of the core issues for me as an artist, for any content-related work I do, is to find the right form. There are artists who develop a style within a medium, stay with that, and work within this focused framework. A work by Dan Flavin will always look like a work by Dan Flavin. I have a different approach. I look for the right form for every new endeavor.

*Why did you use wood for your inlays?*
The representation of power and substance led me to select wood for the inlays. Wood inlays have a 3,000-year-old tradition of craftsmanship and have always been strongly associated with substance. This can be seen in jewelry boxes and entire choir stalls—both are places of worldly and churchly affairs—as well as in the wood inlays in the studiolos of Urbino and Gubbio, which epitomize the marriage between the art of marquetry and the Renaissance. These studiolos are a symbol of the powerful position held by their client, Lord Federico da Montefeltro, as a Renaissance aristocrat. If you follow the history, you see how the intricacy of this architectural symbol of substance was gradually reduced and reduced until it became the wood-paneled executive suites of the 1950s to 1970s. The wood inlay work had vanished. This artistic medium has been completely replaced by a wooden facade, which seems to satisfy the need for substance.

*Do you mean to say that it was impossible to avoid using wood as a material, because you are working with the notion of the art of marquetry as a medium that symbolized power?*
In contrast to the painted, marketable, picture that has established itself and is still present in places of power today, the object- or architecture-related art of marquetry and its pictorial quality has almost completely disappeared. I found this fascinating and my interest in marquetry led me to wood as a pure matter of course. I knew from the beginning that I would not use the figurative aspect, which was originally typical of marquetry. I was looking for a purely abstract, three-dimensional solution, because I wanted to avoid an illustrative image and also wanted to do something in deliberate contrast to the fascinating, two-dimensional wood inlay walls of the studiolos—which look so real that you actually want to grab something from the shelf or sit on the bench. The inlay work in the studiolos is of course a two-dimensional image, but it is also wall covering and makes a room a room. The choir stalls are part of a seating arrangement. The wood inlay pictures I am working on are absolutely images, which is why they end at the edges of the picture surface. But I can create very strong three-dimensional, illusionistic effects using the direction of the veneer's grain, even without the figurative aspect.

*Can you tell us something about how you make the inlays?*
There is always a certain factor of chance: you can plan and consider the properties that are typical of wood, but it will always have a mind of its own. Nonetheless, there are three levels to my inlays: first there is the division of the surface by lighter colored wood, then there's the pattern and direction of the veneer's grain, and thirdly the pattern and direction of the lacewood with its diagonally cut capillaries.

*Can you describe lacewood in more detail?*
Lacewood is stripped in a different way. The medullary rays are cut diagonally. This creates additional slivers on the wood's surface that are not immediately visible. They give my inlay pictures a third level. Oak is perfect for this because it has very distinct medullary rays. I am interested in these additional pictorial levels, their depth effect, and in the relationship between the two different directions of movement of the grain and the slivers of the medullary rays.

*What is the most complex aspect of working with inlays?*
Sanding and waxing are always a difficult and time-consuming job for the carpenter, especially if the inlays are not varnished, because you can only sand the piece along the direction of the grain. That means that every individual surface has to be sanded and waxed in the correct direction, hundreds of times in rotation. Varnished inlays are a bit easier to produce. They only have to be sanded once in the direction of the grain, and after varnishing, only the varnished surface has to be sanded. And that can be done with an electric sander.

*How long does it take you to complete one inlay work?*
It takes about one and a half years, which includes the design phase. The actual production only takes two to three weeks, but this has a lot to do with the special relationship I have with Beck&Pauli carpenters in Leipzig, and the fact that they are interested in my art work.

# JERSZY
# SEYMOUR

**WORKSHOP CHAIR, AMATEUR WORKSHOP**, 2009
PINE, POLYCAPROLACTONE WAX
DEPTH 49 × WIDTH 49 × HEIGHT 77 CM
UNLIMITED EDITION OF UNIQUE PIECES

The aim of this project was to produce a chair without the need for complex industrial technology. The basic elements of the cantilever chair are joined with polycaprolactone, a petroleum-based, biodegradable plastic. The material can be heated with a blow-dryer to make it pliable enough to be molded into shape.

# DJ
# SIMPSON

**FREE ADVICE**, 2006
PLASTICS LAMINATE (FORMICA®) ON BIRCH
PLYWOOD
WIDTH 1.50 × HEIGHT 1.50 M
COURTESY SIES + HÖKE, DÜSSELDORF
PRIVATE COLLECTION RADTKE, KREFELD

DJ Simpson uses an electric milling machine on different materials including Resopal-coated chipboard or aluminum-laminated plywood.
Different abstract lines, forms, and shade variations result in line
with the properties or hardness of the particular material, and give
the work a three-dimensional effect.

# ERNST
# STARK

**BOIS DE BOULOGNE I, LE JOGGEUR**, 2008
CHESTNUT, WATERCOLORS
DEPTH 13.2 × WIDTH 16.5 × HEIGHT 16.2 CM
© 2012, PROLITTERIS, ZURICH

The work is part of a series and was created during a residency in Paris awarded by the Hessische Kulturstiftung (Cultural Foundation of Hesse). The miniature was carved from freshly felled wood using first a chainsaw and then a fine, scalpel-like Japanese woodcarving knife. The tree depicted in the sculpture is a chestnut, and the trunk is taken from the same tree in the Bois de Boulogne.

# WOLFGANG STEHLE

**HILLSIDE**, 2009
SYNTHETIC ENAMEL ON COLORED PAPER, PLYWOOD SUPPORT,
ACRYLIC PAINT
DEPTH 4 × WIDTH 106 × HEIGHT 80 CM
COURTESY GALERIE KUTTNER SIEBERT, BERLIN

**OBSERVATORY CREST**, 2009
COLORED PAPER, COLORED PENCIL, PLYWOOD, ACRYLIC PAINT
DEPTH 4 × WIDTH 30 × HEIGHT 40 CM
COURTESY KUTTNER SIEBERT GALERIE, BERLIN

**POPUPSIDE**, 2009
SYNTHETIC ENAMEL ON PAPER, PLYWOOD
DEPTH 4 × WIDTH 140 × HEIGHT 80 CM
COURTESY KUTTNER SIEBERT GALERIE, BERLIN

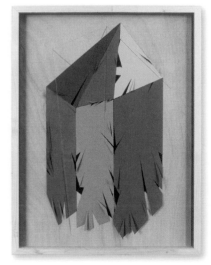

Wolfgang Stehle studied woodwork before attending the
Academy of Fine Arts in Munich. He also uses wood in his
drawings and paintings as a support element or veneer.

*WOLFGANG*
*STEHLE*

**GATEWAY 0.2**, 2009
WOOD VENEER, PLYWOOD SUPPORT, ACRYLIC PAINT
DEPTH 4 × WIDTH 87 × HEIGHT 67 CM
COURTESY KUTTNER SIEBERT GALERIE, BERLIN

**SPACESTATION**, 2009
WOOD VENEER, PLYWOOD SUPPORT, ACRYLIC PAINT
DEPTH 4 × WIDTH 153.5 × HEIGHT 116 CM
COURTESY KUTTNER SIEBERT GALERIE, BERLIN

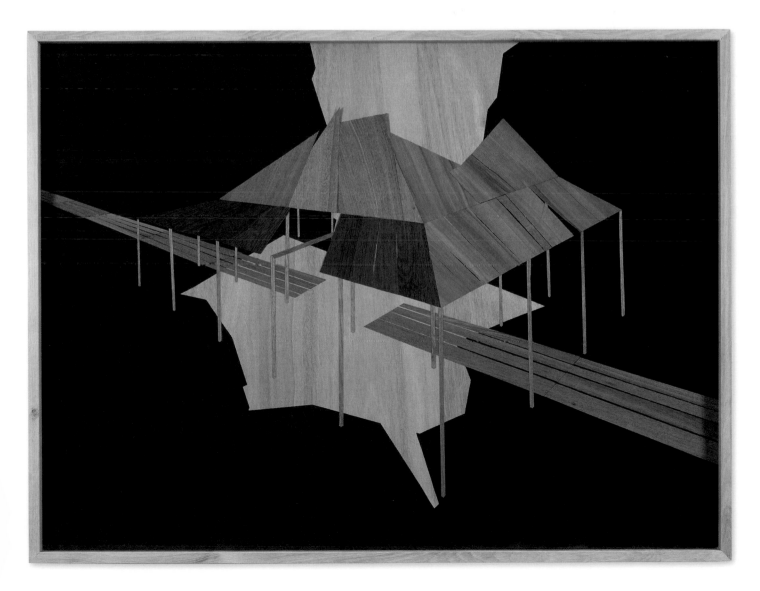

**SPACESTATION**, 2009
WOOD VENEER, PLYWOOD SUPPORT, ACRYLIC PAINT
DEPTH 4 × WIDTH 153.5 × HEIGHT 116 CM
COURTESY KUTTNER SIEBERT GALERIE, BERLIN

# ELISA STROZYK

**ACCORDION CABINET**, 2011
ELISA STROZYK AND SEBASTIAN NEEB
MIXED WOOD, "WOODEN TEXTILE"
DEPTH 43 × WIDTH 100 × HEIGHT 163 CM
PROTOTYPE

Elisa Strozyk joins diverse wooden veneers with a textile support. This combination is the basis of different projects that range from fashion to furniture, accessories, and interiors.

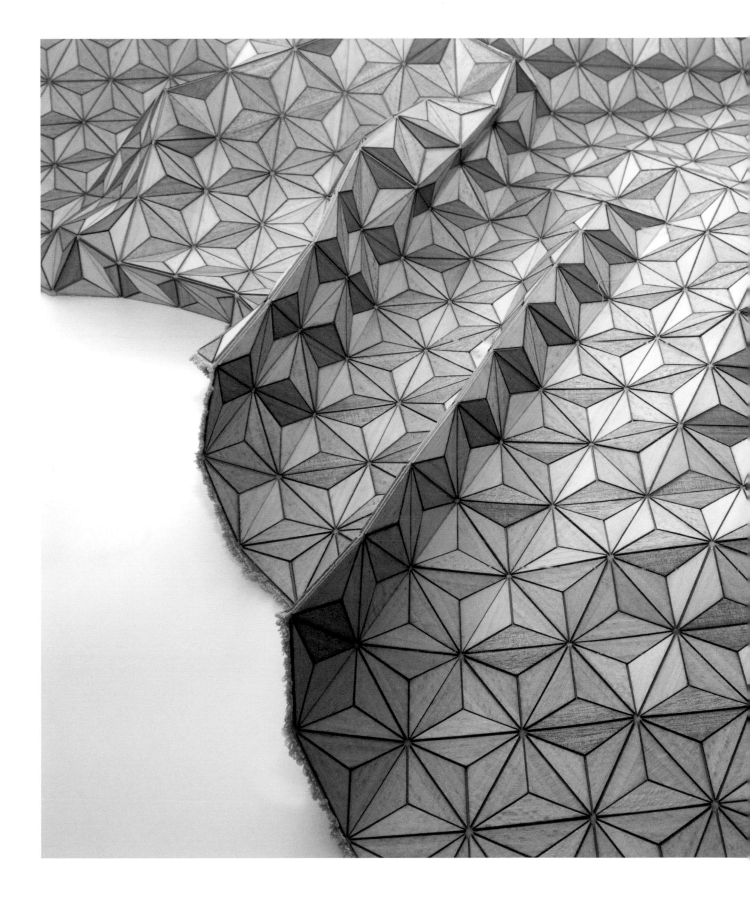

WOODEN CARPET, 2009
THREE-DIMENSIONAL WOODEN CARPET
DIVERSE VENEER ON TEXTILE
UNIQUE PIECE

"WOODEN TEXTILES", 2009
IN THE FASHION COLLECTION
"SIE SPRICHT MIT DEN BÄUMEN"
(SHE TALKS WITH TREES)
BY FASHION DESIGNER NADINE WELCHES

*ELISA
STROZYK*

**STOOL ANIMAL**, 2009
STOOL
DYED PLYWOOD, TEXTILES, SECOND-HAND
STOOL
DEPTH 50 × WIDTH 50 × HEIGHT 33 CM
UNIQUE PIECE

**WOODEN CARPET—SHERWOOD**, 2009
THREE-DIMENSIONAL WOODEN CARPET
VENEER (MAHOGANY, WALNUT, BOG OAK),
LINEN
LENGTH 162 × WIDTH 91 CM
MANUFACTURER: BÖWER

**COFFEE TABLE**, 2009
DISPLAY TABLE
MAHOGANY VENEER, TEXTILE,
SECOND-HAND TABLE
DEPTH 43 × WIDTH 65 × HEIGHT 41 CM
UNIQUE PIECE

**MISS MAPLE**, 2010
HANGING LAMP
MAPLE VENEER, TEXTILES, STEEL
DEPTH 85 × WIDTH 85 × HEIGHT 35 CM
PRODUCT AVAILABLE IN A LIMITED SERIES

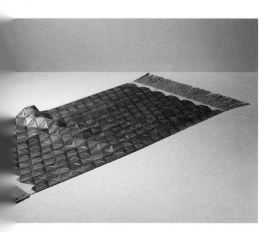

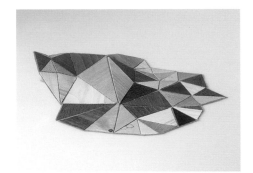

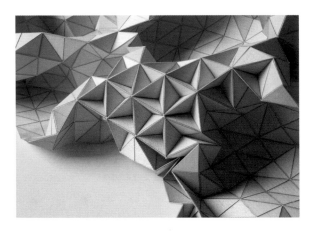

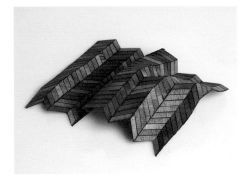

# "BRINGING WOOD TO LIFE"

*You've been working with the combination of wood and fabric for a while. How did you arrive at this idea?*

There were many influences, but one particular aspect was wanting to move from the two-dimensional to the three-dimensional. "Flat" was not enough for me. I come from textiles, and I started out experimenting with all of the textile techniques on wood. But, I have always combined hard and soft materials in order to get the most out of the structures of textiles. I discovered veneers that are thin enough to be used almost the same way as fabric. I started to experiment and soon began breaking down the wood to make it softer and more flexible. The true challenge for me was to find a way to make a fabric-like material from the hard material of wood, which has nothing in common with textiles. I'm interested in borders that cannot be clearly defined, for instance, is it wood or is it fabric?

*Have there been other reasons why you work with wood as a material?*

I'm attracted to the warmth that wood conveys, but I'm also interested in sustainability. Moreover, people tend to hang on to products made from durable materials and that age beautifully for a longer time. Wood is one of the rare materials that actually age beautifully, that do not decay with time. Nowadays, a new product starts going downhill as soon as you remove the wrapping from its perfect finish. It gets scratched, chipped, and so on. But wood does not lose its beauty. It doesn't decrease in value. In fact, it becomes more valuable with time.

*Do you think it's because wood is a natural product?*

Yes, but I'm very impressed by the fact that wood always looks like it has been alive. If it gets wet or moist, it almost comes back to life, it bends and pretty much does what it wants to. At the beginning, I collected a lot of pictures of water-damaged parquet flooring. You could see dramatic warping and splintering. It looked like the water had brought the wood back to life.

*Have you experimented with shrinking and swelling in your "wooden textiles"?*

I tried for a while, but gave up because the way I'm working with wood at the moment is easier.

*Do you glue the materials together?*

Yes, I glue them. But it took a while before I found the right glue. The fact that I use regular veneer means that it breaks very easily. However, I could double glue the veneer to make it more stable, but that would compromise the textile-like structure and the suppleness of the material.

*Which wood do you use?*

Mostly pear, apple, cherry, birch, and maple. They are ordered in a certain way, but the sequence is not always planned out exactly in advance. The pattern develops during the process of gluing.

*You often use the triangle as a form. Is there a special reason for this?*

I have experimented with a variety of forms. I first started with squares, rectangles, and long rectangles. Each one allows you to design a specific kind of movement. But the triangle is the easiest to transform into the third dimension. That's why I experimented more with it. Then I learned that each triangle can also move very differently.

*What market or areas of application do you see for the material?*

The "Wooden Carpet" was actually the original idea. Most homes have wooden floors or carpets. I thought it would be nice to have a wooden floor that you could roll out, and that you can move from one room to another. The "Wooden Carpet" is thicker and more durable than the other wooden textiles, and you can walk on it in high heels. I've also started producing for fashion designers. It's only been an experimental attempt for the runway, but I'm now working on making the material wearable. I think it's interesting to wear the material on the body, especially because it's supple and will move easily with the body. Special veneers exist that can be machine-washed.

*There is still much handcrafted work involved in your pieces. Do you think there could ever be a chance of a series production?*

Everything is developing step by step. At the beginning, I cut the veneer by hand. But it's much easier and faster since I started using laser. Meanwhile, a couple of companies have shown an interest in producing the material, but they're not yet able to produce it industrially. Even Böwer GmbH, who is already manufacturing the material, still largely relies on manual work.

*Do you ever consider other techniques?*

Yes. I'm now beginning to weave and braid wood. I use extremely thin veneers that can actually be laminated onto textiles. They aren't very tear resistant, but have strong fibers. I'll be working with wood for a while.

# STUDIO JOB

**INDUSTRY**, 2008
FURNITURE SERIES
BLACK DYED TULIP TREE, WHITE DYED BIRD'S EYE MAPLE,
POLISHED PU FINISH
TABLE: DEPTH 90 × WIDTH 240 × HEIGHT 76 CM
CABINET: DEPTH 50 × WIDTH 120 × HEIGHT 156 CM
SCREEN: DEPTH 5 × WIDTH 220 × HEIGHT 185 CM
EDITION OF 1/6 + 2 A.P.
COLLECTION GALERIE MITTERRAND CRAMER, GENEVA
EXHIBITED AT PAVILLON DES ARTS ET DU DESIGN, PARIS AND
DESIGN MIAMI/BASEL, MIAMI

The marquetry of the furniture series pays homage to the French
furniture maker André-Charles Boulle (1642–1732), who is considered
a master of marquetry. Studio Job combines this traditional technique with contemporary design. The veneer was cut with a laser
and inlaid by hand. All of the furniture in the series is coated with high
gloss enamel.

# TB&AJKAY

*WITH KARL-JOHAN HJERLING
AND KARIN WIDMARK*

**SPRING TABLE**
(FROM THE "SPRING COLLECTION"), 2010
TABLE
BIRCH, BIRCH PLYWOOD
DEPTH 75 × WIDTH 230 × HEIGHT 72 CM
PROTOTYPE

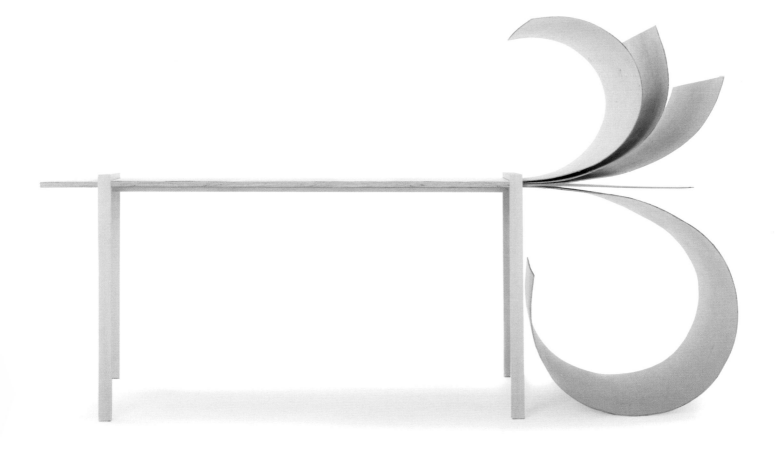

The tabletop is made from thin layers of birch plywood that separate and curl on one side of the table, the way wood shavings do when wood is being planed.

# THE MEDLEY INSTITUTE

*BY JANA PATZ*

**NO. II WHERE SEVEN BECOME ONE,**
**WOODEN OBJECTS,** 2010
FIVE-PIECE JEWELRY AND ACCESSORY
COLLECTION
WALNUT AND SILVER
HANDMADE UNIQUE PIECE

Every piece of the collection is cast from the human form and each is constructed individually using up to seven veneer layers; it is bent, cut, and sanded by hand. The objects can be worn as chains, shoulder objects, or collars.

The combination of fashion design, and materials or ways of working alien to fashion, play a large role in the development of the collection.

# KATHARINA TRUDZINSKI

**ICE CREAM**, 2008
ENAMEL PAINT, ACRYLIC PAINT ON WOOD
DEPTH 75 × WIDTH 80 × HEIGHT 190 CM

The artist, who lives in Hamburg and Berlin, often uses found objects in her work. These include lolly sticks as well as simple DIY materials like plywood boards and roofing lathes.

*KATHARINA*
*TRUDZINSKI*

**UNTITLED**, 2008
ACRYLIC PAINT ON WOOD
LENGTH 1.65 × WIDTH 1.03 M

**DAS HAUS AM HANG**, 2007
ENAMEL PAINT, ACRYLIC PAINT ON WOOD
LENGTH 80 × WIDTH 82 CM

**UNTITLED**, 2006
WOOD, ACRYLIC PAINT, INK, LOLLY STICKS
LENGTH 34 × WIDTH 25 CM

*CHARLOTTE*
*WAGEMAKER*

**MATERIAL ONDERZOEK** (MATERIAL
RESEARCH), 2012
WOODEN TILES
WIDTH 10 × HEIGHT 10 CM
ACRYLIC-BASED PAINT

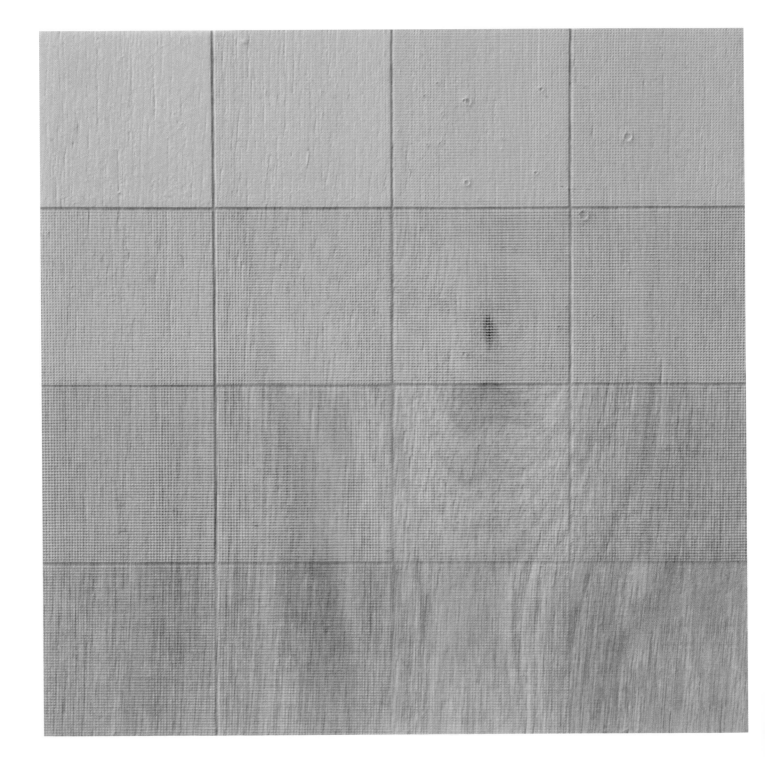

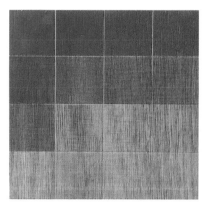

# AI
# WEIWEI

**MAP OF CHINA**, 2004
TIELI WOOD (IRONWOOD) FROM
DISMANTLED TEMPLES OF THE QING DYNASTY
(1644–1911)
Ø 200 CM, HEIGHT 51 CM

For the works entitled "Map of China" and "China Bench," Ai Weiwei
used wood from the Chinese temple ruins of the Qing Dynasty.
His installation entitled "Grapes" consists of chairs also from this era.
Tieli wood is a very hard wood and comes from the iron tree.

AI
WEIWEI

**GRAPES**, 2008
17 CHAIRS FROM THE QING DYNASTY (1644–1911)
DEPTH 1.57 × WIDTH 1.80 × HEIGHT 1.67 M

**BENCH**, 2004
TIELI WOOD (IRONWOOD) FROM DISMANTLED
TEMPLES OF THE QING DYNASTY
(1644–1911)
Ø 55 CM, LENGTH 400 CM
COURTESY FRIEDMAN BENDA GALLERY, NEW YORK

# BETHAN LAURA WOOD

**PARTICLE**, 2010
FURNITURE COLLECTION
DIFFERENT LAMINATES (BY ABET LAMINATI) IN
WOOD LOOK
IN COLLABORATION WITH GIANNINA
CAPITANI

The forms used for this furniture series look like wooden boxes and standardized package materials. The laser-cut laminate is an imitation of the look of oriented strand boards (OSB), and is woven together like a rag carpet.

# RICHARD
# WOODS

**OFFCUT INLAY PICTURE NO. 36**, 2009
WIDTH 90 × HEIGHT 122 CM
GLOSSY ACRYLIC PAINT ON MDF WITH
PLYWOOD
© RICHARD WOODS
COURTESY RICHARD WOODS STUDIO LTD.

**OFFCUT INLAY PICTURE NO. 37**, 2010
WIDTH 90 × HEIGHT 122 CM
GLOSSY ACRYLIC PAINT ON MDF WITH
PLYWOOD
© RICHARD WOODS
COURTESY RICHARD WOODS STUDIO LTD.

Woods' work is a mixture of art, architecture, and interior design. He designs, for instance, facades with cartoon-like patterns or lines floors with oversized artificial wood grain. The plywood pictures are painted using an enamel-based acrylic paint.

# MATERIAL AND TECHNOLOGY GUIDE

*ELEMENTARY PRINCIPLES AND INNOVATIVE
DEVELOPMENTS IN THE AREAS OF WOOD AND
WOOD-BASED MATERIALS, PRODUCTION
PROCESSES AND CONSTRUCTION PRINCIPLES
IN TIMBER BUILDING*

| I | MATERIAL |
|---|---|
| II | TECHNOLOGY: PRODUCTION PROCESSES |
| III | TECHNOLOGY: THE PRINCIPLES OF TIMBER CONSTRUCTION |

# I MATERIAL

**1**    **WOOD—DEFINITION AND CHARACTERISTICS**

What is wood?

Characteristics of wood


**2**    **SOLID WOOD**

**2.1**    Conifers

**2.2**    Deciduous trees


**3**    **VENEER**


**4**    **WOOD-BASED MATERIALS**

**4.1**    **Materials made from solid wood**
**4.1.1**    Solid timber panels
**4.1.2**    Timber construction materials
**4.1.2.1**    Glued laminated timber (glulam)
**4.1.2.2**    Cross laminated timber (CLT)

**4.2**    **Materials made from wood veneer**
**4.2.1**    Veneer plywood, star plywood (veneer panels)
**4.2.2**    Blockboard and laminboard
**4.2.3**    Molded plywood and molded laminate
**4.2.4**    3D-veneer
**4.2.5**    Engineered wood products based on veneers

**4.3**    **Materials made from wood chips**
**4.3.1**    Chipboard
**4.3.2**    Molded chipboard elements
**4.3.3**    Mineral-bound chipboard
**4.3.4**    Engineered wood products based on wood chips

**4.4**    **Materials made from fibers**
**4.4.1**    Fiberboard
**4.4.2**    Fiber shaped elements
**4.4.3**    Engineered wood products based on fibers
**4.4.3.1**    Vapor-permeable MDF panels
**4.4.3.2**    Scrimber
**4.4.3.3**    Shaped wood

**4.5**    **Lightweight panels**

**4.6**    **Composite materials with wood**
**4.6.1**    Wood-glass composites
**4.6.2**    Wood-concrete composites
**4.6.3**    Wood-fiber material composites
**4.6.4**    Wood-steel composites
**4.6.5**    Wood-plastic composites (WPC)

**4.7**    **Other wood composite materials**

**4.8**    **Materials made from woody plants**
**4.8.1**    Bamboo
**4.8.2**    Palm ("palm wood")
**4.8.3**    Lightweight chipboard

**4.9**    **Materials made from non-wood parts of the tree**
**4.9.1**    Cork
**4.9.2**    Bast

## 1 WOOD—DEFINITION AND CHARACTERISTICS

### WHAT IS WOOD?

Trunks, branches and twigs of trees and shrubs consist of wood. Trees are permeated by water transit tissue (xylem) and material transit tissue (phloem) and grow upwards (primary vertical growth), and also in width (secondary thickness growth). Above a certain size the original pathways (medullary rays) can no longer supply the tree. Then, in the course of secondary thickness growth, further pathways (secondary medullary rays) are formed. A separable (embryonal) cellular layer, known as the cambium, is responsible for thickness growth. Tissue that is deposited outwards by the cambium is defined as bast (secondary phloem or inner bark). Bast in turn frequently forms a further (secondary) cambium, the so-called cork cambium (phellogen) that externally forms *cork*, which is excluded from the supply of water and nutrients. Together all cork layers are known as the *bark*. The cork layers of trees are generally thin, for instance in birch trees. Only in those trees where the activity of the cork cambium extends over longer periods, in particular in the cork oak, is a thick cork layer formed. For this reason the bark of the cork oak is often known colloquially as cork.

Tissue transported inwards by the cambium is described as wood (secondary xylem). As it ages and grows (between twenty and thirty years) *sapwood*, young wood that transports water and nutrients, gradually loses the ability to transport water and nutrients. In some species of tree such as Douglas fir, oak, pine or walnut the old internal sapwood changes into heartwood. Sapwood and heartwood are made up of the growth rings of wood known sometimes as annual rings. However, annual rings are only formed in climatic zones with cold periods during which no growth takes place and are therefore generally not found in tropical woods. The trees that do not form any heartwood include maple, birch, alder, lime and hornbeam. Depending on the type of tree, the heartwood contains different tannins and pigments as well as phenolic resins. The greater the amount of phenol in the heartwood, the more resistant it is to attack by fungus or insects, and therefore the more suitable it is for outdoor use.

Wood is made up of cellulose (c. 45 percent), wood polyose also known as hemicellulose—(18-27 percent) and lignin (22-30 percent) as well as further elements such as resins, tannins, and pigments: the cellulose forms the non-woody cell walls which are hardened (made woody) by the wood polyose and lignin. The proportion of lignin, which is decisive for the compressive strength of the wood, is somewhat greater in conifers than in deciduous trees. However, as the production of lignin increases with increased warmth, the lignin content of tropical woods is very much greater than, for example, that of European types of wood.

## CHARACTERISTICS OF WOOD

### Strength

The strength of solid materials is generally described in terms of their gross density and weight. Gross density describes the relationship between mass (kg) and volume ($m^3$). In the case of wood this means the relationship between the cell wall substance and the hollow area. Essentially the rule is: the greater the gross density; the higher the compressive strength, the sound insulation value and the thermal storage capacity of a material. In comparison to construction steel, which has a gross density of 7,850 $kg/m^3$, oak has a gross density of around 700 $kg/m^3$. But despite its relatively low gross density, wood has a comparatively high bending, tensile, and compressive strength, as well as high strength parallel to the direction of the fibers.

### Hardness

Depending on what it will be used for, in addition to strength the hardness of wood also plays a decisive role. The differentiation between hard and softwoods is based on their dry density, the gross density of the wood at 0 percent water content or wood moisture. The boundary between hard and softwoods lies at a dry density of 550 $kg/m^3$. According to this definition most of the conifers are softwoods, such as spruce with a dry density around 430 $kg/m^3$ or Douglas fir, around 470 $kg/m^3$. Many deciduous trees are defined as hardwoods, such as beech and oak with an average dry density of 680 $kg/m^3$. However balsa (on average 90 $kg/m^3$), poplar (average 410 $kg/m^3$), lime and willow (both on average 520 $kg/m^3$) are deciduous trees that are numbered among the soft to very soft woods.

### Swelling and shrinking

An important criterion in the use and processing of wood is its performance as regards swelling and shrinking. In principle, denser wood is more subject to swelling and shrinkage movement than lighter wood with fewer, but larger cell spaces. Exceptions include woods such as teak, afzelia, or mahogany which, despite their high density, are very stable, and woods such as spruce or poplar which despite their low density show marked swelling and shrinkage movement.

### Color

In most kinds of tree the young sapwood is an even, light yellowish or reddish color. When heartwood forms (see above) in conifers and also in most deciduous trees different colored substances are deposited that are produced by the oxidation of various tannins. This results in a wide spectrum of colors ranging from white (larch) to yellow (teak), olive (ash), brown (elm), and to black (ebony). The color of wood can be changed by introducing heat, for instance steaming used in the production of veneers. For example beech which is originally white acquires a salmon tinge as the result of steaming.

### Aroma

The aromas specific to wood depend upon its chemical contents. Coniferous woods in particular contain essential oils and resins (terpenes) whose *scent* induces a feeling of well-being while also functioning as a repellent, for instance against moths (Swiss pine, cedar). Phenolic substances also determine the aroma of wood. These include vanillin which is produced from lignin, benzaldehyde known as bitter almond oil, which is also found in cherrywood, benzyl alcohol, which is found in lignin in spruce, or tannins, which are found in the wood and bark of oak, birch and chestnut.

The chemical content of wood can also influence *taste*, a fact that is exploited in the maturing of wine or whisky in oak barrels (barrique ageing). By "toasting" the inner face of the staves of the barrel over an open fire an abundance of aromas such as vanillin are released and provide the particular taste required. The tannins referred to above evaporate and give the maturing whisky not only its characteristic color but also its slightly smoky taste. In red wines they augment the wine's natural tannin content and with white wines, which are naturally low in tannin, they provide structure.

### Heat

Heat storage and heat insulation capacity are two opposite characteristics of materials. Essentially the rule is: the greater the gross density of a material, the greater its storage and thermal conductivity and the lower its heat insulation capacity. The sole exception is powder snow which, despite excellent insulation properties comparable to those of rock wool, also has the excellent heat storage characteristics of water. This is demonstrated by the heat characteristics of an igloo, for example.

Wood combines both qualities in an ideal way, as it is, after water, one of the best heat storage materials, and after powder snow—and far ahead of many other materials—on account of its poor thermal conductivity, one of the best heat insulators; only a thin surface layer of wood works as heat storage (therefore when used as such only thin layers should be employed). In interior fitting-out wood is therefore ideal for floors. Wood and woodbased materials are also in general an ideal material in harsher climates, in particular: they are natural insulators and comparatively free of condensation.

### Acoustics

On account of its good acoustic properties wood is used to make string and woodwind instruments as well as organs, and is also used in interiors, for instance concert halls, to optimize the acoustics. The spread of sound parallel to the wood fibers is about twice as fast as at right angles to them.

On account of its low weight, solid timber is not a suitable material for (footfall) sound insulation, as it does not sufficiently dampen the spread of sound. For such purposes fiber panels with sound absorbing perforations are more suitable (cf. 4.4.1 fiber insulation board).

### Warning ability

Depending on the respective degree of toughness, certain kinds of timber, when subjected to great buckling stress, give off a cracking sound long before they reach the actual fracture limit. This is called the warning ability and in earlier times led to the use of specific kinds of wood for underground structures in the area of mining (spruce, fir, larch and Scots pine but also oak and acacia have this warning ability). Under certain circumstances—for instance fire—this ability of wood to provide a warning can play a role in modern timber construction.

### Availability

Wood is an economical raw material that is readily available in very many regions of the world, in Central Europe thanks in particular to sustainable forestry which has been carried out there for centuries. Combined with its qualities as a building material this gives wood a considerable advantage over other materials. Due to the short transport routes involved, timber-based materials that, in most cases, are or can be produced in regional proximity offer an economical alternative to other building materials.

### Cradle-to-cradle

Wood is not only a renewable $CO_2$-neutral raw material; if untreated it can be reintroduced 100 percent into the biological cycle (cradle-to-cradle-principle). This natural characteristic, too, gives wood a qualitative advantage over many other materials.

### Age

Age(ing) is of significance for wood in many respects: trees can live for several hundred years, a number for even more than one thousand. Although today, because they are used for timber, few trees reach their natural age, the forestry period (i.e. the period over which a tree grows until its wood is processed) can still be between 100 and 200 years, depending on the species. This means that timber is part of a truly sustainable process that extends over a number of human generations.

Wood—in contrast to all mineral materials and many other materials—does not change its aggregate state as a result of being worked. If it is cared for, which is a relatively simple process, or impregnated, wood does not lose its constructive qualities even after centuries—this too is a special aspect in comparison with many other materials. So wood can be used, restored, and used again several times, in some cases even without recycling, irrespective of its age. Proof of this is offered by, for example, the production of veneers out of old wood, or the further use of reclaimed wood, for instance to make furniture.

### 2 SOLID WOOD

Solid wood is the term used to describe wood that is left with its natural structure, i.e. that is only sawn, milled or planed. A distinction is drawn between logs, which are freed from branches and bark, and sawn timber (construction timber) that is sawn parallel to the axis of the trunk. Logs or round timbers are used as piles, posts and for (peeled) veneers, whereas sawn timber, depending on its dimensions, is used for beams, squared timber, planks, boards or also for veneers.

---

### NOTE

*A variety of criteria can be used to draw distinctions between different kinds of trees, for instance their regional origins (tropical woods), wood-type criteria (trees that form heartwood, those that do not), their size (small trees, medium size trees, tall trees) or their characteristics (hardwood, softwood). Most common is the separation into wood from coniferous and wood from deciduous trees, which is used below.*

---

### 2.1 Softwoods (conifers)

Coniferous trees, which are older in terms of development history, are characterized by quick growth, which makes them particularly suitable for forestry. Conifers—in contrast to deciduous trees—also grow in inhospitable climatic conditions, and their wood has a very even structure. In Europe the conifers most frequently used in the fields of building construction and furniture making are spruce, pine, fir, larch and Douglas fir.

Below are brief descriptions of various conifers and their characteristics, the selection reflects the conifers mentioned in the project section.

### Douglas fir (Pseudotsuga menziesii)

Due to its relatively high dry density (depending upon region c. 520 kg/m³) the wood from the Douglas fir has excellent mechanical properties when subject to bending or tension stress and very high stability. This makes it particularly suitable as construction timber and for hydraulic engineering projects. However, it is also used for railway sleepers or in interiors for floorboards, window frames or wall cladding.
→ *Example: p. 194; Lex Pott*

### Hinoki cypress (Chamaecyparis obtusa)

Hinoki wood is light colored and has a pleasant, lemony scent. It is extremely resistant to rot and needs no additional treatment with wax or oil. In Japan this wood is extremely popular as a construction material for use in temples and shrines.
→ *Example: p. 48; BCXSY*

### Larch (Larix decidua)

Larch is characterized by its durability, even in water. In comparison with other coniferous woods larch is very hard (average dry density 550 kg/m³), durable and tough, it shrinks very little and is largely resistant to attack by fungus. The wood is used for model building, as construction timber both indoors and outdoors (e.g. shingles), and is equally suitable for bridge building and ship building.
→ *Example: p. 252; Wingårdh*

### Pine (Pinus)

As it makes up about 24 percent of the area covered by woodland, pine is, after spruce, the second most common kind of tree in Germany. The wood is durable, somewhat harder than spruce (average dry density 510 kg/m³), and is used above all as construction timber both indoors and outdoors (roof structures, windows, doors, floorboards, furniture making). The sapwood of pine is subject to fungus and insect attack but can be easily impregnated. Like spruce it is frequently used as a raw material for the production of wood-based materials.
→ *Example: p. 52; Beton*

### Silver fir (Abies alba)

Like spruce the wood of the silver fir can be subjected to considerable bending and compression stresses and is therefore highly suitable for construction timber (average density 410 kg/m³). As, compared with other conifers, the wood of the silver fir is more durable under water, it is used primarily for structures in contact with the earth or in hydraulic engineering. A further special quality is its complete freedom from resin, which makes silver fir suitable also for use in interiors and as resonance wood for making musical instruments.
→ *Example: p. 16; Architekten Martenson und Nagel-Theissen*

### Spruce (Picea abies)

The spruce is the most widely grown tree in European forestry. As its wood is not resistant to weathering, unless it is untreated its suitability for outdoor use is limited. The relatively soft spruce wood (average dry density 430 kg/m³) is easy to work and is used as construction timber, for roof beams and battens, for window frames, and also for floors. At the same time spruce is one of the most frequently used raw materials in the manufacture of wood-based materials.
→ *Example: p. 62; Caminada/Ballenberg*

### Swiss or Arolla pine (Pinus cembra)

With a dry density of around 400 kg/m³ the Swiss pine is the lightest native softwood, at the same time its wood has the lowest shrinkage rate of
all coniferous woods. The pinosylvin contained in the wood not only produces a pleasant scent but is also moth-repellent and has an antibacterial effect and is therefore in demand for making furniture. In addition it has been proven that interior fittings or beds made of Swiss pine have a positive impact on the human heart rate in that they lower it perceptibly.

### Western red cedar (Thuja plicata)

The Western red cedar is native to North America. It is said to have healing powers, for instance with asthma. The wood, which has a dry density of c. 350 kg/m³, is light, durable and very resistant to weathering, but if used for building construction can only be subjected to light stresses. Consequently it is used externally for non-structural purposes such as roof shingles, shutters, doors and also for ship building.
→ *Example: p. 11; 24H > architecture*

## 2.2 Hardwoods (woods from deciduous trees)

As they have slower growth rates and do not grow as straight as conifers, deciduous trees have certain disadvantages compared with conifers, however in terms of building construction their qualities are in no way inferior. As a way of strengthening hardwoods are nowadays combined with softwoods—for instance in glued laminated timber. For furniture making and in interior design, hardwood veneers and timber sections are frequently chosen on account of their high quality appearance. In forestry, mixed plantations of conifers and deciduous trees are today preferred to mono-cultures, as the latter are more prone to disease. For this reason attempts are being made to make increased use of hardwood for construction. At present in Austria, for example, hardwood accounts for only 2 percent of the timber used in building.

Below are descriptions of the most common hardwoods with reference to the project section, along with their particular qualities.

### Abachi (Triplochiton scleroxylon)

The wood of the abachi, which is native to Africa, is soft and not weather resistant (dry density c. 350 kg/m³). Abachi wood, which grows quickly, is used mostly for furniture and in interiors and, on account of its good sound qualities, also for making musical instruments. The wood is also said to have an alleviating effect on asthmatic complaints.

→ Example: p. 236; Studio Formafantasma

### Ash (Fraxinus excelsior)

Ash is one of the heaviest and hardest European hardwoods (average dry density 670 kg/m³). It is both strong and elastic. On account of these qualities the wood is used to produce sports equipment, tool handles and ladders. It is also used in furniture making (bentwood furniture), for staircases or parquet flooring in interiors, as well as in building as construction timber. Ash is also very suitable for turning and its interesting grain makes it popular as a veneer.

→ Example: p. 107; Grcic, BD Barcelona

### Balsa (Ochroma pyramidale)

Thanks to its low weight—its dry density is between 70 and 130 kg/m³—balsa wood is traditionally used for model making and in the manufacture of toys, packaging, stage sets and furniture, and also for making surfboards. Balsa wood is also used in the manufacture of lightweight construction panels that are becoming increasingly important in the field of building. Additionally Balsa wood is used in the construction of wind turbines.

→ Example Material Section: p. 266; 4.5, balsa board

### Beech (Fagus sylvatica)

Beech, which is hard and resistant to abrasion (dry density 680 kg/m³), is used above all in interiors for parquet floors or staircases. If untreated it is almost white in color and is also popular as solid wood for furniture making. Beech is increasingly being used in the production of timber construction materials for the building industry.

→ Example: p. 92; Elise Gabriel

### Birch (Betula)

Birch (dry density 640 kg/m³) is one of the heavier woods. Due to its toughness and elasticity this wood can be easily bent. Birch is used primarily for parquet flooring as well as for toys and kitchen utensils. It also serves as the basis for veneer, chipboard and fiber-based materials.

→ Example: p. 239; Tb&Ajkay

### Box (Buxus sempervirens)

With a density of up to 1,100 kg/m³ box wood is the hardest and heaviest European wood. It is highly resistant, ages well, and is suitable for steam bending. It can take substantial loads, and has high compressive and impact strength. It is suitable for engraving and turning and is used to make wind instruments and violins (pegs and tailpiece).

→ Example: p. 166; Idee Liu

### Chestnut (Castanea sativa)

The wood of the chestnut, also known as real chestnut or sweet chestnut, is very resilient and its gold-brown color and grain give it a similar appearance to oak, but it has, however, less strength than oak. This medium weight wood (dry density c. 540 kg/m³) is used as construction timber both indoors and outdoors, as well as in ship building and hydraulic engineering.

→ Example: p. 226; Ernst Stark

### Cocobolo (Dalbergia retusa)

This tree is native to the Pacific coast of Central America. It has a high strength; the dry density is of 800 kg/m³. Cocobolo is used for veneers, inlays and panels, but is also suitable for tool and knife handles.

→ Example: p. 60; Tord Boontje, Cabinet

### Elm (Ulmus)

European and Japanese elms have a dry density of 540 kg/m³, the Wych elm 640 kg/m³. The wood has low bending and compression strength and very low bearing capacity and impact resistance. All varieties are suitable for steam bending. Elm is used to produce veneers, furniture, and parquet and to line walls and ceilings.

→ Example: p. 30; Aldo Bakker

### Honey locust (Gleditsia triacanthos)

The honey locust is native to North America where it is used above all in the manufacture of pallets and boxes but also for furniture making, interior fitting-out and also as construction timber. With a dry density of 720 kg/m³, the wood is comparatively hard and dense.

→ Example: p. 30; Aldo Bakker

### Ironwood (Metrosideros)

The wood of a number of trees, e.g. ipé or tieli, which has a dry density of over 1,000 kg/m³ and is very dense, hard and durable, is known as ironwood. Ironwoods are very suitable for terrace floors or boat jetties. On account of their density and hardness, ironwoods can also be used for turning and for the manufacture of sticks, musical instruments, and furniture.

→ Example: p. 251; Ai WeiWei, Bench

### Lime (Tilia)

The dry density of the European lime (linden) is around 500 kg/m³, whereas the American and Japanese species have a slightly lower density. The wood is yellowish-white in color or often reddish to brownish. Linden wood is frequently used for woodcarving and to make sculptures.

→ Example: p. 162; Khai Liew

### Mahogany (Meliaceae)

Mahogany is a tropical wood tree, various species grow in Africa, Central and South America. Depending on the kind, the dry density varies between 450 and 700 kg/m³. Mahogany ages well and is widely used outdoors, as well as in furniture making, for interior fittings, veneers and for building exclusive boats.

→ Example: p. 60; Tord Boontje, Witches' Kitchen

### Maple (Acer)

With a density of 590 kg/m³ (sycamore—Acer pseudoplatanus) up to 620 kg/m³ (Norway maple —Acer platanoides), maple is regarded as a hard, sturdy and elastic wood with high resistance to abrasion. For this reason and also due to its light color, maple is often used for furniture making and interior fitting-out, as well as for the manufacture of domestic, kitchen and sport appliances and for toys. Maple is widely used in making musical instruments and is especially suitable for wood turning, carving and sculptures.

→ Example: p.86; Laetitia Florin

### Oak (Quercus)

In Europe oak is, along with beech, one of the most frequently used kinds of wood. Oak is heavy—its dry density is 670 kg/m³—resistant and is used as a veneer and solid wood in furniture making, for staircases, doors and windows, as parquet and floorboards and for making barrels (see Aroma). For centuries it has played a major role in building construction, for instance in half-timbered buildings, and its importance in modern building construction is growing.

→ Example: p. 84, Fehling & Peiz

### Padauk (Pterocarpus)

There are various species of padauk (or padouk) tree including the African padauk, Manila padauk and Burma padauk. The wood from Africa is dark brown with violet stripes, the Asian version is golden yellow to brick red and in some cases has a striking grain. This hard wood (dry density 750 kg/m³) is used to make woodwind instruments, in boat building and furniture making as well as for the manufacture of parquet.

→ Example: p. 100; Graft, Restaurant

### Poplar (Populus)

Poplar wood grows quickly, is light and tough (dry density 450 kg/m³) and was used in earlier times for making wooden shoes and is the traditional material for the manufacture of matches, fruit crates or baskets. Poplar was also used for the structure of luxury suitcases (e.g. by Louis Vuitton) and was employed in the manufacture of automobile bodies (for instance of the DKW P15). The trunks are processed to make

chipboard or chipboard panels, laminates and veneers.

→ *Example: p. 52; Beton*

### Rosewood (Dalbergia)

Rosewood is the term used to describe the woods of different members of the genus Dalbergia. Depending on type, the wood is either dark red-black or violet-brown. This dense and hard wood (the dry density is around 800 kg/m³) is used to make marimbas, xylophones and record-ers as well as for the fingerboards, sides and back of guitars. Rosewood is also regarded as an excellent decorative and veneer wood for fur-niture and interior fitting-out, and is very suit-able for inlays too. Black grenadilla wood also belongs to the rosewood family and with a dry density of 1,200 kg/m³ is one of the heaviest woods. It comes from the savannah regions of Africa and is used principally to make flutes, clarinets and oboes. Due to of its hardness this wood is very suitable for turning.

→ *Example: p. 60; Tord Boontje, Cabinet*

### Teak (Tectona grandis)

Teak is among the best known and most valua-ble woods from Asia. Due to its high quality, teak is today cultivated in many tropical countries. It has an average dry density of 630 kg/m³, is pale brown to brown in color and occasionally also has striped markings. Left untreated, teak weathers and turns gray—an effect that is often deliberately exploited. Teak is used for boat-building, for garden furniture, windows and doors as well as for parquet flooring.

→ *Example: p. 127; INCH, Sideboard*

### Tulip tree (Liriodendron tulipifera)

The wood of the tulip tree (also known as white-wood) is used above all in the northeast of the USA in the manufacture of doors, windows, shelving and molds and due to its low weight (average dry density 430 kg/m³) is also used for model building. As a veneer it is frequently used in making pianos.

→ *Example: p. 238; Studio Job*

### Walnut (Juglans regia)

Walnut wood is hard—the dry density is on aver-age around 640 kg/m³—elastic, abrasion resis-tant and it swells and shrinks only slightly. The sapwood is reddish-white in color whereas the heartwood can vary in color from gray to brown. Walnut is valued as a decorative wood for the manufacture of furniture, for interior fitting-out and as parquet, for paneling and turning.

→ *Example: p. 230; Elisa Strozyk, Wooden Carpet, Sherwood*

### Wild cherry (Prunus avium)

The hard wood of the wild cherry is dense, has fine fibers, bends easily, is difficult to split but is not weather resistant. The dry density is around 550 kg/m³. With its shimmering reddish-brown color, cherry wood has been traditionally used for decorative furniture as well as for instru-ments and also in interior fitting-out, for parquet flooring and veneers.

→ *Example: p. 115; Florian Hauswirth, doublefacette*

### Willow (Salix)

The wood of the willow, which dries well, is white or reddish in color. It is flexible, extremely light (average dry density 350 kg/m³), tough and fibrous. Willow rods are used primarily to weave baskets or as fences. In addition willow, like aspen wood, is used to make matches and wooden shoes.

→ *Example: p. 142; Cordula Kehrer, Bow Bin 04*

### Zebrawood (Microberlinia)

The hard tropical zebrawood—its dry density is around 730 kg/m³—has a yellowish gray to brownish color with brown stripes. The strikingly grained wood is used mostly as a veneer in furniture making, but also as solid wood for sculpture and carving.

→ *Example: p. 219; Franziska Schreiber*

## 3 VENEER

Veneers are thin sheets of wood, between 0.05 and 8 millimeters in thickness, which are pro-duced by sawing, cutting or peeling logs. Depend-ing on the technique employed, between 800 and 1,000 square meters of large veneers can be produced per cubic meter of wood. In the pro-duction of sawn veneers, the logs are fixed to a carriage and then slid against either a horizon-tal saw blade (veneer gang saw) or a vertical saw blade (veneer circular saw). The advantages of sawn veneer are that the wood preserves its original color and no cracks or breakage occurs during the production process. This means that sawn veneer is especially recommended for high quality furniture and parquet flooring. The dis-advantage of sawn veneer is that it is an in-efficient and uneconomical way of using wood, as, depending on the thickness of the veneer, between 50 and 80 percent sawdust and waste wood is produced. However, particularly hard woods (e.g. the ironwood tree) or also the hard trunks of palm trees can, from a certain thick-ness, only be used for sawn veneers.

In slicing and peeling the logs are first of all cut to size and then boiled in water or steamed. Boiling influences the suppleness of the wood and the heat changes its color.

A distinction is drawn between different slicing techniques. In longitudinal slicing, which is essentially much the same as planing, a wooden board is pulled flat over a fixed knife and the veneer sheets are planed off from the bottom of the board. In the case of flat cut, flat sliced, crown cut or crown sliced veneer, the log is halved and the core side is fixed to the table or carriage of the cutting machine. The carriage is then led against a fixed blade and the wood is cut from the outside, parallel to the edge of the block (tangential cut). The first slices have a grained (flower-like) appearance, as the blade moves inwards stripes of grain appear. In what is known as true-quarter slicing, the logs are first quartered, also fixed to a car-riage and then cut at right angles to the annual rings, which produces a stripy veneer (rift veneer). In the case of flat quarter or bastard quarter cutting the annual rings of the logs (which are also first cut into quarters) are cut at a flat angle (radial cut), so that first of all a

semi-flowery appearance is obtained, becoming more stripy towards the centre. In those kinds of wood with large pith rays (e.g. oak) these stripes are recognizable as what are called (high) flakes.

In peeling, too, a variety of techniques can be employed. The most frequently used is known as rotary cut. In standard peeling machines, axially positioned brackets hold the wood core and at the same time rotate the flitch against a fixed blade. In this way the veneer is peeled in a spiral from the outside. In a more recently em-ployed process the fixing and drive are separated from each other, which produces a more efficient yield per flitch and also allows logs with a dis-eased core to be used. For veneer-based mate-rials (see relevant section), generally rotary cut veneers are used—the European kinds of wood used here are beech, birch, and poplar, as well as spruce and pine. For eccentric or stay-log cut-ting, the log is halved and fixed eccentrically to a turning beam (stay-log). The veneer is peeled in very flat arcs through the annual rings, pro-ducing a similar appearance to flat cutting. In the technique known as cutting from the heart the halved log is, in comparison with the stay-log process, swiveled through 180° around its long axis and the peeling process begins from the inside. This process produces a particularly "flowery" appearance, especially with wide veneers. For rift cutting, occasionally also known as rift-stay-log cutting, a quarter of a log is fixed to the rotating beam of the stay-log machine. This process is particularly suitable for timber with large pith rays, such as oak, in order to achieve a stripy appearance without recog-nizable "flakes" (see bastard quarter cutting). This is possible by re-fixing the flitch several times so that it is always positioned at about 15° to the cutting position normally used in the production of stripe veneers.

## 4 WOOD-BASED MATERIALS

The term wood-based materials is used to de-scribe all those materials for the production of which solid wood is taken apart by sawing, peeling, splitting, machining, hacking or fraying and then reconstituted using adhesives, screws, dowels, or nails. Wood-based materials have characteristics that solid wood does not possess. For instance, in relationship to their strength, they are relatively light and their mechanical properties are clearly defined or can be precisely calculated. Also, in wood-based materials made from solid wood areas that reduce strength, such as knotholes or incisions in the bark, can be removed thus substantially improving the quality compared with solid wood. In addition wood-based materials are available in the form of large panels and in long lengths and large cross-sections. And, in comparison with solid wood, their swelling and shrinking behavior is less marked. Thanks to all these criteria wood-based materials are especially suitable for industrial production in almost all fields. It should, however, be kept in mind that the amount of energy required to produce a wood-based material in-creases the finer its base particles are.

Engineered wood products (EWP) are construc-tional wood-based materials from the processing

level of veneers upwards. They were specially developed in North America and Scandinavia for use in timber engineering. They represent an alternative to solid timber and—above all from the economic viewpoint—offer an alternative to traditional solid timber-based construction materials such as glulam or cross laminated timber. EWPs are a further development of materials based on veneers, wood chips, and fibers in which particular attention is paid to meeting the requirements of building construction (in terms of strength, fire protection, safety of use etc.). In contrast to standard timber-based materials, EWPs have a very high proportion of artificial resins and are glued under a far higher temperature and with greater pressure. They are characterized by high stability and can be produced in considerable lengths and cross sections with the same constant quality. As they are primarily available in the form of rods (scrimber or parallel strand lumber), or those produced as flat elements (laminated veneer lumber or laminated strand lumber) can be used to form rod-shaped elements, EWPs are frequently referred to as rod-shaped wood-based materials.

*NOTE*

*The various wood-based materials are listed below in ascending order according to the degree of fineness of their elements (solid timber boards/ rods › veneers › chips › fibers). The wood engineered product variations are listed separately. This is followed by the composite materials containing a proportion of wood, further materials made of various combinations of wood with other materials, materials made from woody plants, and materials made from non-wood parts of trees.*

## 4.1 Materials made from solid wood

The term solid wood materials includes all materials manufactured on the basis of solid wood elements (boards or rods) with a minimum thickness of c. 4 millimeters.

### 4.1.1 Solid timber panels

Solid timber panels are produced in single and multi-layer versions. The single layer panels consist of individual 20, 30 or 50 millimeter-wide softwood or hardwood slats that can be extended by means of finger joint connections and glued to create panels of different widths and lengths. In multi-layer solid timber panels, the individual layers are glued together with the grain crosswise up to a total thickness of 60 millimeters. Solid timber panels are used primarily in fitting out interiors and for the manufacture of furniture, internal space dividers and wall linings.

### 4.1.2 Timber construction materials

#### 4.1.2.1 Glued laminated timber (glulam)

Glued laminated timber consists of at least three boards or slats, each up to 45 millimeters thick, which are glued with their fibers parallel. It has a bearing strength up to 50 percent greater than that of normal construction lumber. Glulam is usually made of spruce, occasionally from fir, pine, larch or Douglas fir. More recently glulam made from beech as well as a hybrid of beech and spruce has been approved for construction work. It is expected that other hardwoods such as chestnut, oak, ash, and black locust will be approved in the future. The adhesives used are melamine resin and phenol-resorcinol resin adhesives as well as formaldehyde-free polyurethane adhesives. By gluing together several layers of glulam panels, different forms of T-beams or box-girders can also be made. Glulam is used for roof structures as well as for systems of beams and columns in residential and commercial buildings.

#### 4.1.2.2 Cross laminated timber (CLT)

Cross laminated timber consists of at least three boards of softwood, increasingly also beech and ash, stacked crosswise on top of each other and glued under high pressure to form large solid timber elements. Cross laminated timber is also occasionally known as X-Lam. Where a number of panels are glued together along their narrow ends we speak of multi-layer solid timber panels. Depending on the manufacturer the thickness of the individual panels is normally between 13 and 80 millimeters, with widths of 2 meters and lengths of 5 meters. Slats can be joined by means of finger joints to form large cross laminated timber panels up to 16.5 meters in length. In structural terms, cross laminated timber panels have similar characteristics to prefabricated concrete elements, as, on account of their ability to distribute loads in two directions, they can function simultaneously as columns and beams.

## 4.2 Materials made from wood veneer

In Western Europe—very much in contrast to Asia, for instance—materials made from *wood veneer* make up only a very small percentage of wood-based materials, even though they are characterized by durability and can be used for many different functions. The base material for all veneer materials is generally rotary cut hardwood or softwood veneer with a thickness of between 0.8 and 6 millimeters. Veneer-based materials can be divided up into veneer plywood and (veneer) star plywood, blockboard, molded plywood and molded laminate.

### 4.2.1 Veneer plywood, star plywood (veneer panels)

Veneer plywood consists of an uneven number (minimum three) of glued layers of veneer, that are placed at 90 degrees to each other. The veneer plies can be of the same or different thickness. When the glued layers are swiveled at an angle of between 15° to 45° to each other the material is known as star plywood. Star plywood panels can be loaded in any direction. Veneer plywood sheets with five or more plies of equal thickness and a total thickness of over 12 millimeters are known as multiplex panels. On account of its great stability, veneer plywood

is used in the manufacture of furniture, automobiles and sports equipment, as well as in fitting-out interiors. Synthetic resin compressed wood or densified wood sometimes known under the product name *Pagholz®* (manufacturer: *Pagholz-Formteile*) is a beech veneer plywood saturated with synthetic resin and produced under great pressure which has an extremely high density of up to 1,400 kg/m³. It is used in building motorized vehicles, aircraft and railway cars, as well as for industrial flooring.

### 4.2.2 Blockboard and laminboard

Blockboard consists of at least two cover veneers with a central layer of solid wooden strips that can vary in width between 7 and 30 millimeters. The parallel strips—for instance of spruce—lie alongside each other and are glued only to the two covering plywood sheets. In laminboard the central layer consists of peeled veneer strips up to 8 mm thick that stand on their narrow edge and are glued to each other between the cover sheets. The areas in which they are used include trade fair stands and shop-fitting, as well as the production of vehicles and the manufacture of furniture.

### 4.2.3 Molded plywood and molded laminate

For the production of molded plywood several veneer plies are glued together crosswise under heat (100 °C) and pressure (300 metric tons) and shaped two- or three-dimensionally in press machines. Molded plywood is suitable for the production of stable, rigid parts such as chair seats and backs. For parts subject to greater tensile stress, such as cantilever chairs, *molded laminate* is used. Here the veneer plies are not glued crosswise but with their fibres parallel.

### 4.2.4 3D-Veneer

In this patented process veneer plies are cut into thin strips and then put together again with glue thread on the back. *Reholz® 3D Veneer* (manufacturer: *Reholz®*) can be used to make three-dimensional laminated wood elements (seat shells, elements for fitting-out interiors, or even bath tubs) as well as three-dimensional coatings of surfaces (equipment casings, kitchen unit fronts etc.).

### 4.2.5 Engineered wood products based on veneers

On account of its high tensile and compressive strength, parallel strand lumber (PSL) is suitable for use in traditional as well as modern engineered timber construction. Veneer strips of Douglas fir, longleaf pine, or aspen with a maximum length of 260 centimeters, 13 millimeters wide and 3 millimeters thick are pressed together using phenolic resin at high temperature and under high pressure. The only parallel strand lumber available on the market to date is *Parallam®* (manufacturer: *Weyerhaeuser Company*).

Laminated veneer lumber—LVL is a material that can be used for flat structural elements and as a rod-shaped element for girders, beams, to strengthen beams, or for piers, for instance in bridge building. It is made from rotary cut

spruce or pine veneer around 3 millimeters thick (*Kerto®, manufacturer: Finnforest*, and *Swedlam, manufacturer: Vänerply*) and longleaf pine (*Microllam®, manufacturer: Weyerhaeuser Company*). The veneer plies, mostly with their fibers aligned parallel, are glued with phenolic resin. Due to its similar qualities as a construction material, laminated veneer lumber is regarded as an economic alternative to glulam.

### 4.3 Materials made from wood chips

#### 4.3.1 Chipboard
Chipboard panels are made primarily from wood remnants, the by-products of sawing such as wood shavings and sawdust, as well as forest timber, while used wood is increasingly being employed. Wood chips of different sizes are pressed together and glued in three to five layers. Due to their high dimensional stability, chipboard panels are used above all in furniture making. Chipboard panels are today subdivided according to their use: for example, as well as being used in furniture making what are known as *thin* chipboard panels (thickness 3 millimeters) are also used in the packaging industry or for forming round arches in interiors. In tubular chipboard panels, which are often used in making internal doors, tube-shaped voids are made inside the panel for cost reasons. In Europe chipboard panels account for over 60 percent of the wood-based materials used.

For the production of chipboard panels (and equally for veneer plywood and fiberboard) adhesive resins containing formaldehyde are used. To reduce emissions of carcinogenic formaldehyde, the Fraunhofer Institute for Wood Research—Wilhelm-Klauditz-Institut (WKI) and the Fraunhofer Institute for Silicate Research have investigated a new method in which modified zeolites are introduced to the panel. In the new air cleansing chipboard panels, the synthetic material functions as a filter and, according to the first tests, can absorb up to 70 percent of the formaldehyde.

The production of lightweight chipboard panels is a relatively new area of development. These are manufactured exclusively from remnants (stems etc.) of various crops such as hemp, maize, rapeseed, or sunflowers. Although strictly speaking not wood-based materials, due to their low gross density (between 200 and 500 kg/m$^3$) they represent a future alternative to standard chipboard for interiors and furniture production that also economizes on wood resources.

#### 4.3.2 Molded chipboard elements
Chipboard elements are based on wood chips to which artificial resins are added and then shaped in molds under increased pressure and heat. One widespread such material is *Werzalit®* (*manufacturer: Werzalit*), developed in the 1950s by the eponymous company and registered for a patent. For the production, homogeneous wood chips are worked together with a far higher proportion of adhesive than standard chipboard and at higher density. In what is called the two-phase process, the elements (window sills, door

frames etc.) are produced first in a cold press procedure and subsequently in a hot mold press.

Using the extrusion method, woodchips mixed with adhesive are pressed through heated tubes vertically (Kreibaum process for the production of tubular panels), or horizontally (Hegenstaller process for the production of pallet blocks).

#### 4.3.3 Mineral-bound chipboard
In those areas where stringent fire safety regulations apply, mineral-bound chipboard panels are often suitable due to their fire-retardant qualities. A distinction is drawn between cement-bound chipboard panels such as *Duripanel®* (*manufacturer: Eternit*), which are suitable for back ventilated facades on account of their resistance to weathering and attack by insects, whereas cement-bound chipboard materials such as *Isospan®* (*manufacturer: Isospan, Baustoffwerk*) or woodwool lightweight panels such as *Isolith®* (*manufacturer: ISOLITH M. Hattinger*) and *Heraklith®* (*manufacturer: Knauf Insulation*) offer good insulating properties. Magnesite-bound chipboard panels which are particularly fire-retardant, are used predominantly in ship building but also in interiors. Gypsum-bound chipboard panels are used to clad walls, ceilings or floors as well as for furniture making and interior fitting-out, primarily in public buildings where strict fire protection regulations apply.

#### 4.3.4 Engineered wood products based on wood chips
The engineered wood versions of woodchip-based materials are oriented strand board (OSB) and laminated strand lumber (LSL). These are used as formwork for pouring concrete, as building boards, facade cladding and also in interiors. To produce OSB strands of fresh forest timber—either softwood (spruce, pine) or hardwood—about 75 millimeters long are aligned parallel in the outer layers and glued together, which gives them a high resistance to bending. In waferboard—often popularly called OSB although actually its predecessor—square chips are pressed together arbitrarily, without being aligned parallel.

For laminated strand lumber (LSL), also known under the name Intrallam, strands of aspen are used which are longer than those used for OSB, measuring up to 300 millimeters in length and 25 to 40 millimeters in width. LSL is used above all in fitting-out interiors and in structural timber building.

### 4.4 Materials made from fibers
For the manufacture of fiber-based materials, first of all, like in the production of paper, wood thinnings, waste, and old wood are defibrated by the use of steam. The material is then processed into single or multi-ply fiber panels or pressed into fiber shaped elements under high pressure and at high temperature and with the use of synthetic resin.

#### 4.4.1 Fiberboard
In the production of fiber-based materials, a distinction is drawn between the wet and dry processes. It is primarily soft fiberboard panels

that are produced by means of the wet process. Here the wood fibers are pressed under water with a material such as lignin (which is found in wood) using little or no adhesive. Both soft fiberboard panels as well as wood fiber insulation board have a low density (230 to 350 kg/m$^3$) and are used mostly for acoustic and thermal insulation.

In the dry process, the dried fibers used are coated with resin (diffusion-open MDF panels here form an exception, see 4.4.3.1) and then pressed. This process is used to produce both medium-density fiberboard (MDF) and high-density fiberboard (HDF). MDF and HDF differ only as regards their density. MDF (760 to 790 kg/m$^3$) is used in fitting-out interiors and in the manufacture of furniture, whereas HDF (960 to 1 090 kg/m$^3$) is used above all as the substructure for laminate flooring, but also in model and caravan building.

The material *Kraftplex (wooden sheeting)* (*manufacturer: well.de by FRANZBETZ*), is a special kind of fiberboard. It consists entirely of softwood fibers which, like in the production of paper, are pressed together. Kraftplex can be shaped by deep drawing or canting. It has a similar density to sheet aluminum and is used in the manufacture of furniture and tools and in building vehicles.

#### 4.4.2 Fiber shaped elements
Wood-based shaped fiber elements, for example *Arboform®* (*manufacturer: Tecnaro*), consist of lignin and cellulose, both constituents of wood, that are mixed with further natural fibers such as hemp or flax as well as natural additives. With increased temperature and using the extrusion or injection molding processes, the material can be shaped like a synthetically produced thermoplastic material but can also be processed to form plates or panels. Fiber shaped elements are used in the automobile industry as well as in the packaging, furniture and building industries.

→ *Example: p. 187; Sascha Nordmeyer. Eco-effective table*

#### 4.4.3 Engineered wood products based on fibers

#### 4.4.3.1 Vapor-permeable MDF panels
In building construction, moisture resistant or vapor-permeable MDF panels as well as vapor-permeable wall and roof panels are used to obviate the need for an additional vapor check. Like standard MDF panels, they are manufactured using the dry process but with the following differences: firstly, instead of resin they are bound using moisture-resistant pMDI adhesives, a technical binder based on isocyanate. Secondly, the fibers are more loosely scattered and are pressed using less pressure which means that the panels have a lower density (540-650 kg/m$^3$). Thirdly, the higher proportion of paraffin used ensures strength and dimensional stability under the influence of moisture.

#### 4.4.3.2 Scrimber
In scrimber technology, entire trunks or logs are first of all squashed between rollers which preserves the original orientation of the fibers.

Then the particles are bonded under pressure and heat. This construction material was developed in the early 1970s by the Australian Commonwealth Scientific and Industrial Research Organization (CSIRO). So far it has been used predominantly in Asia, where eucalyptus and bamboo are employed in the manufacture. However at present the Fraunhofer Institute for Timber Research—Wilhelm-Klauditz-Institut (WKI), is examining to what extent scrimber technology, which is largely unknown in Central Europe, could also make use of the weak wood that results from tree diseases such as ash anthracnose. Scrimber is a portmanteau word made up of the words "scrim" and "timber"; it can be processed and used like cut solid wood.

#### 4.4.3.3 Shaped wood
Shaped wood is a new wood-based material in the development of which the TU Dresden played an important role. Like with scrimber, logs and cut wood are crushed under the introduction of heat—but in this case at right angles to the direction of the fibers. In this way the cell walls are pressed together and first of all a foam-like, solid panel material is produced. Under the application of heat this material can then be shaped into various sections, for instance tubes, whereby in the stretched areas the original cell structure is recreated approximately. As 100 percent of the raw wood can be used in this process and thus resource savings of up to 70 percent can be achieved, shaped wood is regarded as an economic alternative for shaping processes that do not involve cutting (rolling, pouring, shaping, deep-drawing, extrusion). In addition, shaped wood can be combined with two-dimensional textile structures as well as with fiber-based materials, (cf. 4.6.3).

#### 4.5 Lightweight panels
Wood-based lightweight panels are sandwich panels in which the cover sheets are made of veneer, chipboard or fiberboard. The center— in multi-ply panels the central layers—consists either of light rod and stick shaped woods such as balsa (balsa board) or honeycomb structures made of recycled paper, cardboard, cellulose fibers, or aluminum. Center layers of natural fiber mats (flax, hemp, kenaf) or of wastepaper fibers (zBoard) are standard. In this context mention should also be made of starchbound lightweight wood-based panels, also known as wood foam or *iwood (developer: innovation wood)*. First of all a paste is made by adding water and starch to sawdust and wood dust. This paste is then foamed with the help of micro-organisms such as yeast or bacteria, and subsequently dried. As the name suggests, the advantage of lightweight panels over solid panels is the fact that they are over 50 percent lighter (density between 50 and 300 kg/m$^3$) but with the same strength. Their disadvantage is their lack of resistance to moisture.

#### 4.6 Composite materials with wood
In order to improve the construction qualities and possibilities of processing wood, above all in the building industry, recently an increasing number of attempts have been made to combine wood with other materials—in particular with glass, concrete, fiber-based materials, steel, and plastics.

#### 4.6.1 Wood-glass composites
Based on the example of the windscreens used in making automobiles, which are connected to the body of the car by means of elastic PU adhesive and as a result are also structurally effective, wood can also be structurally glued to glass. By gluing on all sides the bracing effect of the glass, and consequently the overall strength of the wood-glass composite construction, can be increased. Holzforschung Austria has developed prototypes of a *wood-glass composite element* which was first used in the construction of the solid timber house "Schattenbox" (Hasenauer House in Eichgraben, near Vienna). This house was awarded the Lower Austrian Timber Building Prize in 2009.

#### 4.6.2 Wood-concrete composites
Wood-concrete composites combine the positive characteristics of both materials for building construction. In the compression zone a thin concrete plate is used, in the tension zone the wood, which increases the bearing capacity of the construction as a whole. The decisive aspect is the shear stress resistant connection of the two materials which can either be bolted (more resistant in the case of fire) or glued together. Wood-concrete composites can be used to renovate timber beam ceilings but also in building new bridges, as this construction method allows free spans of over 10 meters.

#### 4.6.3 Wood-fiber material composites
Similar to the combination of wood and concrete, carbon, glass, or aramid fibers—glued parallel to the fibers—can substantially increase the bending strength and stiffness of timber. If bonded at right angles to the wood fibers, this produces transverse strengthening which according to studies results in a breaking load that is up to 200 percent higher than constructions without strengthening. A wood-carbon fiber bridge in Dübendorf (Switzerland) was awarded the Swiss Timber Prize in 2009: in this pedestrian bridge the glulam of the upper construction was pre-stressed at right angles with carbon-fiber strengthened plastics. In the sub-structure carbon-fiber strengthened bands provide pre-stressing in the long direction.

A new combination of wood and fiber materials involves sheathing shaped wood (see entry) in knitted fabric; the materials are connected to each other by means of epoxy and polyester resin. Using this process, branch-like connections can be made that are extremely rigid and stable and meet not only the highest technical demands but also aesthetic expectations.

#### 4.6.4 Wood-steel composites
In this area either wood-steel beams are produced in which the wood is subject to compressive stress and the steel to tensile stress, or wood-steel plates, a hybrid material made of glulam and steel. In the relatively new glued wood-steel composites a wooden construction element is connected with a steel element almost rigidly and yet remains ductile, i.e. plastically malleable. An incision is made in the wood parallel to the direction of the fibers, this is filled with adhesive and the steel element (steel rod, perforated metal etc.) is then inserted.

#### 4.6.5 Wood plastic composites (WPC)
Wood plastic composites (WPC), are the most technologically developed wood composite materials. Today they consist of c. 80 percent wood (wood fibers and particles) and 20 percent plastics (thermoplastics generally polypropylene (PP), in some cases polyethylene(PE)). A major advantage over other wood-based materials is that wood plastic composites can be processed using extrusion and injection molding. Consequently WPCs are increasingly being used where more complex forms are required, for instance in furniture making, for handles, packaging or musical instruments. The numerous materials currently available include *S2 (manufacturer: Werzalit), Arbofill© (manufacturer: Tecnaro), Pallwood® (manufacturer: Pallmann), Fasal® Wood (manufacturer: Fasal), Kupilka® (manufacturer: Joensuu Meskari Oy), Ecogehr® (manufacturer: Gehr) and Xylomer® (manufacturer: Hiendl)*. Due to their toughness and better bursting strength in comparison to plastic-based molded parts, WPC are used in the manufacture of automobiles to line the interiors of vehicles. With the product *Lignoflex®™ (manufacturer: since 2009 the firm Bo-NaFaTec, which was founded by the company Lignotock)* fiber mats are produced which in a second step can be pressed into complex three-dimensional forms under high pressure and at high temperature. In addition WPCs are used outdoors for terrace decks, railings or as facade cladding. The products used in these areas include *Fiberon® (manufacturer: Fiberon), Kovalex® (manufacturer: Kosche) and Megawood® (manufacturer: Novo-Tech)*.

#### 4.7 Other wood composite materials
For non-structural use in furniture making or for accessories, wood is combined with other support materials. One example here is the *wooden textiles* by Elisa Strozyk, for which laser cut veneer plies are bonded to a textile support material. In *Foldtex* from Timm Herok, CNC-milled veneer plywood elements are applied to textiles and also to films. To make the materials *Albeflex (manufacturer: albeflex)* and *MicroWood® (manufacturer: Wood Transformation & Technology bvba)*, thin veneer sheets are bonded to paper so that they can be rolled and folded without breaking. For the material Plytube from Seongyong Lee, which is produced in a similar process to cardboard rolls, veneer is bonded to a metal tube support.

#### 4.8 Materials made from woody plants
Up to the present it is above all in Asia that woody plants such as bamboo, palms or dracaenas have been used in much the same way as wood, or processed to create materials that resemble wood-based materials in terms of their

characteristics and applications. Scrimber technology (4.4.3.2) represents a process that so far has been employed primarily in Asia but is currently being tested in Europe for the production of wood-based materials.

#### 4.8.1 Bamboo

Like maize, rice, or sugar cane, bamboo is one of the woody grasses. Bamboo, which grows very rapidly, is stable and due to the hollow areas in the stems is very light and elastic. It has a relatively high density (ca. 720 kg/m³), is resistant to pressure, and when dry hardly shrinks or swells at all. As regards these qualities it is similar to many kinds of wood, but in terms of its toughness it surpasses them. Bamboo can be used in many different areas, from building construction to fitting-out of interiors (parquet flooring or similar) and from furniture making to the construction of bicycle frames. In addition to being used in the manufacture of the material scrimber, which has already been mentioned above, bamboo is also used to make composites. In these bamboo-plastic composites (BPC), bamboo fibers replace the wood fibers used to produce wood-plastic composites (4.6.5).

#### 4.8.2 Palm ("palm wood")

The woody stems of the palm tree are frequently used in Asia as a construction material or for inlays. "Palm wood", which consists principally of bast fibers, is particularly hard and strong, but due to its rapid growth tends to develop cracks. A special quality is that in palm stems the density increases from inside (c. 400 kg/m³) to outside (c. 800 kg/m³). Rattan (the outer skin of the shoots) and *peddig* (the pulp of the shoots) are gained from the stems of rattan palms. Rattan and peddig are used primarily for the manufacture of wickerwork goods or for woven chair backs and seats. Rattan is also used to make percussion mallets (e.g. for a vibraphone) and staffs (for martial arts).

#### 4.8.3 Lightweight chipboard

As already mentioned under 4.3.1 (chipboard), for the production of lightweight chipboard panels only the wastage of different agricultural plants (some of them woody) such as hemp, maize, rapeseed, or sunflowers is used. They represent a future alternative to wood-based materials.

#### 4.9 Materials made from non-wood parts of the tree

Cork and bast are neither wood nor wood-based, but as they form part of the tree and are widespread materials they are nevertheless mentioned here.

#### 4.9.1 Cork

The best-known material derived from the non-wooden parts of the tree is without doubt the bark of the cork oak, generally known by its abbreviated name cork. It consists largely of suberin, a mix of fatty acids and strong organic alcohol that is produced by cork cambium (see entry) and makes cork impermeable to liquids and gases. Cork also contains lignin, cellulose, polysaccharides, tannins, and waxes. 89 percent of its tissue is gaseous, which means that cork has an extremely low density (0.12 to 0.20 kg/m³). It is due to these qualities that cork has been used for centuries to make bottle stoppers but also as an insulating and sound-absorbing material for floors, walls and ceilings. It is also used for insulation purposes in the form of granulate. If formed into granulate blocks with a suitable binder, cork can be worked very simply, for instance by turning.

#### 4.9.2 Bast

Bast is another part of the bark that can be used as a material. Bast fibers have been used for centuries in the manufacture of nets, cords, ropes, and also textiles. In Africa, until the massive import of cotton materials, fabric made out of bast fibers was widely used to make clothing. In recent times the use of bast fibers to make textiles has again become popular. *Bark Cloth® (supplier: Oliver Heintz)* is produced from the inner bark of the mutuba fig-tree. The bark is first of all detached from the trunk, and then in a longer process it is alternately beaten until it is soft, soaked in hot water and dried again, until at the end of the treatment "cloths" measuring 3 to 6 meters in length and around 2 meters wide are produced. These can then be used to make clothing, decorative fabrics and, after the requisite treatment, decorative panels. To prevent the tree from drying out, banana leaves are wrapped around the trunk after the harvest. The new bark that grows under the layer of leaves can be harvested after about a year. Trees between 50 and 150 years old yield the best harvest.

# II TECHNOLOGY: PRODUCTION PROCESSES

**1**    **RESHAPING**

1.1    Steam bending

1.2    Patented pliable wood, condensed wood

1.3    Kerfing (bending by slitting)

1.4    ZipShaping

**2**    **SEPARATING**

2.1    CNC machining centers

2.2    Cutting processes

2.3    Sandblasting, brushing away, weathering

**3**    **JOINING**

3.1    **Impregnating** (waxing, oiling, storage of resins)

3.2    Timber connections
3.2.1    Bonding
3.2.1.1    Natural adhesives
3.2.1.1.1    Lignin (lignosulfonate)
3.2.1.1.2    Tannins (tannin adhesives)
3.2.1.1.3    Cashew-shell oil
3.2.1.2    Synthetic adhesives
3.2.1.2.1    Phenol formaldehyde resins (PF) and phenol resorcinol formaldehyde resins (PRF)
3.2.1.2.2    Urea formaldehyde resins (UF) and melamine urea formaldehyde resins (MUF)
3.2.1.2.3    Polyvinyl acetate glues (PVA) (white glues)
3.2.2    Mechanical means of connection
3.2.2.1    Timber construction dowels
3.2.2.2    Joinery dowels, friction welding
3.2.2.3    Pin-shaped metal connectors (bolts, clamps, nails, screws)
3.2.2.4    Nail plates
3.2.2.5    Other means of connection and wood connections

**4**    **COATINGS**

4.1    Stains

4.2    Varnishes

4.3    Paints, lacquers

4.4    Films and foils

**5**    **CHANGING THE CHARACTERISTICS OF MATERIALS**

5.1    Chemically modified timber—CMT

5.2    Thermally modified timber—TMT

5.3    Charring (pyrolysis)

The term production process is used to describe those processes by means of which products are made out of raw, semi-finished or other materials. In general, production processes can be subdivided into six main groups. The first is primary shaping, which means the production of a solid body out of a shapeless material—for example, by pouring or casting—whereby cohesion is created. The second main group is reshaping in which a solid volume—which in many cases has already been primary shaped—is altered, for instance by bending, while retaining the cohesion. The third process is separating, in which the cohesion of a solid volume is removed, for instance by sawing or machining. In joining, cohesion is increased or newly created by connecting solid bodies, either with each other or with formless material by means of filling, nailing, bonding etc. Coating describes those production processes in which the application of a metallic (e.g. chrome) or non-metallic (lacquer or similar) layer increases the cohesion. In changing the characteristics, materials are optimized in terms of hardness, elasticity or durability with the aid of processes such as rolling, sintering or irradiating.

In the production of sawn timber (construction timber) and above all in the production of wood-based materials, various production processes are employed. Here, separation or jointing processes (sawing, machining, gluing etc.) play a particularly important role. Different production processes are also employed in the further processing of solid timber and wood-based materials. The processes relevant for the working of timber, which are also dealt with in the project section, are listed below.

## 1 RESHAPING

Essentially there are two processes by means of which wood can be reshaped. These are deep drawing and various methods of bending. Whereas the technique of deep drawing has only begun to be used on wood and wood-based materials fairly recently (cf. Part I wooden sheeting under 4.4.1 Fiberboard), bending techniques have been in use for a long time. On the one hand, there are processes in which shaping tools and forms are required in order to bend rod-shaped pieces of wood or panels. These include steam bending, the manufacture of *patented pliable wood/condensed wood* or the processing of slit materials, such as MDF panels. Shaping tools are also required for the production of molded plywood and molded laminate (see Part I, 4.2.3 Molded plywood and molded laminate). In bending with such shaping tools a distinction is drawn between *elastic shaping*, in which the wood is held permanently in the bent shape (wickerwork, wooden barrels, see also ICD/ITKE, page 132), and plastic shaping in which, after conclusion of the process, the wood itself retains its bent form (furniture, sleigh runners).

The possibilities offered by digital techniques (CNC milling) open up a new category of bending processes that require no shaping tools or forms. These processes include, for example, kerfing and ZipShaping.

### 1.1 Steam bending

Steam bending of wood was already known in ancient Egypt. In the process developed in the first half of the nineteenth century by master joiner Michael Thonet, the piece of wood is heated using steam at a temperature of up to 100°C and is clamped with a shaped steel band so that it cannot move in a longitudinal direction. When it is bent it is also condensed along the inner side and, in comparison with wood that is not condensed, splinters at a far later stage. Consequently, the wood pieces can be bent to a very narrow radius. After bending, the steel band is used as a form in which to dry the bent wood.

### 1.2 Patented pliable wood, condensed wood

Based on the knowledge gained from the steam bending technique, which showed that condensed wood does not split as quickly as stretched wood and can therefore be more easily bent, in the 1920s what is known as the patented pliable wood method was developed. In this process the wood is condensed with the aid of steam along its length by around 20 percent. When cooled and dry it can then be cut, depending on the cross section, by hand or with ratchet steps, or worked on bending machines, and can then be used for handrails or staircase banisters, for example. Patented pliable wood has been produced since the 1990s by Candidus Prugger and has been marketed under the product name *Bendywood®* since 2003. It is available in different kinds of wood (oak, ash, maple, and beech) and in lengths of up to 2.20 meters. Condensed wood is also offered by other manufacturers, but in contrast to patented plywood it springs back after the condensing process (cf. also Part I, 4.4.3.3 Shaped wood).

### 1.3 Kerfing (bending by slitting)

Multiplex or fiber panels can be bent using the kerfing method. Slits are made at regular distances apart on one side of panel materials or wooden strips, which can thus be curved in the direction of the side with the slits (e.g. TOPAN® MDF FORM, manufacturer: Glunz AG). For special uses, such as making musical instruments, the wood is slit on two sides at staggered intervals and can therefore also be bent in the longitudinal direction. One such product is *A4 Kerfing* from the Californian company AST—A4 stands for flexibility on all four axes.

### 1.4 ZipShaping

Like kerfing, ZipShaping also allows wood-based materials to be bent without using shaping tools. By means of a five-axis CNC mill, a panel material (e.g. solid wood panels, plywood panels, MDF panels) is slit on one side and milled so that the grooves and the teeth or fingers between them have a certain angle. In a second panel, the fingers and grooves are milled with the corresponding angles. By bonding the grooved sides of the two panels together, a curvature results whose radius is the product of the difference between the angles at the edges of the teeth. The possibilities of ZipShaping have been explored at the ETH Zurich (see Christoph Schindler, *Ein architektonisches Periodisierungs-*

*modell anhand fertigungstechnischer Kriterien, dargestellt am Beispiel des Holzbaus,* Zurich, 2009) and elsewhere, and have been optimized for the serial production of particularly tight radii of curvature by a number of firms, including designtoproduction.

## 2 SEPARATING

Wood and wood-based materials are generally separated or worked by sawing, milling, turning, drilling, filing, or sanding (see Part I, 3 Veneer and 4 Wood-based materials), processes that all involve producing wood chips. CNC machining centers are frequently used to process materials for structural timber construction as well as in the field of furniture making, in which a number of different tools are integrated that allow complex production processes to be used.

To separate wood and wood-based materials without producing wood chips, modern laser and water jet cutters can be used. Thin plywoods and veneers in particular can be cut very precisely using these cutters.

### 2.1 CNC machining centers

CNC (Computerized Numerical Control) machines with a number of axes allow two- or three-dimensional processing of materials and thus the precise and rapid production of complex building elements and forms. In wood processing, what are called CNC machining centers (trimming machines) are used in which saw, mill, and drill machines are integrated that can be directly controlled by means of CAD-CAM data (plan-to-production process). In addition to the production of carpentry constructions, these machines are also used for prefabrication—of, for instance, furniture parts, digitally carved decorations, building elements in structural timber construction etc. CNC operated machining centers open up new perspectives from the economic viewpoint, too. For example: traditional wood connections such as the dovetail joint are currently experiencing a renaissance as the short time required to equip the machines—the optimal sequence of different work processes can often be organized by attaching just a single work piece—means that such joints can now be made again with high precision and within a competitive cost-benefit framework.

### 2.2 Cutting processes

Water-jet cutting is suitable for the precise cutting of wooden ornaments or inlays. The edges of displays, furniture parts, or components for interior design can also be made using this high pressure cutting technique. Plywood and wood veneer can be cut very well with the help of *lasers*. The most suitable process is sublimation cutting, in which the material is not burnt or melted by the laser but steamed. Extremely high quality edges can be made with this process.

### 2.3 Sandblasting, brushing away, weathering

Annual or growth rings consist of soft early wood and hard late wood. By sandblasting or brushing away the early wood, textured surfaces can be produced. The appearance of this texture or

relief depends on the sand grain and the duration of the process and on the speed and pressure of the rotating brushes. A similar effect (wash-board structure) is also produced by the natural weathering of wood, as early wood weathers more quickly than late wood. Naturally weath-ered wood, for instance from old timber build-ings, is occasionally used to build houses or make furniture (e.g. *Barnwood, producer Ebony and Co.*) (see Part I, 1 Wood—definition and char-acteristics, age).

## 3 JOINING

The category "joining timber" includes the appli-cation of wood preservatives, for instance by impregnating (application processes), as well as connecting processes such as gluing, or pressing together using mechanical means of connection such as clamps, nails, screws, or similar.

### 3.1 Impregnating (waxing, oiling, storage of resins)

In impregnating processes, carbonaceous mate-rials such as waxes, paraffin, or oils and resins are generally introduced as deeply and evenly as possible into the cellular walls of the timber, either by means of tank pressure impregnation (with positive or negative pressure) or by vacuum processes. This makes the wood more resistant to moisture and therefore more dimensionally stable. In addition, it also increases the strength of the wood and makes it more difficult for harm-ful microorganisms to penetrate it. Impregna-tion processes of this kind therefore bring about a modification *of the wood* (see also section 5. Changing the characteristics of the material). For instance *Dauerholz (manufacturer: Dauerholz AG)* is a product manufactured using the patented tank pressure impregnation process. First of all fresh or wet wood is im-pregnated under pressure with paraffin/wax at a temperature of 110°C to 140°C. Due to the high temperature, the water in the wood emerg-es in the form of steam and is replaced throughout the entire cross section (maximum penetration depth) by the impregnation mate-rial. After complete impregnation and with a residual moisture content of less than 20 per cent, the wood is taken out of the still hot impregnation material and gradually cooled. According to specific requirements and use, other materials such as fireproofing agents, color pigments, insecticides, or pesticides can be added to the paraffin or the wax.

At present, the Swiss materials testing and research institute (EMPA) is researching a pro-cess to improve the impregnation of wood. The (dead) wood is deliberately treated with a fungus (physisporinus vitreus/white rot), which ensures that the lignified wood pits (see Part I, 1 Wood—definition and characteristics) that hinder the penetration of wood protection, fireproofing or finishing agents are broken down. The controlled disintegration process caused by the fungus is stopped in time to prevent the breaking down of the cell walls, which are so important for the strength of the wood.

### 3.2 Timber connections

In connecting timber pieces, a fundamental distinction is made between carpentry, joinery, and (engineered) timber constructions. Carpen-try connections is the term used to describe all connections between timber elements that are differentiated according to the form of the connection into lap, comb, or tenon joints, and according to the kind of staggered joint. In traditional carpentry, these connections are generally made without mechanical connectors (screws, bolts etc.). Thanks to the use of CNC machines, in recent times these handmade joints, which are elaborate and therefore costly to produce (above all the comb-type connec-tions such as dovetail joints), have again ac-quired greater importance.

In joinery connections there are different connections along the width, the length and at the corners of the pieces to be connected. The most common width connections are by means of glued joints (e.g. butt joints, dovetail joints, dowel or tenon joints). In addition, tongue and groove connections are used which can also be glued or fixed using nails or clamps.

The most common form of long joint is the finger joint. The wedge-shaped milled fingers of two different pieces of wood engage each other and are glued together. Finger joint connections are also used in engineered timber construction, for instance in the production of cross lami-nated timber (CLT) (see also Part I, 4.1.2.2 Cross laminated timber). For corner connections, for instance in furniture construction, miters as well as tenon and frame connections are common. Corner connections are also additionally strength-ened with connector pieces (dowels, nails etc.) and adhesive.

In modern timber engineering, connections are also made using adhesives and mechanical means. Here a major role is played by special timber-steel connections such as the Greim con-struction method or BSB connections (Blumer-System-Binder), in which (steel) sheets are inserted in slits made in the timber pieces and then connected with bolts, screws, special nails, or pins. Generally speaking, of the traditional carpentry and joinery connections, the only ones suitable for engineered timber are butt joints and notched joints. However, as already men-tioned above, CNC machines now offer increased opportunities to use traditional woodworking joints for structural timber construction also.

### 3.2.1 Bonding

Adhesives are used to solidly connect areas of wood-based materials (solid wood, veneer, or fiberboard). A distinction is drawn between natural adhesives (natural glues, natural resins, lignin etc.) and *synthetic adhesives* (phenolic resins, urea formaldehyde resins etc.).

### 3.2.1.1 Natural adhesives

Although colloquially we still often speak of glu-ing, today natural glues are seldom used in wood processing and very rarely in the building in-dustry. Glutine glues are occasionally still used in furniture making. The natural adhesives that play a role in wood processing are above all

lignin, tannin and also cashew-shell oil as an ad-ditive for synthetic adhesives.

#### 3.2.1.1.1 Lignin (lignosulfonate)

In the manufacture of cellulose pulp by the sulfite process, sulfite liquor results as a waste product that contains lignin in the form of dissolved lignosulfonic acid. In combination with phenolic resins and also with urea resins, sulfite liquor is used to glue chipboard panels.

#### 3.2.1.1.2 Tannins (tannin adhesives)

The wood and bark of different kinds of tree contain tannins (tanning materials) which bind easily with formaldehyde to form what are called tannin adhesives. In combination with phenolic formaldehyde resins, tanning glues are used above all in the production of MDF and HDF panels. In addition, tannins are combined with phenol resorcinol formaldehyde resins (PRF) to create what are called "honeymoon" adhe-sives. These adhesives are particularly suitable for load-bearing building elements (glued lami-nated timber, finger joints) and, in contrast to phenol resins that harden under the application of heat, they can also be used at room temper-ature (cold gluing).

#### 3.2.1.1.3 Cashew-shell oil

The oil obtained from cashew shells contains differ-ent phenolic ingredients (including cardanol and cardol) from which, combined with formal-dehyde, technical adhesives can also be pro-duced. These are ideally suited for the production of plywood and glued laminated timber.

#### 3.2.1.2 Synthetic adhesives

In the production of panel materials today it is principally synthetic condensation resins on a formaldehyde basis (thermosets) that are used. In addition to phenol formaldehyde resins (PF) and the phenol resorcinol formaldehyde resins (PRF) already referred to, it is mostly urea formal-dehyde resins (UF) or melamine urea formal-dehyde resins (MUF) that are used as adhesives in wood processing. For bonding in furniture making, building, and in interior fitting-out, the synthetic thermoplastics created by poly-merization such as polyvinyl acetate glues (PVA) play an important role. Adhesives made from epoxy resin are generally used for repairs, for instance for fissures in glued laminated timber.

#### 3.2.1.2.1 Phenol formaldehyde resins (PF) and phenol resorcinol formaldehyde resins (PRF)

Phenol formaldehyde resins and phenol resorcinol formaldehyde resins, also called phenolic resins, have similar qualities. They are characterized by their high stability and are therefore used pri-marily in engineered timber, in aircraft and ship building, and also as a means of binding wood-based materials. Phenolic resins are dark in color (black, brown, red) and grow even darker on exposure to light. The special quality of phenol resorcinol formaldehyde resins is that they set even when cold, i.e. at temperatures under 30°C. PRF resins can be mixed with other synthetic resin adhesives.

#### 3.2.1.2.2 Urea formaldehyde resins (UF) and melamine urea formaldehyde resins (MUF)

Wood-based materials are generally glued using urea formaldehyde resins and melamine urea formaldehyde resins. Their advantage lies in the many different areas where they can be used, from the production of laminated timber, chipboard, and fiberboard panels, to timber building and vehicle construction. Melamine urea formaldehyde resins show a greater resistance to moisture.

#### 3.2.1.2.3 Polyvinyl acetate glues (PVA) (white glues)

Polyvinyl acetate glues, also known as white glues, are formaldehyde-free dispersion adhesives that can be used in many different areas ranging from the production of panel materials to veneer work, furniture manufacture and interior fitting-out. Polyvinyl acetate glues have good cohesion qualities, but without additives (solvents, hardeners) they are not particularly resistant to heat or moisture.

#### 3.2.2 Mechanical means of connection

Mechanical means of connection include various dowels as well as pin-shaped metal connecting pieces, such as bolts, reamed bolts, dowel pins, clamps, nails, and screws. They are used in joinery connections and, when adapted to meet structural requirements, in structural timber building. Mechanical connections are additionally often glued to the wood (see also Part I, 4.6.4 Wood-steel composites).

#### 3.2.2.1 Timber construction dowels

A variety of dowels are used in timber building. Rectangular dowels made of hard deciduous wood, also known as carpenters' dowels, as well as T-dowels of steel are set, parallel to the fibers, in the wood pieces to be connected and additionally secured with bolts. For timber connections that must transfer loads, what are known as special connectors are employed. These are one-sided for wood-steel connections or two-sided for wood-wood connections. There are special connectors to suit different purposes: ring connectors (two-sided) and plate connectors (one-sided), which are inserted in the wooden pieces to be connected, as well as toothed plate connectors (one- and two-sided versions), which are pressed into the wood.

#### 3.2.2.2 Joinery dowels, friction welding

Joinery dowels are generally made of beech or oak. They are normally used together with polyurethane adhesives or polyvinyl acetate glues. What is called friction welding technology forms an exception in which no adhesive is used and during or after the joining process no further materials foreign to wood are used. It creates what is known as a pure material wood connection which offers, above all, ecological advantages over the usual techniques of connecting wood. In friction welding, a distinction is drawn between vibration welding (VIB), rotation welding (ROT) and orbital welding (ORB). Rotation welding, common in processing plastics, is particularly suitable for connecting wood. A wood dowel is inserted in a pre-bored hole under pressure and with a defined number of revolutions. The resulting heat softens amorphous components of the wood's structure, mainly lignin and hemicellulose. In a short time the softened material stiffens and thus functions like a bonding agent. The surface of the adjacent material is condensed. The strength of the connection achieved varies according to the kind of wood and the difference in the diameters of the hole and the dowel, among other factors.

#### 3.2.2.3 Pin-shaped metal connectors (bolts, clamps, nails, screws)

With pin-shaped metal connectors, the quality of the wood connections depends on the embedment strength. This describes the resistance of the wood to the inserted metal connector and depends upon the gross density of the wood, the diameter of the connector, as well as the angle between the direction of the fibers in the wood and the respective direction of force. Bolts, fitted bolts, and dowel pins are suitable for connecting flat areas and thick walled timber pieces subject primarily to bending stress. In addition, bolts, fitted bolts, and dowel pins can be used to connect different materials, e.g. wood and steel, with each other in a relatively simple and stable way. In contrast to pin dowels and fitted bolts, with standard bolts the diameter of the bore hole is somewhat larger than that of the bolt itself. Thus the tendency of the bolts to deform is somewhat greater and so they are permitted only for temporary buildings (stands, pavilions etc.). Clamps are used in timber construction primarily to secure wood connections. Special wire clamps are used for load-bearing connections in timber engineering, whereby at least half the length of the staple shaft must be given an adhesive coat of resin. In timber building, nailed connections are used primarily for load-bearing constructions in the erection of housing and large sheds/halls. Different kinds of timber construction nails are available for a variety of different uses, a distinction is drawn between timber building nails with or without thread or groove profiling of the shaft. The longer the profiling, the greater the resistance to withdrawal. There are also nails with or without resinated shafts.

For load-bearing wood connections, wood screws made of steel are generally suitable. There are two kinds: those that are screwed into pre-bored holes and those with self-boring hardened full threads. In timber engineering, full thread screws are used as they have greater bearing capacity and stiffness (when extracting them from or pressing them into the wood). Studies (made, for instance, at the faculty for timber engineering and building construction of Karlsruhe University) have shown that the bearing capacity and stiffness of wood connections can be significantly increased by using full thread screws inserted at an incline rather than at right angles to the direction of loading.

#### 3.2.2.4 Nail plates

Nail plates are galvanized or rust-free metal pieces with punched nails between 7 and 21 millimeters in length projecting at an angle of 90° from one side. The plates are used to make connections in roof and wall constructions, in temporary or ancillary constructions, as well as for shuttering and preparatory works. In the factory the nail plate is pressed evenly and across its entire surface into the wood by means of hydraulic presses. The Menig nail plate, named after its Swiss inventor Willi Menig, is a special kind of plate. It has punched nails on both sides and is not pressed into the wood from outside but is placed between the two pieces of timber to be connected.

#### 3.2.2.5 Other means of connection and wood connections

Particularly in the area of furniture making, other means of making joints are also used which have decorative as well as constructional functions. These include, for example, *mechanical connectors* such as differently colored Forex®-platelets (manufacturer: Airex AG) or cable binders, cellulose-based materials such as the extremely robust, pourable, exact fitting and pliable Zelfo® (manufacturer: Zelfo Technology), as well as *plastics*, such as polycaprolactone, a low temperature thermoplastic that has an extremely low hardening temperature (-70°C), and can therefore be handled easily at room temperature.

For structural timber construction, recent research has been carried out into new means of making joints or timber connections. Here, knitted textiles (see Part I 4.6.3 Wood-fibre material composites) should be mentioned, and also new construction principles such as for instance Baubotanik (living plant construction; see Part III, 3 Natural building processes).

#### 4 COATINGS

Coatings are applied to the surfaces of wood and wood-based materials in order to visually upgrade them (decorative surface) or to protect them against damp, moisture, fungus, or UV light. In addition to natural coatings such as veneers or textiles, artificial coating materials are also used, either in liquid form (stains, varnishes, and lacquers) or in solid form (films and foils). In contrast to the saturating impregnation process (see Part II, 3.1 Impregnating), the depth of penetration of liquid coatings into the wood is far shallower. If the wood is to retain its appearance or, as in the case of outdoor use, has to be protected against the weather and fungal attack, such coatings must be renewed at regular intervals. Otherwise the lignin parts gradually disintegrate in a photochemical process and are washed out by the rain. After a certain time, a fungus causes the wood to turn gray. This natural graying can frequently be seen on the wooden facades of buildings in Alpine areas. In combination with constructional measures to protect the wood (the use of dry timber, overhanging roofs to provide protection against the weather) it can, from the ecological viewpoint, offer an alternative worth considering.

## 4.1 Stains

Wood stains are used to protect the surfaces of wood from attack by mold, but also and above all to enhance and to give it color. Staining changes the shade of the wood or evens out differences in its color. The grain and the pores, however, are preserved and remain visible, and a variety of effects can be achieved by different staining processes. By chemical staining, for example, the hard zones that contain lignin (annual rings) react to the stain and change color more intensively than the softer zones (positive stain appearance). With color staining, powder or liquid color pigments are dissolved in water or in a solvent and applied to the wood. Here the softer, more absorbent early wood zones acquire a stronger color than the late wood zones, so that in coniferous woods the grain appears as a negative (negative stain image). Stains can be applied manually with a brush or roller, in industry stains are applied by dipping, spraying, or by industrial rolling.

## 4.2 Varnishes

Varnishes are transparent coatings beneath which the structure and grain of the timber also remains visible, however by adding the appropriate color pigments, more extreme differences of color can be evened out. Outdoors, what are known as wood protection varnishes are used, whose pigments additionally protect the timber against UV light and thus hinder weathering.

## 4.3 Paints, lacquers

Paints and lacquers are coatings that protect wood or wood-based materials against exposure to light and climate, moisture and damp. When it dries and cures, the binding agent in lacquers forms a film (film former) which prevents the growth of algae and mold. Traditional binding agents include natural resin (shellac, urushi lacquer) or lime (lime casein). Shellac is derived from gum resin (a secretion from the female lac bug) and is used to lacquer musical instruments, for example. If shellac is dissolved in high percentage alcohol (e.g. spirit or similar), the resulting product is called French polish. The raw material of urushi or Japanese lacquer is the resin of the lacquer tree. The lacquer is applied in a number of thin layers, each layer is allowed to harden at high humidity and in a dust-free atmosphere. Lime casein combines the qualities of the binding agents lime and casein. Casein paint, which is based on milk proteins (e.g. from low-fat milk or curd cheese), increases resistance to abrasion, the lime paint, which when cured is difficult to dissolve in water, provides the necessary resistance to the effects of weathering.

Modern paints are dissolved either in water (emulsion) or in solvents (gloss paints) and are named after their primary film formers, generally synthetic resins. To coat timber, cellulose nitrate paints (CN paints) are often used on account of their relatively high proportion of solvent, however, in Europe they are increasingly being replaced by water-thinnable paint systems (water-based gloss paints). These include polyurethane gloss paints (PUR paints), which consist of two components (2K), the paint and a hard-

ener, which are first mixed just before use. In addition to their low proportion of organic solvents, a further advantage of these two-component PUR gloss paints is, above all, their resistance to chemical materials, their high resistance to light, and their high resistance to abrasion, scratching, and knocks. In particular in North America and Scandinavia—primarily in furniture production—what are called acid hardening lacquers, frequently also known as sealing lacquers, are used. The film former here is also cellulose nitrate, ester is one of the hardening acids used. The disadvantage of these coatings is that they release formaldehyde while drying, which explains why they are increasingly being replaced by more environmentally friendly lacquers. For high quality applications such as lacquering musical instruments (e.g. pianos), interior fitting-outs of motor car or yacht interiors, polyester lacquers—also known as interior polyester lacquers—are used. In addition to the considerable amount of time required for application, the greatest disadvantage of polyester lacquers is that they emit organic solvents, even after drying.

Here help is provided by the RIM process (Reaction Injection Molding) developed for automobile interiors, in which a two-component polyurethane lacquer is applied with a tool to the surface of the wood or veneer, like in a conventional plastic injection process. The advantages of this process are the shorter hardening time (up to 99 percent) and the reduced amount of vapors (up to 90 percent less).

Short hardening times can also be achieved with radiation hardening or curing lacquers. For instance, under ultra-violet radiation unsaturated polyester lacquers harden in a few seconds to a non-sticky state. Increasingly more environmentally friendly, solvent-free UV lacquer systems, for example UV vacuum lacquers, are being used for lacquering furniture, stairs, or parquet flooring.

## 4.4 Films and foils

Films, generally in the form of high pressure laminates (HPL), are a suitable material for coating door leafs, kitchen worktops etc. Lengths of paper are pressed together, under high pressure, with several layers of melamine or phenolic resins. The coatings are heat, scratch, and solvent resistant. Well known HPL laminated sheets include Dekodur® (manufacturer: Dekodur GmbH & Co. KG), Formica® (producer: Formica Corporation) and Resopal® (manufacturer: Resopal GmbH).

Foil coatings made from PVC (polyvinyl chloride) are suitable for decorative purposes. Various wood-based materials can be covered with the foils. Alternatively, foils on a polyester basis (for instance: Pentadecor® (manufacturer: Klöckner Pentaplast GmbH & Co. KG) are suitable for furniture surfaces.

## 5 CHANGING THE CHARACTERISTICS OF MATERIALS

To permanently change the characteristics of timber, for instance to increase its resistance to attack by mold or to optimize its shrinkage and swelling performance and thus its dimensional stability, there exists the possibility of chemical or thermal modification. As a result of these modification processes, the wood darkens and its appearance then resembles that of many tropical woods. Timber can also be modified by means of complete impregnation of the timber, for instance with resins (see also Part II, 3.1 Impregnating), but in this case no chemical reaction such as, for example, with acetylation, takes place (see Part II, 5.1 Chemically modified timber). Modification processes for timber are more elaborate than impregnation with chemical wood preservatives, but they do not normally require the addition of biocides (bactericides, fungicides, insecticides). Therefore modified timber has no foreign contents and thus with regard to sorting by kind, or reintroduction into the resource cycle, it has a clear advantage over chemically impregnated timber.

## 5.1 Chemically modified timber–CMT

In the chemical modification of timber, first of all reactive chemicals are introduced into the wood. In the next step the timber is heated, causing the chemicals to harden. At present acetylation plays the major role in the area of chemical modification of timber. In this process, the timber is impregnated with acetic anhydride —a derivative of acetic acid created by the elimination of water. In the subsequent heating of the timber under high pressure to over 100°C, the acetic anhydride changes into acetic acid. This acid is then washed out and the timber is dried. This process permanently reduces the timber's ability to absorb moisture, and consequently also reduces the swelling and shrinking of the timber. Various chemical modification processes based on silicon are still at the research and development phase (for instance at the Institut für Holzbiologie und Holztechnologie of Göttingen University). Depending on the particular process, after being treated with silicon (silicates, silanes), timber exhibits greater resistance to fungal attacks or is more water-repellent.

## 5.2 Thermally modified timber–TMT

In contrast to steaming wood, in which temperatures of up to a maximum of 100°C are used to reduce tension (see Part II, 1.1 Steam bending), or, in the production of veneers, to make the wood pliable (see Part I, 3 Veneer), the thermal modification of timber is carried out at significantly higher temperatures.

Essentially in thermal modification the same chemical processes are initiated as in acetylation (see Part II, 5.1 Chemically modified timber). The difference lies in the fact that no acetic anhydride is introduced to the timber from outside but rather, as a result of heating processes, acetic acid is produced by substances in the wood itself. This occurs in the course of

the process at temperatures of around 140°C as a result of the separation of hemicelluloses (timber polyose see Part I, 1 Wood—definition and characteristics). Through the acetic acid and further heating up to 250°C, both the hemicellulose and, in part, the cellulose are removed so that the percentage of lignin (which massively decomposes only at temperatures between 280°C and 500°C) in the timber increases, and with it the strength and hardness of the timber also.

Thermally modified timber, also known as thermowood, can be produced by a number of different processes. They all have in common the gradual heating of the timber to temperatures between 140°C and 250°C over a period of one to two days, as well as subsequent gentle cooling. Particularly widespread are moisture-heat pressure processes, in which the wood is heated using steam under pressure—for instance in the BICOS process (e.g. *Thermoholz Spreewald, manufacturer Thermoholz Spreewald GmbH (THS)*), in the Stellac process (e.g. *Firstwood®, manufacturer Firstwood GmbH*), in the Plato process (*Plato® Wood, manufacturer Plato International BV*)—or in steam saturated nitrogen atmosphere (e.g. *New Option Wood, manufacturer: NEW OPTION WOOD SA*). Further thermal modification processes are the oil-heat process, in which the timber is heated without pressure in a bath of pure vegetable oil (e.g. *Menz OHT®, manufacturer: Menz Holz GmbH & Co. KG*) or vacuum press drying (*Vacu³ process*), in which the heat is applied to the timber by means of hot plates (e.g. *timura Holz, manufacturer: timura Holzmanufaktur GmbH*).

## 5.3 Charring (pyrolysis)

A traditional method of protecting timber still used today, especially in Japan, is charring wood, also called pyrolysis. Under the exclusion of atmospheric oxygen, the wood is heated on one side by means of a gas flame to temperatures of 450°C up to 600°C and then abruptly cooled with water. During the heating process, various substances are released at different temperatures: gases, wood tar, and charcoal. Charring creates a protective layer on the timber which, due to its low thermal conductivity and its ability to prevent the entry of oxygen, considerably delays any further burning. This phenomenon can also be observed in burning timber constructions, which resist the flames far longer than pure steel or concrete constructions (cf. also the point Warning ability, Part I, 1 Wood—definition and characteristics). Although charred timber is also less susceptible to attack by fungi and insects, opinions about protecting wood by charring are divided. The extreme temperature means that during the pyrolysis process not only does the timber lose mass and alter its dimensions, but cracks also occur in the charcoal layer, which means that pests can more easily reach the inside of the timber.

Also employing the pyrolysis process, but in this case using temperatures of up to 900°C, wood-based materials (MDF panels) or bamboo are carbonized to create porous carbon materials (such as wood ceramics or bamboo ceramics). These can be used, for instance, as the base material for catalytic converters or as components for batteries and fuel cells. In the case of flash pyrolysis (wood liquefaction), the timber is heated very rapidly to an average temperature of c. 500°C. In addition to charcoal and gases, this produces mainly pyrolysis oils, which can be used to make biofuel, for example.

# III TECHNOLOGY: THE PRINCIPLES OF TIMBER CONSTRUCTION

1      TIMBER FRAME CONSTRUCTION

2      SOLID TIMBER CONSTRUCTION

3      NATURAL BUILDING PROCESSES

# BIOGRAPHIES

**24H >ARCHITECTURE**
www.24h-architecture.com
The 24H >architecture office was established in 2001 by Boris Zeisser (*1968) and Maartje Lammers (*1963). Both studied at the Delft University of Technology and after graduating, worked at several well-known architectural offices including EEA (Erick van Egeraat associated architects), Mecanoo, and Rem Koolhaas' Office for Metropolitan Architecture. The 24H >architecture team now consists of fifteen employees whose work includes residential and educational buildings.

**WERNER AISSLINGER**
www.aisslinger.de
Werner Aisslinger (*1964) studied industrial design at the Berlin University of the Arts (UdK Berlin). After stints as a freelancer for Ron Arad, Jasper Morrison, and the Studio Delucchi he launched his own studio aisslinger in Berlin in 1993. Werner Aisslinger works are distinguished by their technologically dominated, experimental approach. He is mainly interested in new materials and manufacturing techniques. From 1994 to 1997, Aisslinger was a lecturer at the Berlin University of the Arts and at the Lahti Design Institute, Helsinki. From 1998 to 2005 he was professor at the Academy of Design in Karlsruhe, and since 2006 has been the curator of the Raymond Loewy Foundation and jury member of the Lucky Strike Design Award.

**ALICE** (*Atelier de la conception de l'espace*)
alice.epfl.ch
ALICE is a laboratory connected to the architecture department at the École Polytechnique Fédérale de Lausanne (EPFL) that provides students with experimental access to designing architectural space. The laboratory was founded by Prof. Dieter Dietz (UNDEND Architektur, Zurich) and consists of a team of architects and researchers from all over Europe. "Evolver" in Zermatt is a project from the year 2009 that was headed by Prof. Dieter Dietz and his team members, Katia Ritz (architect, Lausanne), Daniel Pokora (Mazzapokora, Zurich), Olivier Ottevaere (Multiply Studio, London), Aline Dubach, Isabella Pasqualini (architects, Zurich), and Eveline Galatis (secretary, Lausanne). The participating students include Ahmed Belkhodja, Augustin Clement, Nicolas Feihl, Olivier di Giambattista, Eveline Job, Martin Lepoutre, Samuel Maire, Benjamin Melly, Adrian Llewelyn Meredith, and François Nantermod.

**ARCHITEKTEN MARTENSON AND NAGEL-THEISSEN**
www.amunt.info
Björn Martenson (*1966) first trained as a carpenter and then studied architecture at the RWTH Aachen University (Germany), where he has worked as a freelance architect since 2002. Martenson also lectures for the Department and Institute for Housing and Design Basics at RWTH. Sonja Nagel (*1972) studied architecture and design at the Stuttgart State Academy of Art and Design (ABK) and at the University of Stuttgart. Jan Theissen (*1972), after studying product design at the Academy of Fine Arts (HBK Saar) in Saarbrücken and the Design Academy Eindhoven, studied architecture at Pratt Institute in New York and ABK in Stuttgart, where Nagel and Theissen later worked as lecturers. In 2004 they founded Nagel-Theissen in Stuttgart. After completing the "Just K" apartment house collaborative project, Björn Martenson, Sonja Nagel, and Jan Theissen joined forces in 2010 to found amunt—Architekten Martenson und Nagel-Theissen. In 2010, "Just K" was awarded the Weißenhof Architecture Award for young architects and in 2011 the Heinze Architects AWARD, as well as the DETAIL Special Prize for Interior Design.

**YEMI AWOSILE**
www.yemiawosile.co.uk
Yemi Awosile (*1984) is a London-based designer specializing in textiles and material development. She completed her studies at the Royal College of Art in London in 2008. A main focus of Awosile's work is the use of site-specific materials and the merging of traditional craftsmanship techniques and new technologies. For the production and application of cork fabric, Yemi Awosile conducted research in Portugal where she was able to study the range of procedures from harvesting cork to the different ways of processing it.

**SHIN AZUMI**
www.shinazumi.com
Shin Azumi (*1965) runs a design practice in London under the name of "a studio" that specializes in product and furniture design as well as interiors. One of this Japanese designer's best-known pieces is the "LEM" bar stool he designed for the Italian manufacturer Lapalma in 1999. Many works by Azumi, who is a passionate collector of scissors, have been exhibited all over the world in renowned design collections including the Victoria & Albert Museum in London, the Stedelijk Museum in Amsterdam and Die Neue Sammlung in Munich. The stackable multiplex stool "AP" was awarded the International Furnishing Show's (imm cologne) Interior Innovation Award in 2011.

**MAARTEN BAAS**
www.maartenbaas.com
The Dutch designer Maarten Baas (*1978) studied at the Design Academy Eindhoven. The series entitled "Smoke" (2004–2009), which stems from his final degree thesis in 2002, won wide international acclaim and is a favorite in museums and among collectors. The furniture series "Clay Furniture," which he presented at the Milan Furniture Fair in 2006, as well as "Sculpt" (2007), and his hand-carved wooden objects in the "China series" (2008) also won universal recognition. Baas has had numerous solo exhibitions in New York, Miami, Tokyo, and at the London Design Museum. Maarten Baas lives and works in 's-Hertogenbosch, which is south of Eindhoven.

**BERNARDO BADER**
www.bernardobader.com
Bernardo Bader (*1974) studied architecture at Innsbruck University and opened his own practice in 2003 in Dornbirn, Austria. Wood plays a large role in both Bader's renovation commissions and new-build projects. He often uses wood composite element construction for the supporting frames for his new projects. Bader's works have been awarded numerous prizes including the renowned Vorarlberg Timber Construction Award and the Weißenhof Architecture Award in 2007.

**ALDO BAKKER**
www.aldobakker.com
The Netherlands designer Aldo Bakker (*1971) feels bound to an aesthetic that is rooted in craftsmanship and precision. The communicative and associative, rather than the conceptual, aspects of an object are fundamental to Bakker. Bakker's work fluctuates between art and design; the unique choice of materials and the unexpected haptic qualities are among the most exciting aspects of his work. For his "Stool" Aldo Bakker was presented with the design award of the magazine *Wallpaper* in 2011.

**STEPHAN BALKENHOL**
Stephan Balkenhol (*1957) is one of the most important contemporary sculptors. Typical of his work are the markings, notches, and grooves from the sculptural process that he leaves visible on the wood. The sculptures are also painted in a way that allows the structure of the material to remain visible. From 1976 to 1982 Stephan Balkenhol studied at the University of Fine Arts in Hamburg with Ulrich Rückriem. He has taught at the Städelsche Kunstinstitut in Frankfurt, and since 1982 has been Professor at the Karlsruhe University of Arts and Design. Balkenhol lives in Karlsruhe and Meisenthal, France and has a studio in Berlin.

**SHIGERU BAN ARCHITECTS**
www.shigerubanarchitects.com
Japanese architect Shigeru Ban (*1957) uses economical production methods and materials such as cardboard or bamboo. Shigeru Ban is best known in Germany for his cardboard pavilion that was exhibited at the Expo 2000 in Hanover, and which he built in collaboration with architect and lightweight structures specialist, Frei Otto. Ban established his own practice, Shigeru Ban Architects, with offices in Tokyo and Paris, in 1985. He has been a member of the Academy of Arts in Berlin since 2006.

**GEORG BASELITZ**
www.baselitz.com
Georg Baselitz (*1938 in Deutschbaselitz/Saxony as Hans-Georg Kern) is one of the most important German contemporary artists. Baselitz made his name in the 1960s first as a painter, and later with prints, drawings, linocuts, and sculpture. He made his first wooden sculptures in 1979, which he mainly shaped using a chainsaw, ax, and pick. Georg Baselitz lives and works in a house/studio building designed and built by the architects Herzog & de Meuron in Inning/Buch on Lake Ammer, and in Imperia on the Italian Riviera. In 2004, he was awarded the Praemium Imperiale by the Japan Art Association, which is considered the "Nobel prize for art."

**BAUBOTANIK**
*Bureau Baubotanik*
www.bureau-baubotanik.de
Bureau Baubotanik, which specializes in building with live plants, is headed by the architects Hannes Schwertfeger (*1975) and Oliver Storz (*1979). Oliver Storz researches in the field of engineering science with Prof. Dr. Jan Knippers at the University of Stuttgart and Prof. Dr. Thomas Speck at the University of Freiburg. Hannes Schwertfeger researches in the field of design theory with Dr. Gerd de Bruyn at the University of Stuttgart.

*Ferdinand Ludwig*
www.ferdinandludwig.de
Ferdinand Ludwig (*1980) explores and develops support structures in the form of living plant constructions. At the moment, his prototypes deal with living plant construction methods of plant addition. Ludwig researches with Prof. Dr. Gerd de Bruyn at the University of Stuttgart and Prof. Dr. Thomas Speck at the University of Freiburg.

**BCXSY**
www.bcxsy.com
BCXSY is a collaboration project by Israeli designer Boaz Cohen (*1978) and Japanese jewelry designer Sayaka Yamamoto (*1984). Cohen and Yamamoto both studied at the Design Academy Eindhoven, where they also run their practice. They consider their collaboration to be an interdisciplinary experiment that results in concepts, products, furniture, graphic works, and interior design. BCXSY was presented with the design award of the magazine *Wallpaper* for "Join" in 2011.

**BERNATH+WIDMER**
www.bernathwidmer.ch
The architectural practice of Bernath+Widmer was established in 2007 by Roland Bernath (*1973) and Benjamin Widmer (*1978) in Zurich. After an apprenticeship in carpentry, Roland Bernath studied at the Zurich University of Applied Arts in Winterthur. Benjamin Widmer, after his apprenticeship as an architectural draughtsman, also studied architecture at the Zurich University of Applied Arts Winterthur, as well as at the University of Arts (UdK) in Berlin and the ETH Zürich. In addition to their work as architects, Bernath and Widmer began teaching in the fall semester of 2011 at the Lucerne University of Applied Sciences and Arts in the School of Engineering and Architecture.

**BETON**
www.beton-on.com
The Polish design practice Beton has been based in Warsaw since 2007 and was established by architect and fashion designer Marta Rowińska (*1976) and architect Lech Rowiński (*1976). They met each other at the Warsaw University of Technology. Rowińska and Rowiński pursue an interdisciplinary approach within the fields of architecture, fashion, and graphic, industrial, set, and costume design. They received acclaim with their modular cardboard wall "Wall2" at London Design Week. The chapel in Tarnów is their first completed construction.

**PATRICK BLANCHARD**
blanchardsculpt.free.fr
After completing his studies, sculptor and plasterer Patrick Blanchard worked many years for the Louvre and Versailles Museums. In 1992, he opened his own studio in Paris. Patrick Blanchard is also head of the sculpture faculty at the renowned École Boulle and is a member of the Grands Ateliers de France, one of France's largest academies of applied arts. In 1997, he was awarded the distinguished Médaille du Meilleur Ouvrier de France, which selected him as master of his field.

**JÖRG BONER**
www.joergboner.ch
Jörg Boner (*1968) is a product designer and has been running his own practice in Zurich since 2001. Boner's designs are known for their conceptual approach and have been awarded numerous prizes. His chair entitled "Wogg 50" received the Best of the Best of the Interior Innovation Award at the imm cologne in 2011. In addition to his work as a designer, Jörg Boner began teaching at the ECAL (École Cantonale d'Art de Lausanne) in 2002. Boner is also the art director for the furniture and lamp collection "nanoo," a spinoff from Schweizer Faserplast AG. The Schweizerische Eidgenossenschaft awarded the "Grand Prix Design 2011" to Jörg Boner for his ongoing contributions to Swiss design and his commitment as both designer and teacher.

**TORD BOONTJE**
tordboontje.com
Tord Boontje (*1968) studied industrial design at the Design Academy Eindhoven and at the Royal College of Art in London. He established his practice in London in 1996 where he now lives and works, after a short stay in Bourg-Argental, France. Boontje attempts to provide a sensual experience for the user through his designs, as well as to connect the present with tradition. Since 2009, Tord Boontje has also served as Professor and Head of the Department of Product Design at the Royal College of Art in London.

**GION A. CAMINADA**
www.arch.ethz.ch/darch/entwurf/caminada/
Gion A. Caminada (*1957) is considered one of the most important proponents of Swiss building culture. He has focused on the *Strickbau* technique since 2000 (a method popular in Alpine regions of "knitting" together layers of wooden beams or logs) in his hometown of Vrin in the Canton of Graubünden, and, as its village planner, aims to maintain the historical image of the village. In addition to this practical work as an architect, he also teaches architecture and design as a guest professor at the Swiss Federal Institute of Technology (ETH) in Zurich, where, above all with the project "Orte schaffen", he devotes himself to the dialogue between science, business, politics, handcraft, architecture and other disciplines.

**NICK CAVE**
www.soundsuitshop.com
Nick Cave (*1959) was born in Missouri and lives in Chicago, Illinois. He designed his first "Soundsuits" as kinetic sculptures in response to the race riots in Los Angeles in 1991 that were a reaction to the murder of Rodney King by the police. The Soundsuit designs are inspired by African ceremonial costumes, Tibetan textiles, and pop culture figures. Nick Cave is a trained dancer, has danced for the New York Alvin Ailey American Dance Theater, and is now head of the fashion department at the School of the Art Institute of Chicago (SAIC).

### GEHARD DEMETZ

www.geharddemetz.com

Gehard Demetz (*1972) is from South Tyrol and is a wood carver and sculptor. He debuted in 2005 as an artist and became internationally successful almost overnight. His sculptures are almost always of children and although he leaves the work as a whole in a very rough, almost sketch-like state, the surfaces are finely polished and highly detailed. In 2010, Demetz was commissioned to make a sculpture of the founder of the sporting goods manufacturer Nike, William "Bill" Jay Bowerman, for their European headquarters.

### MARCO DESSÍ

www.marcodessi.com

Marco Dessí (*1976) from South Tyrol studied design at the University of Applied Arts in Vienna, graduating in 2007. In that year, he founded his own design practice in the same city and has since worked in the fields of furniture design, objects, retail, and exhibition design. His clients include renowned companies such as Lobmeyr, Augarten, and Richard Lampert. In 2006, he was awarded second place in the Rosenthal Design Award for his design "Chaos Theory."

### STEFAN DIEZ

www.stefan-diez.com

Stefan Diez (*1971) was born in Freising near Munich and studied at the Stuttgart State Academy of Art and Design after completing an apprenticeship in carpentry. He established his practice in Munich in 2003 and has since worked in different design fields, ranging from furniture and tabletop design to industrial and exhibition design. His clients include Authentics, Bree, e15, Merten, Moroso, Rosenthal, Thonet, and Wilkhahn. His products have received international design awards, such as the German Design Award four times (2006, 2008, and 2010), as well as the iF gold award in 2009. His plywood chair "Houdini" was awarded the German Design Prize in Gold in 2012. Diez has been a professor of industrial design at the Karlsruhe University of Arts and Design (HfG) since 2007.

### DOSHI LEVIEN (NIPA DOSHI AND JONATHAN LEVIEN)

www.doshilevien.com

The London-based design practice of Doshi Levien was established in 2000 by Nipa Doshi (*1971) and Jonathan Levien (*1972). Nipa Doshi first studied design at the National Institute of Design in Ahmedabad (India), before she completed her master's degree in furniture design at the London Royal College of Art (RCA). Doshi Levien offers consultation on a global scale to international clients such as Intel, Swarovski, Nokia, Authentics, Moroso, and Cappellini. The "Rocker" rocking horse for the Richard Lambert furniture company was awarded Best of the Best by the Interior Innovation Award Cologne.

### DUTCH INVERTUALS

www.dutchinvertuals.nl

Dutch Invertuals Collective was established by the Dutch conceptual designer Wendy Plomp (*1977) in 2009. The group consists of graduates of different design disciplines from the renowned Design Academy Eindhoven. Members of the Dutch Invertuals Collective's project "Matter of Time" (2010) are Carolina Wilcke, Daphna Isaacs & Laurens Manders, Edhv, Juliette Warmenhoven, Julien Carretero, Max Lipsey, Mieke Meijer, and Raw Color.

### PIET HEIN EEK

www.pietheineek.nl

Piet Hein Eek (*1967) graduated from the Design Academy Eindhoven and made his name in the early 1990s with a series of monumental cupboards made from recycled wood. He founded his studio in 1992, which, since 1993, he has operated under the name Eek & Ruijgrok BV together with his partner, designer Nob Ruijgrok. The Netherlands designer creates and produces very successful unique pieces from recycled wood. He likes to create works that are not products of mass production. His pieces are exhibited in the collection of the Museum of Modern Art (MoMA) in New York.

### FEHLING & PEIZ

www.kraud.de

After an apprenticeship in carpentry, Yvonne Fehling (*1972) studied product design at the Karlsruhe University of Arts and Design (HfG). She began collecting practical experience during her studies working for Marcel Wanders in Amsterdam as well as Colin Ross and Young Lin in Taipei and China, among others. Jennie Peiz (*1976) also studied at the HfG in Karlsruhe and has worked in Rotterdam, Sydney, New Delhi, and London. They both became freelancers in 2006 and run a design studio in Karlsruhe as well as the product label "Kraud." In addition to designing furniture, bags, and lamps, Fehling & Peiz also develop exhibition concepts. In 2010 Fehling & Peiz were among the five finalists in the Design Prize of the Federal Republic of Germany in the category "Next Generation."

### HANS-PETER FELDMANN

The artist Hans-Peter Feldmann (*1941) is a cult figure according to insiders of the contemporary art scene. He started off painting, after studying at the Arts Academy in Düsseldorf, however in 1968 he began working conceptually with the medium of photography and with everyday objects. Feldmann, who never signs his works, does not distinguish between the materials that he makes himself or materials that he finds. In 2010, he was awarded $100,000 in the Hugo Boss Prize of the Solomon R. Guggenheim Foundation. In 2011, he will be honored with a solo show of his work in the prizewinner exhibition at the New York Guggenheim Museum. Hans-Peter Feldmann lives and works in Düsseldorf.

### LAETITIA FLORIN

www.laetitiaflorin.ch

The product designer Laetitia Florin (*1988) graduated in 2010 with a bachelor's degree from the ECAL (École Cantonale d'Art de Lausanne). The Dutch magazine *Frame* (edition 78) named her one of the ten best design graduates of the year. In 2011 she exhibited "Bidum," her series of baskets made from textile coatings and spring steel strips, at the competition "[D3] Contest" at the imm cologne.

### MALCOLM FRASER ARCHITECTS

www.malcolmfraser.co.uk

Malcolm Fraser (*1959) studied architecture at the University of Edinburgh in Scotland. After working first as a community architect in Wester Hailes in south Edinburgh, and in the practice of architect and theoretician Christopher Alexander in Berkeley, California, Malcolm Fraser established his own architectural practice in 1993 in Edinburgh. The portfolio of his practice includes diverse building types, including public buildings, residential buildings, art and education facilities, commercial buildings, community buildings, as well as the master planning of large construction projects.

### FRONT

www.frontdesign.se

The Swedish designers Sofia Lagerkvist (*1976), Charlotte von der Lancken (*1978), and Anna Lindgren (*1977) all studied at the Konstfack University College of Arts, Crafts and Design in Stockholm. They have been working together in their Stockholm studio on the island of Södermalm under the name of Front. Their conceptual design has received much attention, because with each new product, they question their role as designers as well as the conventions associated with design itself. They integrate elements into their design process that are alien to the concept, such as magic tricks or living animals that help them convey their ideas. Their clients include Kartell, Moooi, Moroso, Established & Sons, Skitsch, and Porro.

### TERUNOBU FUJIMORI

Japanese architect and author Terunobu Fujimori (*1946) is professor at the Institute of Industrial Science at the University of Tokyo. He designed his first building, the Jinchokan Moriya Historical Museum in Nagano, in 1991 at the age of forty-four. He often uses charred wood as a material for his architecture, which is the traditional Japanese method of wood conservation, called Yakisugi. In 2010 for the "Raiding Project," Terunobu Fujimori designed one of ten temporary residences for the 2011 Franz Liszt anniversary year.

### ELISE GABRIEL

www.gabrielise.fr

The French designer Elise Gabriel (*1985) works in the fields of fashion, furniture, jewelry, and set design. She conceived the project "Zelfo Embrace" for her master's thesis at the École Normale Supérieure in Cachan, France. Elise Gabriel lives and works in Paris, and has run Atelier Bancal together with the designer Bertrand Gravier since 2009.

### MARTINO GAMPER

gampermartino.com

After completing an apprenticeship as a furniture designer, South Tyrolean Martino Gamper (*1971) studied sculpture and product design at the University of Applied Arts Vienna and Academy of Fine Arts Vienna. He completed his master's degree in 2000 at the Royal College of Art in London, the city in which he has since based his practice. Gamper often fluctuates between art and design in his work. He received international acclaim with his exhibition "100 Chairs in 100 Days," which has been exhibited worldwide in museums and design festivals since 2007. For this project, Gamper dissected old chairs into small pieces and put them back together again within 100 days as new chair creations.

### LIAM GILLICK

www.liamgillick.info

Liam Gillick (*1964) is one of today's most versatile contemporary artists. His work includes painting, sculpture, object art, and music. Gillick is also a writer, critic, and curator. His works can be seen in major museums around the world and in the context with important art exhibitions. In 2002, Gillick was nominated for the Turner Prize. In 2009 he designed the German Pavilion at the 53rd Venice Art Biennale. Liam Gillick lives and works in London and New York.

### GLASS HILL

www.glasshill.co.uk

The London-based design studio, Glass Hill, was established at the beginning of 2010 by British Joe Nunn (*1980) and Swedish Markus Bergström (*1979). Nunn and Bergström met each other in 2005 while studying at the Royal College of Art (RCA) in London. They design furniture, accessories, and products for their clients, who include Woodfinch Rare Books, the RCA, Phillips de Pury, and the Institute of Contemporary Arts (ICA) in London. They are also involved in architectural and interior design projects.

### GRAFT

www.graftlab.com

The architectural practice GRAFT was established in Los Angeles in 1998 by Lars Krückeberg (*1967), Wolfram Putz (*1968), and Thomas Willemeit (*1968). In 2007 M. Alejandra Lillo (*1972) joined as a partner. GRAFT have won several international architecture and design awards. They are not only renowned for their architecture projects: in 2010, their exclusive design for the design department store Stilwerk, of nine "Phantom Tables" made from fiberglass reinforced plastic, was on show at the Miami/Basel Design Fair. The architectural practice has offices in Los Angeles, Berlin, and Beijing and employs approximately one hundred architects, designers, and artists.

### GRAMAZIO & KOHLER

www.gramaziokohler.com

The Swiss architects Fabio Gramazio (*1970) and Matthias Kohler (*1968) established their practice in Zurich in 2000. They use computer and digital production as design tools but mix these with traditional design, construction, and building methods. In addition to their architectural activities, Gramazio & Kohler work as urban planners and lighting planners. Both are also architecture and digital production professors at the Department of Architecture at the ETH in Zurich. In 2012 Gramazio & Kohler were presented with the Best Architects Award for the Tanzhaus Zürich.

### KONSTANTIN GRCIC

konstantin-grcic.com

Konstantin Grcic (*1965) is one of the most internationally renowned, contemporary German designers. He completed an education in furniture making at Parnham College, after which he studied design from 1988 to 1990 at the Royal College of Art in London. Konstantin Grcic lives in Munich where he has run his design practice, KGID Konstantin Grcic Industrial Design, since 1991. His best-known designs include the chairs "Chair_One" (2004) and "Myto" (2008) as well as the lamp "Mayday" (1999). In addition to his work as a product designer, Grcic curates and designs exhibitions and interiors, such as for the Parrish Art Museum on Long Island, a project by the architects Herzog & de Meuron.

### GUALLART ARCHITECTS

www.guallart.com

Vicente Guallart (*1963) is a Spanish architect who established his practice in Barcelona in 1992. His works are influenced by nature, technology, and architecture, and he also involves such disciplines as geology, sociology, engineering, production technology, and software design. In addition to his architectural activities, Vicente Guallart is the director of the Institute for Advanced Architecture of Catalonia (IAAC) which is based in Barcelona.

### MAX AND HANNES GUMPP

www.hannesgumpp.com

Hannes and Max Gumpp are twin brothers (*1977) and have previously worked collaboratively on projects. Hannes Gumpp first studied architecture and design at the Stuttgart State Academy of Art and Design and then graduated with a degree in industrial design. In 2007, he established his design practice together with architect Andreas Meyer. Max Gumpp studied sculpture at the Academy of Fine Arts in Munich. The brothers live and work in Munich.

### FLORIAN HAUSWIRTH

www.florianhauswirth.ch, www.postfossil.ch

Florian Hauswirth (*1970) studied industrial design at the University of Applied Sciences Northwestern Switzerland, after completing his degree as a technical model builder. From 2000 to 2006 he worked as a freelancer in the development department of the Swiss furniture manufacturer Vitra in Birsfelden. Since 2006, Florian Hauswirth has been a freelance designer in Biel and member of the design collective, postfossil. His work focuses on consumer goods, furniture, packaging, objects, retail, exhibitions, and cultural projects. His designs have won several awards and have been exhibited internationally. In 2010, Hauswirth was awarded a New York studio residency by the Bernese Foundation for Applied Arts.

### STUART HAYGARTH

www.stuarthaygarth.com

British designer, Stuart Haygarth (*1966), has worked since 2004 on design projects that deal with collecting objects such as PET bottles, eyeglass lenses, table fireworks, and so on. Haygarth categorizes the objects he collects from the streets or flea markets and uses them to make chandeliers or installations, giving the objects a new meaning. For this reason, Haygarth considers his work to be on the edge of design and art. In 2008 he was honored at the British Design Awards by being named best newcomer.

### HEIDE UND VON BECKERATH ARCHITEKTEN

www.heidevonbeckerath.com

Architects Tim Heide (*1959) and Verena von Beckenrath (*1960) run a practice together in Berlin. Andrew Alberts was also a partner from 1996 to 2008. Their work focuses on designing and planning interior spaces and buildings, evaluations in the field of urban planning, design concepts for exhibitions and trade fairs, as well as consultancy for corporations. Their work has won numerous awards and has been exhibited and published internationally. In the German Timber Building Prize 2011 Heide und von Beckerath Architekten received a recognition for the house in Oderbruch.

### STAFFAN HOLM

www.staffanholm.com

Staffan Holm (*1977) completed his master's degree at the School of Design and Crafts in Gothenburg and established his practice in the same city. Holm attempts to connect functional and emotional aspects in his work in order to encourage the user to bond with the product. Together with the designer Dan Sunaga, Staffan Holm was awarded the 2009 Nordic Design Prize for the "Newton Coffee Table," and in 2010 received the prize awarded by the Swedish magazine, *ELLE Decor* for best piece of furniture.

### BENJAMIN HUBERT

www.benjaminhubert.co.uk

The British designer Benjamin Hubert (*1984) studied industrial design and technology at Loughborough University and received his bachelor degree in 2006. Shortly thereafter, in 2007, he opened a studio in London and specialized in designing furniture and lamps. He is mainly interested in the materials ceramics, wood, and cork. Benjamin Hubert's works quickly received international acclaim and have won numerous prizes, including British Design Award 2010 (Design of the Year) and the *ELLE Decor* International Design Award—EDIDA (International Young Designer of the Year 2010).

### ENRIQUE ILLÁNEZ SCHÖNENBERGER

www.enriqueillanez.com

The Swiss-Ecuadorian, Enrique Illánez Schönenberger (*1981) completed his education as a furniture maker after which he studied at the ECAL (École Cantonale d'Art de Lausanne). The Netherlands magazine *Frame* (edition 78) chose him as one of the best ten graduates of 2010. "Brigitte," his series of outdoor furniture, was exhibited in 2011 in the competition "[D³] Contest" at the imm cologne.

### INCHFURNITURE

www.inchfurniture.ch

INCHfurniture was established in 2004 by Thomas Wüthrich (*1975) and Yves Raschle (*1974) in Basel. During a long research visit to Indonesia, the two designers were able to get to know the woodworking technical school, PIKA. The workshop that now produces INCHfurniture's products also contains a teaching facility that is highly acclaimed in Indonesia. The wood used to manufacture the furniture comes from a sustainable teakwood plantation. For the Swiss pavilion at the EXPO 2010 in Shanghai, Wüthrich and Raschle designed a furniture line, which they called "The Shanghai Series," to furnish the entire pavilion.

### THE INSTITUTE FOR COMPUTATIONAL DESIGN (ICD) AND THE INSTITUTE OF BUILDING STRUCTURES AND STRUCTURAL DESIGN (ITKE), UNIVERSITY OF STUTTGART

icd.uni-stuttgart.de / www.itke.uni-stuttgart.de

The Institute for Computational Design (ICD), under the leadership of Prof. Achim Menges, deals with the possibilities of integrating diverse architecture-related requirements and complex relationships between material, form, structure, and environment into generative, computer-based processes. The Institute of Building Structures and Structural Design (ITKE), under the leadership of Prof. Jan Knippers, has a long experience with consultation, inspection, and evaluation of buildings made from fiber-reinforced plastic. At the end of 2010, the two institutes worked collaboratively on a temporary research pavilion made of wood, which was to demonstrate state of the art computer-based design, simulation, and production processes in the architectural context, and convey these into a complex supporting structure made from pliable, formed plywood strips. In 2011 a second pavilion followed, which explored transferring to architecture the biological structural formation principles exhibited by sea urchins' endoskeletons using new, computer-based design and simulation processes, as well as computer-operated production methods for implementing these in building.

### IWAMOTOSCOTT ARCHITECTURE

www.iwamotoscott.com

The San Francisco based architectural practice was established in 1998 by Lisa Iwamoto and Craig Scott. Both graduated with a master's degree from Harvard University. In addition to architecture, IwamotoScott Architecture also works in the fields of design and exhibition design. Their projects have received numerous awards and have been displayed in renowned museums and exhibitions worldwide. Both architects also teach: Lisa Iwamoto as Assistant Professor at the University of California, Berkeley and Craig Scott as Associate Professor for Architecture at California College of the Arts.

### HELLA JONGERIUS

www.jongeriuslab.com

Hella Jongerius' (*1963) work fluctuates between the borders of design and its associated disciplines, craftsmanship, and art. Jongerius interweaves historical and contemporary forms, motifs, and techniques. She designs limited editions and series of objects that include mainly vases, dishes, furniture, and textiles. Jongerius received international acclaim for her designs for Droog. In 2000, she established Jongeriuslab in Rotterdam, which she moved to Berlin in 2008. Hella Jongerius works for distinguished companies such as Vitra, Ikea, Belux, Porzellan Manufaktur Nymphenburg, and Royal Tichelaar Makkum, and is represented by Galerie Kreo in Paris. In addition she also develops color concepts for various clients such as Camper or Deutsche Bank.

### CORDULA KEHRER

www.cordulakehrer.de

Cordula Kehrer (*1981) has worked since 2008 as a freelance product designer in the fields of furniture design, accessories, and exhibition design. She studied product design at the Karlsruhe University of Arts and Design. Kehrer was a scholar of the Studienstiftung des deutschen Volkes (The German National Academic Foundation) in 2005, won the RecyclingDesignAward in 2010, and was awarded the Cultural Grant of the City of Karlsruhe in 2011. She has presented her works at international trade exhibitions such as the imm cologne, the Tendence in Frankfurt, and the Maison&Objet in Paris.

### STEFFEN KEHRLE

www.steffenkehrle.com

Steffen Kehrle (*1976) gathered practical experience with BMW, Busse Design, Starczewski Design, and Frédéric Dedelley, even while he was studying industrial design at the University of Applied Arts in Vienna. From 2007 to 2009 he worked as a designer at Stefan Diez, and was among those responsible for many product developments. His "Atelier Steffen Kehrle" has been based in Munich since 2009, and is focused on product, exhibition, and interior design. Since October 2009, Steffen Kehrle has been a lecturer at the Art Academy in Kassel in the fields of furniture design and architecture exhibition.

### KO-HO

www.Ko-ho.fi

The Finnish design practice, Ko-Ho, is currently in the start-up phase. Both founders, Timo Hoisko (*1982) and Matti Korpela (*1985), completed an apprenticeship as cabinetmakers before studying Industrial Design at the Seinäjoki University of Applied Sciences.

### KRAUS SCHÖNBERG ARCHITEKTEN

www.kraus-schoenberg.com

Architects Tobias Kraus (*1969) and Timm Schönberg (*1971) founded their practice in 2006 with offices in Constance and London. They quickly made a name with their projects and are now counted among the most influential representatives of a generation of architects who feel committed to designing and realizing buildings that are sustainable and consider the needs of the residents and users. Their Haus W. in Hamburg, which was completed in 2009, won the German Timber Construction Award, and is also considered by architects to be an icon of new construction.

### KENGO KUMA & ASSOCIATES

www.kkaa.co.jp

Japanese Kengo Kuma (*1954) studied architecture at the University of Tokyo and founded the architectural practice Kengo Kuma & Associates in 1990. The practice now employs more than 100 people in locations in Tokyo and Paris, and focuses on using natural materials to create airy, light, and open spaces. They apply methods with great flexibility to create structures that harmonize with the human body. Kengo Kuma is a professor of architecture at Tokyo University.

### MAYA LAHMY

lahmy.dk

Danish architect, Maya Lahmy (*1975), first studied at the Irwin S. Chanin School of Architecture at Cooper Union in New York and then at the School of Architecture at the Royal Danish Academy of Fine Arts in Copenhagen. Since 2004, together with architect Gudrun Krabbe (*1976), Maya Lahmy has worked under the name of krabbelahmy design in the field of exhibition design.

### LASSILA HIRVILAMMI ARKKITEHDIT

www.lh-ark.fi

Lassila Hirvilammi Architects Ltd. was founded in 2001 under the name of Lassila Mannberg Architects Ltd. in Oulu (Finland). In 2004, Anssi Lassila (*1973) and Teemu Hirvilammi's (*1974) practice moved to Seinäjoki (Finland). The architects design apartment and public buildings as well as interiors. In 2010, Lassila and Hirvilammi were given the Pietilä Award, and their design for the Kuokkala Church received the Finnish Wood Prize.

### LE BRICCOLE DI VENEZIA

www.veneziabriccole.com

The "Briccole di Venezia" is a project by the Italian furniture manufacturer Riva 1920. It involves 29 designers and architects who were invited to design art and furniture objects using the wooden stakes salvaged from the canals of Venice. The surface of these oak stakes displays a typical water-worn quality, which results in an extraordinary collection of furniture consisting of unique pieces.

### SEONGYONG LEE

www.seongyonglee.com

South Korean Seongyong Lee (*1976) first studied design at Seoul National University, after which he graduated with a master's degree from the Royal College of Art in London in 2010. In 2009, he won the iF concept award for his floating soup ladle "Floater" and the International Design Excellence Award (IDEA) in bronze. He has presented his stool, "Plytube," which originated from his master's thesis work, at numerous trade exhibitions and design festivals where it received wide acclaim. Seongyong Lee lives and works in London.

### HANS LEMMEN

www.hanslemmen.nl

The Netherlands artist Hans Lemmen (*1959) studied at the Academy of Fine Arts in Maastricht. His drawings, site-specific works, and sculptures have made him one of the most diverse representatives of contemporary art in the Netherlands. There was a solo exhibition of Hans Lemmen's work in 2011 at CAAM (Centro Atlántico de Arte Moderno) in Las Palmas on the Canary Islands that travelled to other venues in Spain, the Netherlands, and Germany. Hans Lemmen lives and works in Maastricht and Waltwilder (Belgium).

### KHAI LIEW

www.khailiewdesign.com

The Malaysian designer Khai Liew (*1952) first made his name as a restorer of old Australian furniture after emigrating to Australia. At the beginning of the 1990s, he started to become interested in Danish furniture. In 1997, he established his practice Studio Khai Liew Design, which was a combination of workshop and shop. He sold his own designs along with imported Danish furniture. Khai Liew is also a professor at the School of Art, Architecture and Design of the University of South Australia. He lives and works in Adelaide.

### KAI LINKE

www.kailinke.com

Kai Linke (*1980) studied architecture at Darmstadt University of Technology and studied product design at the Academy of Art and Design in Offenbach (Germany). In 2005, Linke was a scholar of the Studienstiftung des deutschen Volkes (The German National Academic Foundation). He has run a practice in Offenbach since 2009. In 2010 and 2011 Linke was nominated for the Newcomers Design Award of the Federal Republic of Germany.

### IDEE LIU

www.yiidesign.com

After his studies at the National Yunlin University of Science and Technology (NYUST) in Yunlin (Taiwan) and at Da-Yeh University in Changhua (Taiwan), the Taiwanese designer Idee Liu (*1973) worked for a number of renowned design studios around the world, including Designaffairs in Munich, Pentagram Design in London, Ignition Design, and Globe Union. He now works for JIVA Design in Taipei.

### LOCALARCHITECTURE

www.localarchitecture.ch

localarchitecture is based in Lausanne and was established in 2002 by Manuel Bieler (*1970), Antoine Robert-Grandpierre (*1972), and Laurent Saurer (*1971). All three partners have a master's degree in architecture from the École Polytechnique Fédérale de Lausanne (EPFL). Their work aims to achieve a symbiosis with the local context by taking into consideration the specific situation's sounds, smells, weather, and seasons. localarchitecture's work has been awarded numerous architectural prizes, including the Holzpreis Schweiz (Swiss wood prize) several times.

### PAUL LOEBACH

www.paulloebach.com

Furniture designer Paul Loebach (*1972) comes from a German family of furniture makers and grew up in Cincinnati, Ohio. Loebach studied industrial design at Rhode Island School of Design (RISD) and opened a studio in New York after graduating in 2002. He works as a designer and consultant with numerous American and European furniture companies, including Areaware and Roll & Hill.

### PHILIPPE MALOUIN

www.philippemalouin.com

The Canadian Philippe Malouin (*1982) studied industrial design at the University of Montreal, the École Nationale Supérieure de Création Industrielle (ENSCI) in Paris, and at the Design Academy in Eindhoven. After his studies he was first a freelancer for Tom Dixon. In 2009, he founded his own studio in London. Since then his work has been presented in the most important design galleries worldwide. Malouin often experiments with materials and manufacturing techniques, but his primary interest is the actual design process.

### ENZO MARI

The Italian designer and object artist Enzo Mari (*1932) made a name for himself far beyond the borders of Italy with his designs for companies such as Danese, Gavina, Artemide, Olivetti, and Castelli. In 1968, he participated in the 4. documenta in Kassel. In addition to his design work, Mari has also taught through his working career, for institutions such as the Politecnico di Milano,

at the Centro Studi e Archivio della Comunicazione (CSAC) in Parma, and at the Accademia di Belle Arti in Carrara. He is also honorary professor for design at the Academy of Fine Arts in Hamburg. Enzo Mari lives and works in Milan.

**MICHAEL MARRIOTT**
www.michaelmarriott.com
The English designer, author, curator, and teacher, Michael Marriott (*1963) studied furniture design first at the London College of Furniture and then at the Royal College of Art. In 1993, he opened his own design studio and has since designed furniture, accessories, and lamps. He also develops ideas for installations, exhibitions, and art projects. His clients include Established & Sons, SCP, move, and modus.

**JÜRGEN MAYER H.**
www.jmayerh.de
Jürgen Mayer H. (*1965) studied architecture at the University of Stuttgart, at the Cooper Union in New York, and at Princeton University. In 1996 he established his own architectural practice in Berlin. In addition to his architectural designs, Jürgen Mayer H. works with the patterns of encoded data and number columns as well as with color. He has been teaching at several universities since 1996, including the Berlin University of the Arts, the Graduate School of Design (GSD) of Harvard University, the Architectural Association in London, and, now, Columbia University in New York. He was awarded the Mies van der Rohe Prize in 2003 in the category of "Emerging Architect" and in 2005 the Holcim Award Bronze Europe for sustainable architecture. In 2010, he won the Audi Urban Future Award. His projects are included in collections such as the New York MoMA and the MoMA in San Francisco. In 2011 on the occasion of BODW he conceived the German Design Loft for the German Design Council.

**JUNICHI MORI**
The Japanese artist and sculptor Junichi Mori (*1965) received his master's degree from the Graduate School of Fine Arts of Tokyo National University of Fine Arts and Music. His wood and marble sculptures with which he attempts to capture the flowing motion of nature have received wide acclaim in the art world. Junichi Mori's works have been displayed since the mid 1990s in numerous group and solo exhibitions. In 2010 he participated, for instance, in the exhibition "Neo-Ornamentalism from Japanese Contemporary Art" at the Museum of Contemporary Art Tokyo (MOT) and was represented at the VOLTAShow in Basel. Junichi Mori lives and works in Kanagawa (Japan).

**PAOLA NAVONE**
www.paolanavone.it
Paola Navone (*1950) graduated in 1973 with a degree in architecture from the Polytechnic University in Turin. Over the course of her long and varied career, she has also worked as a designer, art director, critic, teacher, and exhibition curator. Her international clients include Abet Laminati, Armani Casa, Knoll International, Alessi, Driade, Molteni, porcelain factory Reichenbach, and Swarovski. Navone's work is characterized by the combination of Asian craft traditions and European influences. In 1983, Paola Navone was awarded the prestigious International Design Award in Osaka and in 2000, she was named Designer of the Year by the German magazine *Architektur & Wohnen*. Navone lives in Milan and Hong Kong.

**NENDO**
www.nendo.jp
Oki Sato (*1977) grew up in Toronto and studied architecture at Waseda University in Tokyo, where he established his design studio Nendo in 2002. In 2005 he opened another studio in Milan. Nendo is now one of the most internationally prominent design studios in Japan. The focus is on product, furniture, and packaging design, as well as architecture and interior architecture. His international clients include Swedese, Moroso, Cappellini, Boffi, Quodes, Puma, and Toyota.

**SASCHA NORDMEYER**
www.saschanordmeyer.com
Sascha Nordmeyer's (*1977) mother is French and his father German. He grew up near Frankfurt am Main and moved to France in 1998, where he studied at the École Supérieure d'Art et de Design (ESAD) in Reims. After his studies, Nordmeyer worked as a designer for the French luxury brand S. T. Dupont, where he designed high-tech accessories for the James Bond film "Casino Royale." In 2008, Sascha Nordmeyer became a freelance designer with his own practice in Reims (France).

**HENRIQUE OLIVEIRA**
www.henriqueoliveira.com
Brazilian artist Henrique Oliveira (*1973) graduated from the University of São Paulo in 2007 with a master's degree in visual poetics. His works have been shown internationally in numerous solo and group exhibitions—for instance in 2008 at the Contemporary Arts Center, New Orleans and in 2010 at the 29th Bienal Internacional de São Paulo and the IX Bienal Monterrey FEMSA, Casa de la Cultura de Puebla, Mexico. Oliveira lives and works in São Paulo.

**JENS OTTEN**
www.jepada.de
Jens Otten (*1974) studied product design at the School of Art and Design in Kassel. He was awarded the Lucky Strike Junior Designer Award for his degree thesis work, the chair "Experimentelle Elastostatik." At the moment Jens Otten is a lecturer at the Saar School of Architecture at the Saarland University of Applied Sciences in Saarbrücken (Germany).

**HARRY PARR-YOUNG**
www.harryparr-young.com
Harry Parr-Young (*1988) was born in Portugal. He completed his studies in furniture and product design at Buckinghamshire New University in 2010. He designs cleverly devised experimental products using a wide variety of materials. His works have been shown in numerous exhibitions such as at the Victoria & Albert Museum in London. His stool "Rattan Splice Mark I" was exhibited at the "Tent Selects" event as one of the best graduate works of 2010. Harry Parr-Young lives and works in England and Portugal.

**PATTERNITY**
www.patternity.co.uk
The London-based design studio Patternity was established in 2009 by the architects Anna Murray (*1983) and Grace Winteringham (*1985), designers of textiles and surfaces. The studio specializes in designing patterns for fashion and interior design. Patternity is divided into three core parts: an archive of constantly updated patterns from around the world, a design studio that also offers consultations, and an online shop that offers limited design editions and pattern designs. The furniture designed by Patternity is done in collaboration with Grace's father, the furniture maker Toby Winteringham (*1955).

**LEX POTT**
www.lexpott.nl
Dutch designer Lex Pott (*1985) completed his studies in 2009 at the Design Academy Eindhoven. During his studies he worked for different design practices including Scholten & Baijings and Jongeriuslab. His works have been shown internationally in museums and trade fairs, including Dutch Design Week in Eindhoven, the Museum für Angewandte Kunst in Frankfurt am Main, and gallery 21_21 Design Sight in Tokyo.

**RAY POWER**
www.raypowerdesign.com
Irish designer Ray Power (*1975) studied ceramics at Crawford College in Cork and specialized in designing furniture and lamps. In 2007, Powers presented his "Sweet Pendant Light" made from wine glasses at the furniture fair in Milan and created an uproar in the design world. In 2009 he was awarded the Good Design Award of the Chicago Athenaeum for his lamp "Air." Ray Power lives in Barcelona where Ray Power Design is based.

**PHILIPPE RAHM ARCHITECTES**
www.philipperahm.com
Philippe Rahm (*1967) studied architecture at the EPFL in Lausanne and the ETH Zurich. Rahm aims to stimulate awareness of sustainable and environmentally friendly architecture with his work on "meteorological architecture," which emphasizes the importance of the interaction between meteorology, architectural space, and human organism. Rahm's designs have been awarded international prizes, and his work has been exhibited around the world, for instance in 2002 and 2008 at the Architecture Biennale in Venice and in 2007 in a solo exhibition at the Canadian Centre for Architecture in Montreal. Philippe Rahm has run his architectural practice in Paris since 2008, and is also a guest lecturer at different European academies.

**RAW EDGES**
www.raw-edges.com
Yael Mer and Shay Alkalay of Raw Edges were born in Tel Aviv in 1976. The husband and wife team both graduated with a master's degree from London's Royal College of Art. Their official professional collaboration began after years of shared life. They want to develop unprecedented products collaboratively. Raw Edges have received many awards including British Council Talented Award, the iF gold award, the Dutch Design Award, and the Wallpaper Design Award 2009. Their clients include Cappellini, Established & Sons, and Arco. They also design unique and limited editions in their London-based studio.

**STEFFEN REICHERT**
icd.uni-stuttgart.de
Steffen Reichert (*1984) studied product design at the Academy of Art and Design in Offenbach and completed his master's degree in design and computation at the School of Architecture at the Massachusetts Institute of Technology (MIT). Reichert was a scholar of the Studienstiftung des deutschen Volkes (The German National Academic Foundation), and his works have won awards including the Bavarian State Award and the Materialica Award. At the moment, Steffen Reichert is a research assistant and doctoral student at the Institute for Computational Design (ICD) in Stuttgart.

**ROLU**, rosenlof/lucas, ro/lu
www.ro-lu.com
The Minneapolis, Minnesota-based Studio ROLU, rosenlof/lucas, ro/lu was established in 2003 by Matt Olson (*1967) and Mike Brady (*1973) and now has four employees. Their field of activity includes the design and construction of furniture, landscape design, architectural projects, urban planning, and art in public spaces. They search out references to the everyday in their work and aim to design products that are affordable and accessible to the widest possible public.

**ADRIEN ROVERO**
www.adrienrovero.com
The Swiss industrial designer and scenographer Adrien Rovero (*1981) studied at the ECAL (École cantonale d'art de Lausanne). In 2006, he opened his studio in Renens (Switzerland). Rovero's work is based on the close observation of elementary needs, which results in unexpected and often surprising solutions. Adrien Rovero was awarded the jury prize of the Villa Noailles, the French art and design festival, as well as the Federal Award for Design of the Swiss Cultural Affairs Office. In 2011 he received the Design Prize of the Schweizerische Eidgenossenschaft. Adrien Rovero teaches at the ECAL in Lausanne.

**MARC SADLER**
www.marcsadler.it
Austrian-born Marc Sadler (*1946) studied industrial design at l'École Nationale Supérieure des Arts Décoratifs (ENSAD) in Paris and first specialized in designing sports equipment. Sadler designed the patented "Shell" system for the Italian ski manufacturer, Caber, and developed sports shoe soles for the sporting goods manufacturers Nike and Reebok. After having lived in many places in Europe, North America, and Asia, Sadler now lives in Milan and is a consultant for companies in the fields of furniture, household appliances, lamps, technology and sport. His best-known products include the lamps "Twiggy" and "Mite" for Foscarini, the lamp "Drop" for Flos, and the "Alukit" kitchen for Boffi. His back protector for motorcycle riders, which he designed for Dainese, was purchased by the permanent collection of MoMA in New York.

**STEFAN SAGMEISTER**
www.sagmeister.com
Austrian-born Stefan Sagmeister (*1962) is one of the most renowned and influential graphic designers in the world. He established his practice, Sagmeister Inc., in New York in 1999. Sagmeister's CD covers for Lou Reed, the Rolling Stones, and the Talking Heads have achieved cult status. Sagmeister was nominated for a Grammy five times, and he won it in 2004 for his cover design of the album "Once in a Lifetime" by Talking Heads. In 2009, Stefan Sagmeister was honored with the Lucky Strike Designer Award. His most recent exhibition "Sagmeister: Another Exhibit About Promotion And Sales Material" was shown in a number of European museums in 2011/2012.

**COLIN SCHAELLI**
www.colinschaelli.com
The Swiss product designer and art director Colin Schaelli (*1980) studied at the Zurich University of the Arts and opened his design practice in 2006 under the name DBCSC with offices in Zurich and Tokyo. Schaelli designs products that he explains are as simple as possible, unpretentious, and variable. Schaelli received the Swiss Design Prize in the category of "New Comer" in 2009 for the display and storage concept "V30 Freitag Skid." In 2009, he also won the red dot award: communication design for the publication *Urban Myth*, on which he worked as art director.

**ALBRECHT SCHÄFER**
The artist Albrecht Schäfer (*1967) studied at the Braunschweig University of Art, at Chelsea College of Art & Design in London, and at the Academy of Fine Arts in Munich. Schäfer has been the recipient of numerous grants and art prizes and his work has been shown in group and solo exhibitions worldwide. Since 2010, Albrecht Schäfer, who lives and works in Berlin, has served as sculpture professor at the Berlin Weißensee School of Art (KHB).

**SCHOLTEN & BAIJINGS**
www.scholtenbaijings.com
Stefan Scholten (*1972), who studied at the Design Academy Eindhoven, and self-educated Carole Baijings (*1973), founded their collaborative design practice in 2000 in Amsterdam. They are among the most successful young Netherlands designers. Their product and furniture designs often refer to craftsmanship traditions, such as hand-painted, handmade paper. For their tableware series "Paper Table," Scholten & Baijings received the Dutch Design Award in 2010 and in 2011 the Wallpaper Design Award.

**FRANZISKA SCHREIBER**
franziskaschreiber.com
Fashion designer Franziska Schreiber (*1977) majored in German and American studies at Humboldt University in Berlin and clothing design at the University of Applied Sciences (HTW) in Berlin. In 2003, Franziska Schreiber was awarded the Lucky Strike Junior Designer Award for her degree work, the collection: "body meets dress meets wood." From 2003 to 2007 she managed the label "Pulver" together with her fellow students Elisabeth Schotte, Therese Pfeil, and Franziska Piefke. Since 2006, Franziska Schreiber has also worked as artistic assistant in the fashion department of the Industrial Design Department at the Berlin University of the Arts.

### TILO SCHULZ
www.tiloschulz.com
Tilo Schulz (*1972) is an artist, exhibition curator, and lecturer. He was one of the curators of the exhibition "squatting. erinnern, vergessen, besetzen" at the Temporäre Kunsthalle in Berlin in 2010. His work deals with the clichés and political implications of the abstract and formalist aspects of Modernism. At the beginning of the 1990s, as a self-educated artist, Schulz began to paint non-representationally. Since 2005, he has been designing small format works of marquetry that he makes out of grained veneer and thin, light colored strips of wood. Schulz has been the recipient of numerous residences and grants; his work has been shown in solo and group exhibitions in museums and galleries all over the world. Tilo Schulz lives and works in Berlin and Leipzig.

### JERSZY SEYMOUR
www.jerszyseymour.com
Canadian Jerszy Seymour (*1968) was born in London, studied industrial design at the Royal College of Art, then went to Milan, and has lived in Berlin since 2004. He has worked for renowned manufacturers such as Magis and Moulinex, but his interests mainly lie in his own conceptual projects, such as "Workshop Chair," the construction principles of which are communicated in workshops at museums and design festivals. Seymour is also a lecturer at the Royal College of Art in London, the Domus Academy in Milan, and at the ECAL in Lausanne to name a few. At the moment he is guest professor at the Academy of Fine Arts (HBK) in Saarbrücken (Germany).

### DJ SIMPSON
English artist DJ Simpson (*1966) comes from Lancaster and lives in London. He first studied at Reading University and then completed his master's degree at Goldsmiths College in London. He calls his works paintings, although he uses a hand-held electric milling machine to process the surfaces of chipboard or plywood, which are finished with a monochrome laminate (also known as "routing"). His works have been internationally exhibited at art fairs, in museums, and galleries, and have received numerous awards.

### ERNST STARK
www.ernststark.de
The artist Ernst Stark (*1965) first attended the Vocational School for Wood Sculptors in Bischofsheim/Rhön. His miniature sculptures capture things, moments, and situations that have impressed him and stuck in his memory. Ernst Stark has received numerous grants and awards as well as various residencies, including in 2007 the Paris studio grant of the Hessische Kulturstiftung (Hesse State Cultural Foundation) where he created the series "Bois de Boulogne." Ernst Stark lives and works in Paris.

### WOLFGANG STEHLE
www.wolfgangstehle.com
The artist Wolfgang Stehle (*1965) completed an apprenticeship as a wood sculptor at the Job Training Center for Construction and Design in Munich, then studied at the Academy of Fine Arts in Munich, before receiving his master's degree at the Chelsea College of Art & Design in London. His sculptures, video works, drawings, and pictures deal with processes of transformation, forms of movement, patterns, and progressions. Since 2007, Stehle has been an artistic assistant at the Academy of Fine Arts in Munich where he also lives and works.

### ELISA STROZYK
www.elisastrozyk.de
Elisa Strozyk (*1982) studied textiles and surface design at the KHB in Berlin and at the ENSAD in Paris. In 2009 she completed her master's degree in future textiles at Central Saint Martins College of Art & Design in London. During her studies, she completed internships at the wallpaper design studio of Andrea Pößnicker and at Samsonite. She also created wall designs for Circus Hotel and the Buffalo Shop in Berlin. In 2010, Elisa Strozyk was awarded the Design Prize of the Federal Republic of Germany in the category of "New Comer." Elisa Strozyk lives in Berlin where she also has her studio. The "Accordion Cabinet" was created in collaboration with the artist Sebastian Neeb (*1980), who studied with Daniel Richter at the Berlin University of the Arts (UdK). Sebastian Neeb also lives and works in Berlin. Under the title "Craft Alchemy" in the framework of Design Miami 2011, Strozyk and Neeb staged a design performance for the fashion label Fendi.

### STUDIO FORMAFANTASMA
www.formafantasma.com
The Italian designers Andrea Trimarchi (*1983) and Simone Farresin (*1980) run their Eindhoven-based practice under the name of Studio Formafantasma. Their collaboration began during their studies in communication design, later they discovered their interest in product design during their respective master's studies at the Design Academy Eindhoven. Their master thesis work, delivered in 2009, dealt with traditional Sicilian craftsmanship. Their work is rooted in the desire to connect craftsmanship and industrial production processes in both their own projects as well as in cooperation with other companies.

### STUDIO JENS PRAET
www.jenspraet.com
The Belgian industrial designer Jens Praet (*1984) opened his practice in Panzano near Florence after studying in Florence and at the Design Academy Eindhoven. His designs aim to connect traditional craftsmanship techniques with innovative production methods. His "Shredded Collection," a series of furniture made from shredded paper, was shown at the beginning of 2011 during Praet's first solo exhibition in the United States at the Industry Gallery in Washington, DC.

### STUDIO JOB
www.studiojob.nl
Antwerp-based Studio Job is headed by Belgian Job Smeets (*1970) and Dutch Nynke Tynagel (*1977). Both studied at the Design Academy Eindhoven: Tynagel, graphic design, and Smeets, product design. Since it was established in 1998, Studio Job has operated on the fine line between art and design. In collaboration with design galleries such as Moss and manufacturers such as Royal Tichelaar Makkum, Smeets and Tynagel design complexly handcrafted, ironic installations as limited editions or unique pieces, and—as is the case with their furniture series "Industry" —often use provocative elements such as gas masks or nuclear waste barrels. In 2011/2012 Groninger Museum devoted a solo exhibition to Studio Job.

### TB&AJKAY
www.tb-ajkay.com
Industrial designer Therése Broberg (*1981) who studied at Lund University (Sweden), and textile designer Susanne von Ajkay (*1981), who graduated from the University of Borås (Sweden), established their practice in 2009 under the name of Tb&Ajkay, which is part of the Stockholm-based design cooperative Headoffice. Broberg and von Ajkay design furniture, lamps, and accessories, as well as wallpaper and patterns.

### THE MEDLEY INSTITUTE BY JANA PATZ
themedleyinstitute.com
Jana Patz (*1977) studied fashion design in Berlin and Stockholm. In 2007, together with Amélie Riech, she founded the jewelry label "Uncommon Matters," before establishing the Medley Institute in Berlin, which is a platform where artists and designers of all disciplines can collaborate to create products, objects, concepts, and accessories that cannot be clearly categorized as either art or design. Since 2007, Jana Patz has worked as an artistic assistant in the fashion section of the Industrial Design Department at Berlin University of the Arts.

### KATHARINA TRUDZINSKI
www.katharinatrudzinski.de, hui-hui.de
Artist Katharina Trudzinski (*1977) lives in Hamburg and Berlin. She studied textile design at the University of Fine Arts in Hamburg (HFBK) and graduated from the same institution with a postgraduate degree in art. Her sculptural works and pictures, which Trudzinski mostly creates from found wood, are meant to enter into a dialog with their environment. Katharina Trudzinski sees her art as a source of inspiration for her Hamburg- and Antwerp-based fashion label "Hui-Hui," which she has run together with her sister Johanna Trudzinski and Anne Schwätzler since 2002.

### XAVIER VEILHAN
www.veilhan.net
French artist Xavier Veilhan (*1963) is one of the most established artists of his generation. His work comprises sculpture, painting, photography, film, and performance. In addition to his archetypical sculptures, which he creates from different materials such as wood, aluminum, or stainless steel using 3D scanners, he is also well known for his motorized vehicle designs, such as the "RAL 5015" boat (2010). Xavier Veilhan has received numerous international awards and his work has been shown in group and solo exhibitions throughout the world, for instance, in 2008 in Versailles. Xavier collaborated with designers Ronan and Erwan Bouroullec for an installation for the opening exhibition "Chefs-d'oeuvre?" at the Centre Pompidou Metz in 2010.

### CHARLOTTE WAGEMAKER
www.charlottewagemaker.com
The Dutch designer Charlotte Wagemaker (*1986) completed her studies in product design in 2011 at the HKU, Hogeschool voor de Kunsten Utrecht. As part of her material research for her thesis, she experimented with treating wood with staining and laser techniques.

### WAUGH THISTLETON ARCHITECTS
www.waughthistleton.com
Architects Andrew Waugh (*1966) and Anthony Thistleton (*1967) met in 1991 at college and decided to establish a practice together, based in London. Waugh and Thistleton now enjoy an excellent reputation in Great Britain and North America. For each project, they typically begin by observing its cultural, social, and historical context. Their urban house "Murray Grove" in London received the RIBA (Royal Institute of British Architects) President's Award for Research in 2010.

### AI WEIWEI
www.aiweiwei.com
Ai Weiwei (*1957), Chinese conceptual artist, sculptor, and curator, is one of the most influential artists today—especially because of his political and social activities. He first made a name for himself in the 1970s with the dissident group "Stars." From 1981, Ai Weiwei lived in New York and studied at Parsons School of Design. In 1993, he returned to China where he has since supported his country's experimental art in his gallery, China Art Archives and Warehouse. Ai Weiwei also works in the fields of architecture and urban planning and acted as consultant to architects Herzog & de Meuron in their design of the "Bird's Nest" 2008 Olympic Stadium in Beijing.

### WINGÅRDH ARKITEKTKONTOR
www.wingardhs.se
Swedish architect Gert Wingårdh (*1951) studied at Chalmers University of Technology in Gothenburg (Sweden), where he has been a professor since 2007. He established his practice in 1977 in the same city. Gert Wingårdh is also a member of the Swedish Royal Academy of Fine Arts and the Royal Academy of Engineering and Science. His designs have received numerous international awards. At the moment, Wingårdh Arkitektkontor boasts approximately 150 employees in its offices in Gothenburg and Stockholm. Their self-acclaimed architectural mission is a strong commitment to the artistic and poetic dimensions of architecture.

### MARTIN WÖHRL
Artist Martin Wöhrl (*1974) studied at the Academy of Fine Arts in Munich, at Edinburgh College of Art, and at the Glasgow School of Art. His work has won numerous awards. In 2007, he was a grant holder of the Internationales Künstlerhaus Villa Concordia, in 2004 he was awarded the USA scholarship residency of Bavaria, and in 2002, a DAAD scholarship. His artistic work makes use mainly of materials such as chipboard, construction foam, styrofoam, or plaster, making reference to history, art history, the domestic world, and architecture. For Wöhrl's work entitled "Cantina Sociale" (2010), the artist visited the last professional cooper, a maker and repairer of casks and barrels, to interview him about his work. Martin Wöhrl lives and works in Munich.

### BETHAN LAURA WOOD
www.woodlondon.co.uk
English product designer Bethan Laura Wood (*1983) first studied at the University of Brighton and then at the Royal College of Art in London. She established her practice under the name of WOOD while still studying. Bethan Laura Wood's work recontextualizes parts of everyday products. Her portfolio ranges from furniture, accessories, and lamp objects to jewelry, ceramic works, as well as set design and installations in public spaces.

### RICHARD WOODS
www.richardwoodsstudio.com
British artist Richard Woods (*1966) is a graduate of the Slade School of Fine Art. His designs refer to the clichés of traditional British interiors and architectural style by, for instance, imitating the wooden grain of fishbone parquet flooring, red bricks, flowered wallpaper, or timber framing, and using these to cover floors, walls, or entire facades. For the London-based design firm Established & Sons, Woods created a hand-woven wool carpet with a pattern of wooden paneling.

# INDEX

2K-PUR paints. See polyurethane gloss paints
3D-veneer 264
3D wood. See 3D-veneer

**A**

A4 kerfing 270
abachi 262
abies alba 261
acacia 261
acer 262
acer platanoides 262
acer pseudoplatanus 262
acetylation 273
acid hardening lacquer 273
acoustics 260
acoustic insulation 265, 267
acoustic property 260
Acrodur® 12
adhesives 263, 264, 265, 269, 271, 272
adhesive resins 265
afzelia 260
ageing 113, 235, 261
air cleansing chipboard panel 265
aircraft construction 264, 271
Albeflex 266
alder 54, 260
American walnut 108
annual rings 260, 263, 270, 273
anti-bacterial effect 261
apple 235
application process 271
aramid fiber 266
Arbofill© 266
Arboform® 187, 265
arolla pine 261
aroma 260, 262
artificial coating 272
artificial resin 264, 265
ash 30, 56, 107, 108, 110, 116, 118, 122, 144, 156, 197, 245, 260, 262, 264, 270
ash anthracnose 266
ash plywood 107
ash veneer 198
aspen 263, 264, 265
asthma 261, 262

**B**

back ventilated facade 265
bacteria 266
bactericides 273
balloon frame 276
balsa 260, 262, 266
bamboo 36, 103, 106, 111, 213, 259, 266, 267, 274, 278
bamboo ceramics 274
bamboo fiber 267
bamboo-plastic composite (BPC) 267
bark 260, 261, 267
Bark Cloth® 40, 41
Barktex® 40, 41
barnwood. See reclaimed wood
barrels 262
barrique ageing 260
basket 262
bast 142, 259, 260, 267
bastard quarter cutting 263
bast fiber 267
bast weave 142
Baubotanik 43, 46, 47, 272, 276. See also living plant load-bearing structure
beams 261, 264, 276
bearing capacity 262, 272
bearing strength 264
beech 30, 92, 98, 119, 197, 260, 262, 263, 264, 270
beech plywood 76
beech veneer 187
beech veneer plywood 264
bending 111, 122, 240, 269, 270
bending method 270
bending process 270
bending strength 260, 262
bending stress 261, 272
Bendywood® 270
bentwood. See steam bending
bentwood chair. See steam bending
benzaldehyde 260
benzyl alcohol 260
betula 262
BICOS process 274
bicycle frame construction 36, 267
binding agent 273
biocides 273
biofuel 274
bionics 276
birch 76, 85, 98, 132, 190, 235, 239, 244, 260, 262, 263
birch plywood 28, 72, 132, 176, 225, 239, 245
birch plywood sheets 72
bird's eye maple 238

bitter almond oil 260
black locust 264
black walnut 108
blockboard 259, 264
block building 276
block building 276
board 261, 264, 276
boat-building 263
boat jetty 262
bolts 269, 271, 272
bond 181
bonding 269, 271
box 262
box-girder 264
boxwood 166, 182, 183
braiding 235
breaking load 266
bridge building 261, 264, 266
brushing away 269, 270
BSB connections (Blumer-System-Binder) 271
buckling stress 261
building 262, 271
building construction 261, 262, 265, 267
building industry 262, 271
bursting strength 266
butte 217
butt joint 271
buxus sempervirens 262

**C**

cabin construction 62
cabinetmaker 54
cable binder 272
cable ties 136, 176
CAD 105
cambium 260
camphor 25
Candidus Prugger 270
canting 265
capillary 223
caravan building 265
carbon 266
carbon-fiber strengthened plastic 266
carbonization 27, 90, 252, 274
cardanol 271
cardol 271
carpentry dowel 272
carpentry 271
carpentry connection 271, 276
carpentry joint 276
carving 262
casein 273
cashew-shell oil 269, 271
castanea sativa 262
cast resin 139, 140
catalytic converter 274
cedar 32, 35, 42, 90, 192, 260
cellulose 260, 265, 267, 274
cellulose-based bioplastic 92
cellulose-based materials 272
cellulose nitrate paint (CN paint) 273
cement-bound chipboard 265
central layer 264, 266
chamaecyparis obtusa 261

changing characteristics 270
charcoal. See charring
charring 269, 274, 279
chemically modified timber (CMT) 269, 273
chemical modification 273
chemical staining 273
chestnut 197, 226, 260, 262, 264
chip 259, 264, 265
chipboard 225, 237, 253, 259, 262, 263, 265, 266, 267, 282
chipboard panel 263, 265, 271, 272
cidori 152
clamp 269, 271, 272
CNC 37, 59, 77, 181, 266, 269, 270, 276, 279
CNC machine 271, 276
CNC machining center 269, 270, 276
CNC milling 56, 72, 105, 168, 176, 190, 215
CNC technology 108. See also CNC
coarse particle board 204
coating 269, 270, 272, 273
cocobolo 60, 262
cold gluing 271
color 260
color staining 273
columns 264
comb joint 271, 276
comb-type connection 271
composite material with wood 259
compression stress 261
compression zone 266
compressive strength 260, 262, 264
concrete 264
concrete construction 265
concrete plate 266
condensed wood 269, 270
conifers 259, 260, 261, 262
coniferous wood 260, 261, 273
connecting process 271
constructional wood-based material 263
construction lumber 264
construction timber 261, 262, 270
contouring 103
cork 20, 124, 259, 260, 267, 278, 280
cork cambium 260
cork fabric 278
cork granulate 267
cork layer 260
cork mats. See cork
cork oak 267
corner connection 271
cornus 68
covering plywood sheet 264
cover sheet 266
cover veneer 264
cradle-to-cradle 187, 261
cross-laminated pine. See cross laminated timber (CLT)
cross laminated timber (CLT) 150, 168, 248, 259, 264, 271, 276
crown cut 263
crown sliced veneer 263
curing lacquer 273
cutting 263, 266
cutting process 269, 270
cut wood 266
cypress 48, 152

**D**

dalbergia 60, 263
dalbergia retusa 262
Dauerholz 271
deciduous trees 259, 260, 261, 262
deciduous wood 88
decorative surface 272
deep drawing 265, 266, 270
defibrating 265
degree of toughness 261
Dekodur® 273
densified wood 264
density 265, 266
depth of penetration 272
diffusion-open MDF panel 265
dimensional stability 265
dogwood tree 68
door 262
door frame 265
door leaf 273
Douglas fir 108, 150, 194, 195, 260, 261, 264
dovetail joint 270, 271
dowel 263, 271, 272
doweling 59
dowel joint 271
dowel pin 272
dowel welding 119
dracaena 266
drilling 270
dry density 260, 261, 262, 263
dry process 265
durability 270
Duripanel® 265

**E**

early wood 270
ebony 260
eccentric cutting 263
Ecogehr® 266
elasticity 262, 270
elastic shaping 270
elm 30, 260, 262
embedment strength 272
emulsion 273
engineered timber 271
engineered timber construction 264, 271
engineered wood product (EWP) 259, 263, 264, 265
engraving 262
epoxy resin 26, 27, 236, 266, 271
eucalyptus 266
extrusion 266
extrusion method 265
extrusion molding process 265, 266

**F**

facade cladding 266
facade shingles. See shingles
fagus sylvatica 262
Falun paint 121
[illegible]
fiber 259, 264, 265
fiber-based material 262, 265, 266
fiberboard 259, 265, 266, 271
fiberboard panel 272
fiber mat 266
Fiberon® 266
fiber panel 260, 265, 270
fiber shaped element 259, 265
file-to-factory process 105, 132, 168
filling 270
film 269, 272, 273
film former 273
finger joint 264, 271, 276
finishing agents 271
fir 28, 261, 264
fireproofing agents 271
fire protection 261, 264, 265, 266, 276
fitted bolt 272
flake veneer 263
flash pyrolysis (wood liquefaction) 274
flat cutting 263
flat quarter cutting 263
flat shell structure 276
flat sliced 263
flax 265, 266
floorboards 261, 262
foil 269, 272, 273
foil coating 273
folded structure 168
Foldtex 266
footfall sound insulation 260
forestry 261, 262
forestry period 261
Forex® disks 86
Forex®-platelets 272
form 264
formaldehyde 265, 271, 273
formaldehyde free dispersion adhesive 272
Formica® 114, 225, 273
forming 103
frame connection 271
frame construction 15, 120, 156, 276
[illegible]
frame timber construction 276
fraxinus excelsior 262
fraying 263

French polish 273
friction welding 116, 119, 269, 272
friction welding technology 272
fruit crate 262
FSC label 131
fuel cell 274
full thread screw 272
fungal attack 261, 272, 273
fungicides 273
fungus (physisporinus vitreus) 271
furniture 262, 270
furniture making 261, 262, 263, 264, 265, 266, 267, 270, 271, 272

**G**

girder 264
glass 266
glass fiber 266
gleditsia triacanthos 262
gloss paint 273
glue 235
glued crosswise 264
glued joint 271
glued laminated timber (glulam) 259, 264, 271
glued wood-steel composite 266
glue thread 264
gluing 271
glutine glue 271
gold leaf 120, 161
grafting fruit trees 276
grain 213, 273
graying 272
gray discoloration 263
Greim construction method 271
grenadilla wood 263
groove joint 28
gross density 260, 265
grow over 44, 47
growth 261, 267
growth ring 270
gum resin 273
gypsum-bound chipboard panel 265

**H**

hacking 263
half-timbered construction 119, 262, 276
handrail 270
hardness 270, 274
hardwood 119, 260, 261, 262, 264, 265
HDF 114
HDF panel 271
heart-free beams. See heart-free hardwood
heart-free hardwood 50
heart-free oak. See heart-free hardwood
heart rate 261
heartwood 260, 261, 263
heat insulation capacity 260
heat insulator 260
heat storage 260
heat storage characteristic 260
heat storage material 260
Heggenstaller process 265
hemicellulose 116, 119, 260, 274
hemp 12, 148, 265, 266, 267
Heraklith® 265
high-density fiberboard (HDF) 265
high pressure laminate (HPL) 273
hinoki cypress 48, 261
honey locust 30, 262
[illegible]
hornbeam 99, 260
hot mold press 265
HPL laminated sheet 273
hydraulic engineering 261, 262

**I**

impact resistance 262
impact strength 262
impregnation 261, 269, 271, 272, 273
impregnation material 271
incision in the bark 263
industrial flooring 264
injection molding process 208, 265, 266
inlay 223, 262, 267, 270
insecticides 271, 273
insulating property 265
intarsia 140, 174, 192, 236
interior fitting-out 260, 262, 263, 264, 265, 267, 271, 272, 273
interiors 261, 262, 265, 273
internal space dividers 264
Intrallam 265
ipé (ironwood) 112, 262
ironwood 250, 262, 263. See also ipé
irradiating 270
isocyanate 265
Isolith® 265
Isospan® 265
iwood 266

**J**

Japanese lacquer tree. See Urushi lacquer
joinery 103
joinery connection 271, 272
joinery dowel 269, 272
joining 269, 270, 271
joists 276
juglans regia 263

**K**

kenaf 12, 266
kerfing 269, 270
Kerto® 265
kitchen appliances 262
kitchen worktop 273
knife handle 262
knitted fabric 266
knitted textiles 272
knothole 263
Kovalex® 266
Kraftplex 265
Kreibaum process 265
Kupilka® 266

**L**

[illegible]
lacewood 223
lacquer 269, 270, 272, 273
lacquer tree 273
laminate 107, 122, 254, 263, 282
laminated spruce 215
laminated strand lumber (LSL) 264, 265
laminated timber 272
laminated veneer 181
laminated veneer lumber (LVL) 264
laminated zebrawood veneer 219
laminate flooring 265
laminboard 259, 264
lap joint 271, 276
larch 88, 252, 260, 261, 264
larix decidua 261
laser 245, 266, 270
laser beam technology 23, 154, 236, 238
laser cut technology 254
laser cutting 136
lasing 245
late wood 270, 273
lathing 124, 174
LenoTec® 276
lightweight building panels 259
lightweight chipboard 259, 267
lightweight chipboard panel 265, 267
lightweight construction panel 262
lightweight panel 266
lignin 116, 119, 187, 260, 265, 267, 269, 271, 272, 273
Lignoflex®™ 266
lignosulfonate 269, 271
lignosulfonic acid 271
Lignotrend® 276
lime casein 62, 273
lime paint 273
lime-wood 42, 54, 69, 70, 71, 156, 162, 171, 172, 260, 262, 273
linden. See lime-wood
LiquidWood® 214
liriodendron tulipifera 263
living plant load-bearing structure 47, 276
load-bearing structure 52
log 261, 265, 266, 276
[illegible]
log cabins 67
log construction 276
longitudinal slicing 263
long joint 271
longleaf pine 264, 265

**M**

machining  171, 263
magnesite-bound chipboard panels  265
mahogany  54, 61, 260, 262
mahogany veneer  233
maize  265, 267
maple  42, 54, 86, 119, 170, 174, 185, 235, 260, 262, 270
maple veneer  202, 233
marquetry  238, 282
match  262, 263
matched joint  28
material transit tissue  260
MDF  100, 114, 180, 187, 214, 255
MDF panel  270, 271, 274
mechanical connection  269, 271, 272
medium-density fiberboard (MDF)  265
medullary rays  223, 260
Megawood®  266
melamine resin adhesive  264
melamine urea formaldehyde resin (MUF)  269, 271, 272
meliaceae  262
Menig nail plate  272
Menz OHT®  274
metrosideros  262
microberlinia  263
Microllam®  265
MicroWood®  266
milling  59, 261, 270
milling machine  181, 282
mineral-bound chipboard  265
mineral-bound chipboard panel  265
miter  271
mixed plantation  262
model building  261, 262, 263, 265
moisture/heat pressure process  274
mold  90, 265
molded chipboard element  265
molded laminate  264, 270
molded plywood  56, 59, 76, 259, 264, 270
molded wood  259
motor car body construction  262
multi-axis CNC technology. See CNC
multi-layer solid timber panel  264
multiplex  24, 278
multiplex panel  264, 270
musical instruments  266
musical instrument making  260, 261, 262, 263, 267, 270, 273
mutuba fig-tree  267

**N**

nails  175, 263, 269, 271, 272
nailed connection  272
nail plate  269, 272
nail plate joints. See nail plates
natural adhesive  271
natural building process  275, 276
natural coating  272
natural construction process  276
natural glue  271
natural resin  271, 273
natural weathering  271
negative stain image  273
New Option Wood  274
non-wooden part of the tree  259, 264, 267
Norway maple  262
notched joint  271

**O**

oak  24, 66, 80, 84, 93, 121, 144, 174, 192, 197, 200, 218, 223, 260, 261, 262, 263, 264, 270, 280
oak barrel  260
oak cork. See cork
oak veneer  74, 217, 236
obechi veneer  236
ochroma pyramidale  262
oil  260, 261, 271
oiled  127, 128, 129
oil-heat process  274
oiling  35, 84, 269, 271
old wood  261, 265
oriented strand board (OSB)  204, 236, 254, 265
osier. See willow
oxidation  260

**P**

packaging  262, 266
padouk  60, 102, 103, 262
Pagholz®  264
paint  120, 273
painting. See coating
pallet  262
pallet block  265
Pallwood®  266
palm wood  81, 259, 263, 266, 267
panels  262
panel construction  276
panel element  276

panel materials  271, 272
panels (timber frame building)  276
paraffin  265, 271
Parallam®  264
parallel strand lumber (PSL)  264
parquet flooring  262, 267
patented pliable wood  269, 270
pathways  260
pear  235
pectin  148
peddig  267
peeled veneer  261
peeled veneer strip  264
peeling  263
PEFC  7
Pentadecor®  273
pesticides  271
phellogen  260
phenol  260
phenol formaldehyde resin (PF)  269, 271
phenolic ingredients  271
phenolic resin  260, 264, 265, 271, 273
phenol-resorcinol resin adhesive  264
phenol resin bond  72
phenol resin glue  72
phenol resorcinol formaldehyde resin (PRF)  269, 271
phloem  260
picea abies  261
pigment  260
pile  261
pin  271
pine  89, 98, 114, 119, 175, 197, 224, 261, 263, 264, 265
pine infill  50
pinecone  202
pine plywood  204
pinosylvin  261
pin-shaped metal connectors  269, 272
pinus  261
pinus cembra  261
pith ray  263
planing  59, 239, 261, 263
plank  261
plastic-coated veneer  196
plastic injection process  273
plastic shaping  270
plate connectors  272
plate structure  276
platform frame  276
Plato process  274
Plytube  160, 266
plywood  24, 38, 56, 74, 132, 154, 160, 204, 225, 228, 229, 233, 255, 270, 271, 280, 282
plywood panel  270
pMDI adhesive  265
polycaprolactone  224, 272
polycaprolactone wax  224
polyester lacquer  273
polyester resin  266
polyethylene (PE)  266
polypropylene  78, 110, 184

polypropylene (PP)  266
polysaccharide  267
polytetrafluorethylene (PTFE)  39
polyurethane  177, 178, 181
polyurethane adhesive  264
polyurethane foam  198
polyurethane gloss paint (PUR paints)  273
polyvinyl acetate glue (PVA)  269, 271, 272
Polywood®  196
poplar  93, 260, 262, 263
populus  262
pores  273
porous carbon material  274
post  261, 276
post and beam construction  50, 67. See also timber-frame construction
post building  276
pouring  266
prefabrication  16, 28, 150, 175, 248, 276
prefabrication level  276
preparatory works  272
pressing together  271
press machine  264
primary shaping  269, 270
principles of timber construction  275
production process  269, 270
prunus avium  263
pseudotsuga menziesii  261
pterocarpus  262
PU adhesive  266
PVC-film. See PVC (polyvinylchloride)
PVC (polyvinyl chloride)  273
pyrolysis. See charring
pyrolysis oil  274

**Q**

quercus  262

**R**

radial cut  263
radiation hardening lacquer  273
railing  266
railway car construction  264
railway sleeper  261
rapeseed  265, 267
rattan  142, 191, 209, 213, 267
rattan palm  267
rattan tubes. See rattan
rattan weave  142
real chestnut  262
reamed bolt  272
reciprocal frame  276
reclaimed wood  30, 80, 188, 189, 250 261, 265, 279, 282
recycled wood  279
rectangular dowel  272
red beech  42
Reholz®  264
reshaping  270
resin  30, 138, 141, 260, 261, 265, 271, 273
resonance wood  261
Resopal®  225, 273
Rhus vernicifera  30
ribbing  103
rice  267
rift cutting  263
rift-stay-log cutting  263
rift veneers  263
RIM process (reaction injection molding)  273
ring connectors  272
robot-controlled production. See CNC
rod  264
rod shaped wood  266
rollers  265
rolling  266, 270
roof construction  272
roof shingle  261
roof structure  261, 264
rosewood  60, 263
rotary cut  263
rotary cut veneer  265
round rods  181
round timber  261

**S**

S2  266
safety of use  264
salix  263
sandblasting  163, 269, 270
sand blasting (sanding)  163
sanding  270
sandwich panel  266
sapwood  260, 261, 263
sawdust  263, 265, 266
sawing  261, 263, 270
sawing by-product  265
sawn timber  261, 270
sawn veneer  60, 263

scent 260, 261
Scots pine 261
screw 263, 269, 271, 272
screw joints. See pin-shaped metal connectors
scrimber 259, 264, 265, 266, 267
sculpture 262
sealing lacquer 273
sectioning 103
self-supporting frame 276
separating 269, 270
shaped wood 266
shaping 266
shaping tool 270
shear stress resistant connection 266
shellac 273
shell structure 276
shingles 11, 52, 261
ship building 261, 262, 265, 271
shop-fitting 264
shrinkage cracks 51. See also shrinking
shrinking 35, 111, 260, 261, 263, 267, 273
shutter 261
shuttering works 272
silanes 273
silicates 273
silicon 273
silver fir 16, 261
sintering 270
skeleton frame 276
skeleton frame construction 276
slats 264
sleigh runners 270
sliced veneer 77
slicing 263
slit material 270
smoked oak 192
soft fiberboard panel 265
softwood 119, 260, 261, 264, 265
solid constructions 67
solid timber 260, 264
solid timber board 264
solid timber construction 275, 276
solid timber construction system 276
solid timber elements 264, 276
solid timber panels 264
solid wood 59, 259, 261, 262, 263, 264, 266, 271
solid wood elements 264
solid wooden strips 264
solid wood materials 264
solid wood panels 259, 270
sound. See acoustics
sound absorbing perforations 260
sound quality 262
special connectors 272
splitting 263
spread of sound 260
spruce 14, 16, 62, 66, 88, 105, 121, 156, 163, 181, 248, 252, 260, 261, 263, 264, 265
spruce plywood 134
spruce shingles. See shingles
squared timber 261
square section 276
stage set 262
staggered joint 271

stain 144, 269, 272, 273
staining 24, 72, 110, 218
staircase 262
staircase banister 270
starch-bound lightweight wood-based panel 266
star plywood 259, 264
stay-log cutting 263
steam bending 262, 269, 270, 273
steaming 260
steel 181, 266
Stellac process 274
stem-forming plant 276
stick shaped wood 266
stiffness 272
storage of resin 269, 271
strand lumber 265
strength 260, 262, 263, 264, 272, 274
strength of wood 271
Strickbau 67, 278
strips 264
strip veneer 263
structural timber building 265, 272
structural timber construction 270, 271, 272
suberin 267
sublimation cutting 270
sulfite liquor 271
sulfite process 271
sunflower 265, 267
supplier of prefabricated construction systems 276
surfboard 262
Swedlam 265
sweet chestnut 262
swelling 235, 260, 263, 267, 273
Swiss pine 260, 261
sycamore 262
sycamore veneer 203
synthetic adhesive 271
synthetic condensation resin 271
synthetic resin 111, 264, 265
synthetic resin compressed wood 264
system of beams 264

T
tangential cut 263
tank pressure impregnation 271
tannin 260, 267, 269, 271
tannin adhesive 269, 271
tar smoldering. See carbonization
taste 260
tategu 48
T-beam 264
T-dowel 272
teak 93, 127, 128, 129, 131, 210, 211, 213, 260, 263, 280
teak veneer 198
tectona grandis 263
temperature 111
tenon connection 271
tenon joint 271
tensile strength 260, 264
tensile stress 261, 264
tension zone 266
terpene 260
terrace deck 266
terrace floor 262
textiles 272
thermal conductivity 260
thermal insulation 103, 265, 267
thermally modified timber (TMT) 269, 273
thermal modification 269
thermoplastics 266
thermoplastic material 265
thermoset binder 12
thermosets 271
thermowood 274
thickness growth 260
thin chipboard panel 265
three-dimensional coating of surfaces 264
three-dimensional forming 266
three-dimensional laminated wood element 264
three-dimensional processes 103
three-dimensional shaping 264
three-ply panels 168. See also glued laminated timber
thuja plicata 261
tieli 250, 251, 262
tilia 262
timber 261
timber-based construction material 264
timber-based material 261, 264
timber building 62
timber connection 269, 271
timber construction 275, 276
timber construction dowel 269, 272
timber construction material 259, 262, 264
timber engineering 264, 272
timber-frame construction 121, 275, 276
timber polyose 274
timber section 262

timber-steel connection 271
timura Holz 274
tongue and groove framework 121
tongue and groove connection 271
tool handle 262
tool making 265
toothed plate connectors 272
TOPAN® MDF Form 270
toughness 262, 266, 267
trade fair construction 264
traditional woodworking 69
transparent coating 273
transverse strengthening 266
treehouse 88
trimming machine 270
triplochiton scleroxylon 262
tropical wood 260, 261, 263
true-quarter slicing 263
trunk 265
tubular chipboard panel 265
tubular panel 265
tulip tree 238, 263
turning 262, 267, 270
two-component polyurethane lacquer 273
two-phase process 265

U
ulmus 262
Umgebindehaus (Upper Lusatian House) 276
unsaturated polyester lacquer 273
upright 276
urea formaldehyde resin (UF) 269, 271, 272
urea resin 271
urushi lacquer 30, 273
UV lacquer systems 273
UV vacuum lacquer 273

V
Vacu³ process 274
vacuum press drying 274
vacuum process 271
vanillin 260
vapor-permeable MDF panel 265
vapor-permeable wall and roof panel 265
vehicle construction 264, 265, 266, 272
vehicle interior 266
veneer 60, 103, 136, 160, 192, 196, 223, 228, 235, 240, 259, 261, 262, 263, 264, 266, 271, 272, 282
veneer-based material 263, 264
veneer circular saw 263
veneer gang saw 263
veneer panel 259, 264
veneer ply 264, 266
veneer plywood 259, 264
veneer production 260, 273
veneer sheet 263, 266
veneer strip 264
veneer work 272
vertical growth 260

**W**

waferboard 265
wall cladding 261
wall construction 272
wall lining 264
walnut 100, 137, 140, 240, 260, 263
walnut veneer 138
warmth 235
warning ability 261
washboard structure 271
waste wood 263. See also reclaimed wood
water-based gloss paint 273
water-jet cutting 270
water transit tissue 260
wax 261, 267, 271
waxing 98, 269, 271
weak wood 266
weathering 35, 269, 270, 272, 273
weaving 235, 263, 267
Werzalit® 265
western red cedar 11, 78, 261
wet process 265
white rot 271
whitewood 263
wicker 142. See also rattan
wicker weave 142
wickerwork 267, 270
wild cherry 263
willow 46, 260, 263
willow rods. See willow
window 262
window sill 265
wind turbine 262
wine corks 23. See also cork
wire clamp 272
wood based element 276
wood-based material 259, 260, 261, 263, 264, 265, 266, 267, 270, 271, 272
wood ceramics 274
woodchip 264, 265
woodchip-based material 265
wood composites 266
wood-concrete composite 259, 266
wood connection 269, 270, 272
wood core 263
wood dowels 74, 116
wood dust 266
wooden barrel 270
wooden constructions 181
wooden dowels 119, 276
wooden fibers 235
wooden shingles. See shingles
wooden shoe 262, 263
wooden slat 264
wooden structure 181
wooden textiles 235, 266
wooden tubes. See Plytube
wood fiber 260, 265, 266, 267
wood fiber insulation board 265
wood-fiber material composite 259, 266
wood fiber panel 260
wood foam 266
wood-glass composite 259, 266
wood grain 111
wood growth. See growth
wood inlays. See inlay
wood intarsia. See intarsia
wood joints 119, 181
wood materials 77
wood modification 271
wood plastic composite (WPC) 77, 78, 184, 208, 259, 266, 267
wood polyose 260
wood protection varnish 273
wood remnant 265
wood screw 272
wood shavings 206, 239, 265
wood-steel beam 266
wood-steel composite 259, 266
wood-steel plate 266
Woodstock® 184
wood tar 274. See also carbonization
wood turning 262
wood veneer. See veneer
woodwool lightweight panel 265
woodworking joint 271
woody agricultural plants 267
woody grass 267
woody plants 259, 264, 266, 276
WPC. See wooden plastic composite

**X**

X-Lam 264
xylem 260
Xylomer® 266

**Y**

Yakisugi. See charring
yeast 266
yellow pine 98

**Z**

zBoard 266
zebrano 219
zebrawood 263
Zelfo® 92, 272
zeolite 265
ZipShaping 269, 270

# PICTURE CREDITS

**11  24H >
ARCHITECTURE**
Christian Richters

**12  WERNER
AISSLINGER**
Studio Aisslinger

Michel Bonvin

**14  ALICE**
Adrian Llewelyn Meredith

Nicolas Feihl

**16  ARCHITEKTEN
MARTENSON UND
NAGEL-THEISSEN**
Brigida González

Architekten Martenson
und Nagel-Theissen

**20  YEMI
AWOSILE**
Lilybeth King

Yemi Awosile

**25  MAARTEN
BAAS**
Contrasts Gallery, Shanghai

Bas Prince

moss gallery

Maarten Baas
www.maartenbaas.com

**28  BERNARDO
BADER**
Adolf Bereuter

**30  ALDO
BAKKER**
Erik and Petra Hesmerg

Aldo Bakker

**32  STEPHAN
BALKENHOL**
Stephan Balkenhol

Stefan Seitz

**36  BAMBOOSERO**
Jason Finch

Bamboosero

**37  SHIGERU BAN ARCHITECTS**
Blumer-Lehmann AG

designtoproduction

Julien Lanoo
www.ju-la.be

**40  BARK
CLOTH**
Bark Cloth Europe

ARTE

**42  GEORG
BASELITZ**
Photo: Jochen Littkemann, Berlin
Lithography: Farbanalyse

**43  BAUBOTANIK**
Ferdinand Ludwig

Oliver Storz

Ferdinand Ludwig

Britta Biermann

**48  BCXSY**
BCXSY

Hiromi Yokoi

**50  BERNATH+
WIDMER**
Bruno Altenburger

Roland Bernath

**52  BETON**
Jakub Certowicz

**54  PATRICK
BLANCHARD**
Lee Mawdsley, Courtesy Meta

**56  JÖRG
BONER**
Milo Keller, Paris
www.milokeller.com

**60  TORD
BOONTJE**
Meta

Angela Moore and artecnica

**62  GION A.
CAMINADA**
Lucia Degonda

Alig Schreinerei Zimmerei Fensterbau, Vrin

Lucia Degonda

**68  NICK
CAVE**
James Prinz

**69  GEHARD
DEMETZ**
Luca Reffo, Wanda Perrone Capano, Francesca Todde

**72  MARÇO
DESSÍ**
Tobias Schlorhaufer

Marco Dessí

**74  STEFAN
DIEZ**
Stefan Diez Industrial Design

Martin Url

Stefan Diez Industrial Design

Constantin Meyer

Thonet

Myrzik Jarisch

78 *DOSHI LEVIEN*
Moroso

Doshi Levien

80 *DUTCH INVERTUALS*
Bart Hess

Laurens Mulkens

81 *PIET HEIN EEK*
Fair Trade Original

84 *FEHLING & PEIZ*
Horst Bernhard, Hardheim

86 *LAETITIA FLORIN*
Laetitia Florin

87 *MALCOLM FRASER ARCHITECTS*
Kristian Buus

90 *TERUNOBU FUJIMORI*
Edmund Sumner

Adam Friedberg

92 *ELISE GABRIEL*
Maxime Champion

93 *MARTINO GAMPER*
Angus

Anne Heslop

96 *LIAM GILLICK*
Courtesy Three Star Books, Paris

98 *GLASS HILL*
Glass Hill

100 *GRAFT*
GRAFT

Ricky Ridecos

104 *GRAMAZIO & KOHLER*
ETH-Studio Monte Rosa/Tonatiuh Ambrosetti

Gramazio & Kohler

106 *KONSTANTIN GRCIC*
Skitsch

BD Barcelona

Gerhardt Kellermann

Plank

112 *GUALLART ARCHITECTS*
Laura Cantarella, Nuria Díaz

114 *MAX AND HANNES GUMPP*
ABR

115 *FLORIAN HAUSWIRTH*
Nici Jost

Philipp Hänger

Florian Hauswirth

Max Yawney

120 *STUART HAYGARTH*
Stuart Haygarth

121 *HEIDE UND VON BECKERATH ARCHITEKTEN*
Maximilian Meisse
www.meisse.de

122 *STAFFAN HOLM*
Kalle Sanner

Staffan Holm

124 *BENJAMIN HUBERT*
Benjamin Hubert

126 *ENRIQUE ILLÁNEZ SCHOENENBERGER*
ECAL

127 *INCHFURNITURE*
Hans-Jörg Walter

Mark Niedermann

INCHfurniture

132 *ICD + ITKE*
Steffen Reichert

Simon Schleicher

Achim Menges

134 *ICD*
ICD Institute for Computational Design, University of Stuttgart

136 *IWAMOTOSCOTT ARCHITECTURE*
IwamotoScott Architecture

137 *HELLA JONGERIUS*
Fabrice Gousset

142 *CORDULA KEHRER*
Evi Künstle

144 *STEFFEN KEHRLE*
Pixelgarten
www.pixelgarten.de

Atelier Steffen Kehrle

Stattmann Neue Möbel

148    **KO-HO**
Ko-Ho

150    **KRAUS
SCHÖNBERG
ARCHITEKTEN**
Kraus Schönberg Architekten

152    **KENGO
KUMA
& ASSOCIATES**
Daici Ano

154    **MAYA
LAHMY**
Laura Stamer

156    **LASSILA
HIRVILAMMI
ARKKITEHDIT**
Jussi Tiainen

158    **LE BRICCOLE
DI VENEZIA**
RIVA1920

160    **SEONGYONG
LEE**
Seongyong Lee

161    **HANS
LEMMEN**
Christian Grovermann

Hans Lemmen

162    **KHAI
LIEW**
Grant Hancock

163    **KAI
LINKE**
Kai Linke, Adrian Niessler
and Catrin Altenbrandt

Kai Linke

166    **IDEE
LIU**
William Chen

167    **LOCALARCHITECTURE**
Milo Keller, Paris
www.milokeller.com

170    **PAUL
LOEBACH**
Jeremy Frechette

Jeremy Frechette

Paul Loebach

170    **PHILIPPE
MALOUIN**
Ad Achkar

Rami Chahine

175    **ENZO
MARI**
Jouko Lehtola

176    **MICHAEL
MARRIOTT**
Guido Fantuzzi

Mark Whitfield

177    **JÜRGEN
MAYER H.**
David Franck, Ostfildern

Fernando Alda
www.fernandoalda.com

Ludger Paffrath

182    **JUNICHI
MORI**
Keizo Kioku

Kei Miyajima

184    **PAOLA
NAVONE**
eumenes

185    **NENDO**
Yoneo Kawabe

187    **SASCHA
NORDMEYER**
Sascha Nordmeyer

188    **HENRIQUE
OLIVEIRA**
Eduardo Ortega

Nash Baker

Galeria Millan

190    **JENS
OTTEN**
Kati Liebert

191    **HARRY
PARR-YOUNG**
Des Carrington
www.carrington-photography.com

192    **PATTERNITY**
Toby Winteringham

Nick Downey

194    **LEX
POTT**
Lex Pott

196    **RAY
POWER**
Santiago Relanzón

197    **PHILIPPE RAHM
ARCHITECTES**
A. Dupuis/VIA

198    **RAW
EDGES**
Raw Edges

Ed Reeve

202    **STEFFEN
REICHERT**
Steffen Reichert

Boris Miklautsch

204   *ROLU*
ro/lu

206   *ADRIEN ROVERO*
VIA/Marie Flores

Adrien Rovero

202   *MARC SADLER*
Skitsch

209   *STEFAN SAGMEISTER*
Karim Charlebois-Zariffa

214   *COLIN SCHAELLI*
Noë Flum

Anita Baumann

216   *ALBRECHT SCHÄFER*
Uwe Walter

217   *SCHOLTEN & BAIJINGS*
Peter Guenzel

Takumi Ota

219   *FRANZISKA SCHREIBER*
Anne Amzoll

220   *TILO SCHULZ*
Uwe Walter, Berlin

Holger Albrich

224   *JERSZY SEYMOUR*
Markus Jans

225   *DJ SIMPSON*
Achim Kukulies, Düsseldorf

226   *ERNST STARK*
Gilles Hirgorom, Paris

Ernst Stark

230   *ELISA STROZYK*
Sebastian Neeb

Photography KHB Berlin, photographer Heike Overberg,
model agencies: Splendide, Izaio (fashion photographs)

Böwer

Elisa Strozyk

236   *STUDIO FORMAFANTASMA*
Studio FormaFantasma

237   *STUDIO JENS PRAET*
Studio Jens Praet

Davide Farabegoli

238   *STUDIO JOB*
Robert Kot

239   *TB&AJKAY*
Alexander Pihl

240   *THE MEDLEY INSTITUTE BY JANA PATZ*
Sabrina Theissen

242   *KATHARINA TRUDZINSKI*
Florian de Bruen
www.floriandebruen.com

Katharina Trudzinksi

244   *XAVIER VEILHAN*
André Morin

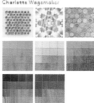

245   *CHARLOTTE WAGEMAKER*
Charlotte Wagemaker

248   *WAUGH THISTLETON ARCHITECTS*
Will Pryce
www.willpryce.com

KLH UK Limited

250   *AI WEIWEI*
Ai Weiwei

Steve Benisty

252   *WINGÅRDH ARKITEKTKONTOR*
Åke E:son Lindman

Gert Wingårdh

254   *BETHAN LAURA WOOD*
Ellis Scott

### I Books

- **Asenbaum, Stefan/Hummel, Julius/Mang, Karl et al. (eds.)** *Gebogenes Holz. Konstruktive Entwürfe. Wien 1840–1910.* Vienna 1979
- **Bablick, Michael** *Holz und Holzwerkstoffe – Oberflächenbehandlung und Schutz.* Munich 2009
- **Bangert, Albrecht/Ellenberg, Peter** *Thonet-Möbel. Bugholz-Klassiker 1830–1930. Ein Handbuch für Liebhaber und Sammler.* Munich 1993
- **Becker, Gerhard W./Braun, Dietrich** *Kunststoff-Handbuch*, 2nd fully revised edition. Munich, Vienna 1988
- **Blaser, Werner** *Joint and Connection: Ideas in Furniture Design and their Background.* Basel 1992
- **Bruyn, Gerd de/Ludwig, Ferdinand/Schwertfeger, Hannes (eds.)** *Lebende Bauten – Trainierbare Tragwerke.* Berlin 2009
- **Büren, Charles von (ed.)** *Kurt Naef. Der Spielzeugmacher. The Toymaker.* Basel, Boston, Berlin 2006
- **Cassina (eds.)** *Le Corbusier Authentic Wood.* Meda 2010
- **Cerliani, Christian/Baggenstos, Thomas** *Sperrholzarchitektur*, 2nd edition. Dietikon 2000
- **Evers, Dietrich** *Holzzeit – Überleben dank Holz.* (Exhibition at the Historische Museum Blumenstein in Solothurn/Switzerland, 9 May–5 November 1989). Wiesbaden 1989
- **Flade, Helmut** *Intarsia – europäische Einlegekunst aus sechs Jahrhunderten.* Munich 1986
- **Friedrich-Schoenberger, Mechtild** *Holzarchitektur im Detail. Konstruktion und Design moderner Einfamilienhäuser.* Stuttgart 2003
- **Fritz Becker KG (ed.)** *Der Becker – Formholzkompendium*, 2nd edition. Brakel 2010
- **Graubner, Wolfram** *Woodworking Joints.* London 1992
- **Håkanson, Sven-Gunnar** *Blockhäuser und Hütten selbst gebaut*, 4th edition. Hanover 2007
- **Hablützel, Alfred/Büren, Charles von/Blaser, Werner et al.** *Die Birke. Bedeutung und Werkstoff in Design und Kunst.* Sulgen 1996
- **Herzog, Thomas/Natterer, Julius/Volz, Michael et al.** *Wood Construction Manual.* Basel, Boston, Berlin 2004
- **Kalweit, Andreas/Paul, Christof/Peters, Sascha et al. (eds.)** *Handbuch für Technisches Produktdesign.* Berlin, Heidelberg 2006
- **Kaufmann, Hermann/Nerdinger, Winfried (eds.)** *Building with Timber: Paths into the Future.* Munich, London, New York 2011
- **Kolb, Josef** *Systems in Timber Engineering: Loadbearing Structures and Component Layers.* Basel 2008 (3rd revised German edition: *Holzbau mit System.* Basel 2010)
- **Krackler, Verena/Keunecke, Daniel/Niemz, Peter** *Verarbeitung und Verwendungsmöglichkeiten von Laubholz und Laubholzresten.* IfB project study. Zurich 2010
- **Landesgewerbeamt Baden-Württemberg (eds.)** *baumstark! Wald, Holz, Kultur.* Stuttgart 2001
- **Lefteri, Chris** *Holz. Material, Herstellung, Produkte.* Ludwigsburg 2003
- **Lohmann, Ulf et al.** *Holzlexikon*, 4th edition. Hamburg 2010
- **Mang, Karl** *History of Modern Furniture.* London 1979
- **Mari, Enzo** *autoprogettazione?* Mantua 2002
- **Müller, Christian** *Holzleimbau. Laminated Timber Construction: Development, Aesthetics, and Building Practice of a Modern Technology.* Basel 2000
- **Nabors, Murray W.** *Introduction to Botany.* London 2004
- **Niemz, Peter** *Holztechnologie II. Holzwerkstoffe*, 2nd revised edition. Zurich 2003
- **Nothhelfer, Karl** *Massivholz, Sperrholz, Gussholz? Das Gebrauchsmöbel der Zukunft.* Ravensburg 1947
- **Peters, Sascha** *Material Revolution: Sustainable Multi-purpose Materials for Design and Architecture.* Basel 2010
- **Pfeifer, Günter/Liebers, Antje/Reiners, Holger** *Der Neue Holzbau: Aktuelle Architektur. Alle Bausysteme. Neue Technologien.* Munich 1998
- **Prieto, Jorge/Keine, Jürgen** *Holzbeschichtung.* Hanover 2007
- **Röttger, Ernst/Klante, Dieter/Sagner, Alfred** *Creative Wood Design.* Creative Play Series, volume 2. New York 1961 *Die Säge. 100 Jahre Geschichte und Geschichten der Altendorf-Formatkreissäge.* Heidelberg 2006
- **Sauer, Christiane** *Made of ... : New Materials Sourcebook for Architecture and Design.* Berlin 2010
- **Schindler, Christoph** *Ein architektonisches Periodisierungsmodell anhand fertigungstechnischer Kriterien, dargestellt am Beispiel des Holzbaus.* Zurich 2009
- **Schönburg, Kurt** *Holzoberflächen am Bauwerk. Eigenschaften, Bearbeitung, Gestaltung.* Stuttgart 2009
- **Seeland, Klaus/Schmithüsen, Franz (eds.)** *Man in the Forest. Local Knowledge and Sustainable Management of Forests and Natural Resources in Tribal Communities in India.* New Delhi 2000
- **Spannagel, Fritz** *Der Möbelbau*, reprint of 10th edition from 1954. Hanover 1983
- **Villegas, Marcelo** *New Bamboo. Architecture and Design.* Bogotá 2003
- **Wagenführ, André/Scholz, Frieder (eds.)** *Taschenbuch der Holztechnik.* Munich 2008
- **Wagenführ, Rudi** *Holzatlas*, 6th newly revised and expanded edition. Munich 2007
- **Waugh, Andrew/Weiss, Karl Heinz/Wells, Matthew (eds.)** *A Process Revealed – Auf dem Holzweg.* London 2009
- **Weiß, Susanne** *Kunst + Technik = Design? Materialien und Motive der Luftfahrt in der Moderne.* Cologne 2010
- **Zwerger, Klaus** *Wood and Wood Joints: Building Traditions of Europe and Japan*, 2nd revised and expanded edition. Basel 2012

### II Essays

- **Arndt, Ulrich** "Naturbelassenes Holz im Freien." In: *Detail*, No. 10, 2006, pp. 1136–1140 "Auf Zementfüßen – Holz und Eternit – eine ungewöhnliche Möbelfamilie von Jörg Boner." In: *Design-Report*, No. 1, 2010, pp. 63–66
- **Barlovic, Ingo** "THEMEN – Von Gläubigen und Wissenden – Naturwissenschaftliche Altersbestimmung von Holz – Erfahrungen eines Sammlers afrikanischer Kunst." In: *Restauro*, No. 7, 2009, pp. 446–451 "DESIGN – Holz fordert Kreative heraus." In: *GZ*, No. 11, 2009, pp. 78–81
- **Enns, Jonathan** "Intelligent wood assemblies: incorporating found geometry & natural material complexity." In: *Architectural Design*, vol. 80, No. 6, 2010, pp. 116–121
- **Hartwig, Joost /John, Viola/Zeumer, Martin** "Nachhaltiger Materialeinsatz: Holz und Holzwerkstoffe." In: *Detail Green*, No. 2, 2009, pp. 56-59
- **Houseley, Laura** "I wood." In: *Pop*, No. 22, 2010, pp. 171–187
- **Idenburg, Florian/Gallanti, Fabrizio** "Nido di legno./Wood nest." In: *Abitare*, No. 503, 2010, pp. 58–67
- **Kaltenbach, Frank** "City of Wood – Aktuelle Geschosswohnungsbauten aus Holz." In: *Detail*, Nr. 10, 2010, pp. 1056–1064
- **Kato, Takashi** "Discussions and dialogs concerning the earth by scientists and designers." In: *Axis*, No. 146, 2010, pp. 93–97
- **Klee, Doris** "Wald und Holz: Eine Spurensuche in alten Zuger Akten." In: *Kunst + Architektur in der Schweiz*, No. 1, 2010, pp. 24–30
- **Kremer, Birgit** "Taschenuhren aus Holz. Die Erfolgsstory der Uhrmacherfamilie Bronnikov." In: *Weltkunst*, No. 12, 2008, pp. 28–30
- **Martin, Fabian/Schegk, Ingrid** "Holz und Holzwerkstoffe in der Landschaftsarchitektur – Holzschutz: Heimische Hölzer, Tropenholz und Kunst-Holz im Test." In: *Garten + Landschaft*, No. 11, 2009, pp. 15–18
- **McCloud, Kevin** "Branching out." In: *Grand Designs*, No. 62, 2009, pp. 104ff. "Milk & Honey. (A selection of furniture combining wood with white hard materials.)" In: *Frame*, No. 74, 2010, pp. 200ff.
- **Modlmayr, Hans-Jörg** *Speerspitze der Archäologie – Die Erforschung der Holz-Zeit.* Transcript of broadcast "Deutschlandradio Kultur – Forschung und Gesellschaft" on 27 August, 2009
- **Müller, Burkhard** "Die Schönheit des Waldbaus. Die Forstakademie Tharandt feiert ihren zweihundertsten Geburtstag – und die Entdeckung der Nachhaltigkeit." In: *Süddeutsche Zeitung*, No. 140, 20 June 2011, p. 9
- **Quiroga, Grace/Jormakka, Kari** "Naturholz : Kulturholz – Holz und sein geheimnisvoller Nimbus." In: *Detail*, No. 11, 2008, pp. 1242–1248 "Report – Selbstkleber – Lineares Vibrationsschweißen verklebt Holz ohne Kunststoffe." In: *Design-Report*, No. 4, 2008, p. 54ff.
- **Schindler, Christoph** "Das neue Bild vom Holz – Digitale Holzbearbeitung zur Umsetzung gekrümmter Formen." In: *Detail*, No. 11, 2008, pp. 1310–1316
- **Spohr, Kathrin** "Venedig am Rhein./Venice at stakes." In: *form – The Making of Design*, No. 237, 2011, p. 90ff.
- **Stravrinaki, Maria** "The African chair or the charismatic object." In: *Grey Room*, No. 41, 2010, pp. 88–109
- **Thun, Matteo** "Holz in Architektur, Interior- und Produktdesign – Hommage an einen Baustoff." In: *Detail*, No. 10, 2010, pp. 982–994
- **Tilson, Jake** "Norwegian Wood: Stavanger." In: *Blueprint*, No. 276, 2009, pp. 42–48
- **Tommasini, Maria Cristina** "Frida: legno vs plastica." In: *Domus*, No. 927, 2009, pp. 96–98
- **Tönges, Christoph** "Bauen mit Bambus." In: *Detail*, No. 6, 2008, pp. 652–662
- **Uhlmann, Steffen** "Luxusyachten statt Schrankwände. Der traditionsreiche Möbelhersteller Deutsche Werkstätten Hellerau musste sich neu erfinden, um in der hart umkämpften Branche zu überleben." In: *Süddeutsche Zeitung*, No. 14, 19 January 2011, pp. 21

### III Journals

- *Arch+*, Nr. 193, special issue 'Wood'. September 2009: www.archplus.net
- *Bauen mit Holz – Fachzeitschrift für Konstrukteure und Entscheider*: www.bauenmitholz.de
- *European Journal of Wood and Wood Products* (Holz als Roh- und Werkstoff): www.springer.com/life+sciences/forestry/journal/107
- *exakt – Einrichten, Ausbauen, Modernisieren*: www.exakt-magazin.de
- *HK – Holz- und Kunststoffverarbeitung*: www.hk-magazin.com
- *Holz-Zentralblatt – Unabhängiges Organ für die Forst- und Holzwirtschaft*: www.holz-zentralblatt.com
- *More Woodturning* (ed. Fred Holder): www.morewoodturning.net
- *Zuschnitt* (ed. proHolz Austria): www.zuschnitt.at

### IV Websites

- American Craft: www.americancraftmag.org
- American Hardwood Export Council (AHEC): www.americanhardwood.org/de
- APA – The Engineered Wood Association: www.apa-europe.org
- Berner Fachhochschule Architektur, Holz und Bau. Standort Biel: Fachbereich Holz, angeschlossene Technikerschulen HF Holz Biel: www.ahb.bfh.ch
- Bundesverband Deutscher Fertigbau e.V. (BDF): www.bdf-ev.de
- Bureau Baubotanik: www.bureau-baubotanik.de
- École Polytechnique Fédérale de Lausanne (EPFL), Prof. Dr. Yves Weinand: http://ibois.www.epfl.ch
- Eidgenössische Materialprüfungs- und Forschungsanstalt (EMPA): www.empa.ch
- Fachgebiet Tragkonstruktion, Fachbereich Architektur, Universität Kassel: http://cms.uni-kassel.de/asl/fb/fgs/fgsa/tk/fachgebiet.html
- Fraunhofer-Institut für Fabrikbetrieb und -automatisierung (IFF): www.holzlogistik.iff.fraunhofer.de
- Fraunhofer-Institut für Holzforschung – Wilhelm-Klauditz-Institut (WKI): www.wki.fraunhofer.de
- Fraunhofer-Institut für Silicatforschung (ISC): www.isc.fraunhofer.de
- Holzforschung Austria: www.holzforschung.at
- Infoholz.at: www.infoholz.at, www.dataholz.com
- Informationsdienst Holz: www.informationsdienst-holz.de
- Informationssystem Nachwachsende Rohstoffe (INARO): www.inaro.de
- Initiative Furnier + Natur e.V. (IFN): www.furnier.de
- Institut für Baustatik und Konstruktion (IBK), Fachbereich Stahl-, Holz- und Verbundbau, ETH Zurich: www.ibk.ethz.ch/fo
- Institut für Holzbiologie und Holztechnologie, Universität Göttingen: www.uni-goettingen.de/de/131929.html
- Institut für Tragkonstruktionen und Konstruktives Entwerfen (ITKE), Universität Stuttgart: www.itke.uni-stuttgart.de
- Institute for Computational Design (ICD), Universität Stuttgart: http://icd.uni-stuttgart.de
- Institut Grundlagen moderner Architektur und Entwerfen (IGMA), Universität Stuttgart: www.uni-stuttgart.de/igma
- Katalog bauphysikalisch ökologisch geprüfter Holzbauteile: www.dataholz.com
- Kuratorium für Waldarbeit und Forsttechnik e.V. (KWF): www.kwf-online.org
- Landesforsten Rheinland-Pfalz: www.wald-rlp.de
- Lignum – Holzwirtschaft Schweiz: www.lignum.ch
- Material Archiv: www.materialarchiv.ch
- proHolz Austria – Arbeitsgemeinschaft der österreichischen Holzwirtschaft: www.proholz.at
- Stiftung Unternehmen Wald: www.wald.de
- Verband der Deutschen Möbelindustrie e.V. (VDM): www.hdh-ev.de, www.raumausstattung.de
- WECOBIS – Ökologisches Baustoffinformationssystem: www.wecobis.de/jahia/Jahia/Home/Bauproduktgruppen/Holz-Holzwerkstoffe
- WonderWood: www.wonder-wood.de

### V Additional sources on design

- Baunetz: www.baunetz.de
- core 77 – design magazine and resource: www.core77.com
- designboom: www.designboom.com
- Designlines: www.designlines.de
- dezeen – design magazine: www.dezeen.com
- domus: www.domusweb.it
- FRAME magazine: www.framemag.com
- Frieze magazine: www.frieze.com
- nextroom – architektur im netz: www.nextroom.at
- PIN-UP Magazine for Architectural Entertainment: www.pinupmagazine.org
- Sight Unseen: www.sightunseen.com
- Viewpoint: www.view-publications.com

Thank you!

We greatly appreciate the contributions made by the designers, architects, and artists whose outstanding works are presented in this book. Sincere thanks go to the photographers for the excellent images, as well as to the gallerists, art institutions, and the staff members of the studios, design and architecture practices that supported us in researching and acquiring image material.

Very special thanks go to Charles von Büren, Berne, for his excellent professional consultation regarding the manuscript and for his ever-valuable suggestions.

*We were fortunate to have many enthusiastic, patient, interested, and astute people to assist us with this project, but above all, we would like to sincerely thank*
Helge Aszmoneit, Frankfurt am Main; Cornel Bigliotti, Lucerne; Ursula M. Geismann, Bad Honnef; Susanne Krieg, Basel; Berit Liedtke, Basel; Odine Oßwald, Basel; Marina Previsic, Lucerne; Ulrike Ruh, Basel; Sarah Schwarz, Basel; Katharina Sommer, Basel; Robert Steiger, Basel; Peter Wesner, Frankfurt am Main; Christina Wittich, Frankfurt am Main.

*We especially thank our interview partners, who not only invested time, but who also shared with us their expertise on wood and their enthusiasm for the material:*
Stephan Balkenhol, Jörg Boner, Gion A. Caminada, Stefan Diez, Konstantin Grcic, Florian Hauswirth, Hella Jongerius, Wolfram Putz/GRAFT, Stefan Sagmeister, Andre Santer/Büro Jürgen Mayer H., Tilo Schulz, Elisa Strozyk, Thomas Wüthrich and Yves Raschle/INCHfurniture.

*For their inspiration, for the information they provided, and for their tireless commitment we would also like to thank*
Bernardo Bader, Dornbirn; Jörg Boner, Zurich; Siska Diddens, Berlin; Marianne Goebl, Miami; Kathleen Granados/Friedman Benda Gallery, New York; Dominik Hammer, Munich; Florian Hauswirth, Biel; Oliver Heintz/Bark Cloth, Ebringen; Franziska Holzmann, Athens; Connie Hüsser, Zurich; Milo Keller, Paris; Galerie Kreo, Paris; Rainer Lienemann, Munich; Sophie Lovell, Berlin; Prof. Achim Menges, Stuttgart; Maarten Statius Muller/Studio Job; Jana Patz/The Medley Institute, Berlin; Raw Edges, London; Andre Santer, Berlin; Fabian Scheurer/designtoproduction, Zurich; Tilo Schulz, Berlin; Hannes Schwertfeger/Bureau Baubotanik, Stuttgart; Mathias Siebert/Kuttner Siebert Galerie, Berlin; Ernst Stark, Paris; Elisa Strozyk, Berlin; Ragna van Doorn/Studio Ai Weiwei, Beijing; Vicky Wang/Galerie Jochen Hempel, Leipzig; Andrew Waugh, London; Julia Westner/Büro Georg Baselitz, Munich.

*We thank the sponsors of this book project for their generous support:*

Lignum, Holzwirtschaft Schweiz
www.lignum.ch

German Association of Prefabricated Building Manufacture (BDF)
Bad Honnef, Germany
www.bdf-ev.de

The Authors

Barbara Glasner (*1970) holds a master's degree in interior design and works as a consultant and freelance curator for design and architecture in Frankfurt am Main, Germany. From 2001 to 2007, in collaboration with the German Design Council, she supervised the various editions of the highly successful design project "ideal house cologne," where internationally renowned designers such as Zaha Hadid, Hella Jongerius, Patricia Urquiola, Fernando and Humberto Campana, Konstantin Grcic, Ronan and Erwan Bouroullec, Naoto Fukasawa, Stefan Diez, and Dieter Rams presented their visions of future living at the International Furniture Fair (imm cologne) in Cologne, Germany. In 2008, she published the book *Patterns 2. Design, Art and Architecture* together with Petra Schmidt and Ursula Schöndeling, and in 2009 *Chroma. Design, Architecture, and Art in Color* in cooperation with Petra Schmidt, both published by Birkhäuser Verlag.
www.barbara-glasner.de

Stephan Ott (*1962) holds an MA in German Studies, History, Politics and Theater, Film and Television Studies and works as a freelance author, journalist and editor with a key focus on design. Between 1999 and 2012 Ott worked for the German Design Council and initially headed their press and publicity department. Until recently he was responsible there for communications strategy and conception as well as the editorial department. Since July 2012, Stephan Ott has been editor-in-chief of the design journal form. He also teaches text design at the Academy of Visual Arts (AVA) Frankfurt.
www.design-international.net

# IMPRINT

*Idea and conception:*
Barbara Glasner and Stephan Ott

*Texts:*
Stephan Ott

*Interviews:*
Barbara Glasner and Stephan Ott

*Picture editor:*
Barbara Glasner

*Translation from German into English:*
Laura Bruce (Introduction, Projects, Interviews, and Biographies),
James Roderick O'Donovan (Materials and Techniques)

*Copy editing:*
Julia Dawson

*Project management:*
Berit Liedtke, Odine Oßwald, Ulrike Ruh, Sarah Schwarz,
Katharina Sommer, Robert Steiger

*Layout and cover design:*
Modulator, Lucerne; Marina Previsic, Cornel Bigliotti

*Typography:*
Birkhäuser Verlag

*Cover material:*
Savanna Limba, Gmund

*Image processing:*
Photolitho AG, CH-Gossau ZH

A CIP catalogue record for this book is available from the Library
of Congress, Washington D.C., USA.

Bibliographic information published by the German National
Library. The German National Library lists this publication in the
Deutsche Nationalbibliografie; detailed bibliographic data are
available on the Internet at http://dnb.d-nb.de.

This book is also available in a German language edition
(ISBN 978-3-0346-0673-8).

© 2013 Birkhäuser Verlag GmbH, Basel
P.O. Box 44, CH-4009 Basel, Switzerland
Part of De Gruyter

Printed on acid-free paper produced
from chlorine-free pulp. TCF ∞

Printed in Germany

ISBN 978-3-0346-0674-5

9 8 7 6 5 4 3 2 1
www.birkhauser.ch